THE POLITICAL ECONOMY OF THE RAJ 1914-1947

CAMBRIDGE COMMONWEALTH SERIES

Published in association with the Managers of the Cambridge University Smuts Memorial Fund for the Advancement of Commonwealth Studies

General Editor: E. T. STOKES, *Smuts Professor of the History of the British Commonwealth, University of Cambridge*

TITLES PUBLISHED BY THE CAMBRIDGE UNIVERSITY PRESS

John S. Galbraith: Mackinnon and East Africa, 1878–1895
C. H. Grant: The Making of Modern Belize: Politics, Society and British Colonialism in Central America
G. Andrew Maguire: Toward 'Uhuru' in Tanzania
Ged Martin: The Durham Report and British Policy
John McCracken: Politics and Christianity in Malawi 1875–1940
Ronald Robinson (editor): Developing the Third World
Philip G. Wigley: Canada and the Transition to Commonwealth: British–Canadian Relations 1917–1926

TITLES PUBLISHED BY MACMILLAN

Roger Anstey: The Atlantic Slave Trade and British Abolition, 1760–1810
T. R. H. Davenport: South Africa: A Modern History
B. H. Farmer (editor): Green Revolution? Technology and Change in Rice-Growing Areas of Tamil Nadu and Sri Lanka
Partha Sarathi Gupta: Imperialism and the British Labour Movement, 1914–1964
Ronald Hyam and Ged Martin: Reappraisals in British Imperial History
B. R. Tomlinson: The Indian National Congress and the *Raj*, 1929–1942: The Penultimate Phase
B. R. Tomlinson: The Political Economy of the Raj 1914–1947: The Economics of Decolonization in India.
John Manning Ward: Colonial Self-Government: The British Experience, 1759–1856.

THE POLITICAL ECONOMY OF THE RAJ 1914–1947

The Economics of Decolonization in India

B. R. Tomlinson

© B. R. Tomlinson 1979

All rights reserved. No part of this publication may be reproduced or transmitted, in any form or by any means, without permission

First published 1979 by
THE MACMILLAN PRESS LTD
London and Basingstoke
Associated companies in Delhi
Dublin Hong Kong Johannesburg Lagos
Melbourne New York Singapore Tokyo

Printed in Great Britain
By Unwin Brothers Limited
The Gresham Press Old Woking Surrey

British Library Cataloguing in Publication Data

Tomlinson, Brian Roger
    The political economy of the Raj, 1914–1947
    (Cambridge Commonwealth series)
    1. India – Economic conditions – 1918–1947
    I. Title II. Series
    330.9′54′035   HC435

    ISBN 0–333–22361–6

This book is sold subject
to the standard conditions
of the Net Book Agreement

Contents

List of Tables	vi
Preface	ix
Abbreviations	xiv
1 THE POLITICAL ECONOMY OF THE RAJ IN 1913	1
2 INDIA AND THE WORLD ECONOMY, 1919–1939	30
3 THE COLONIAL GOVERNMENT AND THE INDIAN ECONOMY: Central Government Economic Policy, 1914–1947	57
4 THE IMPERIAL GOVERNMENT AND THE INDIAN ECONOMY: The Official Mind of Decolonization 1914–47	104
Statistical Appendix to Chapter 4	153
5 Postscript: The Economics of Decolonization	157
Notes	168
Bibliography	186
Index	197

List of Tables

1.1	Government of India Expenditure in England 1913–14	18
2.1	India's Industrial Progress in Import Substitution 1919–1936	32
2.2	Indices of Industrial Production, India and World 1920–1938	32
2.3	Indices of Indian Industrial Production 1925–1937	33
2.4	Indices of Internal Economic Activity 1920–1939	35
2.5	Partial Estimate of Allocation of Internal Savings in India 1930–1939	38
2.6	Branches of Commercial Banks in India 1929–1952	41
2.7	Percentage Share of British Goods in India's Imports 1913–1938	47
2.8	British Production, Total Exports and Exports to India by Major Heads 1924 and 1935	48
2.9	Nominal British Overseas and Expatriate Investment in India 1921 and 1938	49
2.10	Racial Composition of Rupee Company Boards listed in *Indian Investors' Year-Book* 1925–6 and 1938–9	54
3.1	Government of India Expenditure and Receipts in UK 1925–1934	82
3.2	Defence Expenditure in India 1939–1945	93
3.3	Indices of Relative Price Movements 1939–44	94
3.4	Indices of Indian Industrial Production 1939–1945	95
3.5	Indices of Goods Available for Civil Consumption in India 1939–40 to 1945–6	97
4.1	Government of India and British Government Net Defence Expenditure in India 1913–1920	109
4.2	Central Government Revenue and Expenditure 1914–1945	153
4.3	Central Government Debt 1913–1945	155

| 4.4 | Percentage of Revenue and Expenditure by Major Heads: Central Government 1919–1940 | 155 |
| 4.5 | Percentage of Revenue and Expenditure by Major Heads: all Provincial Governments (excluding Burma) 1924–1940 | 156 |

Preface

Decolonization is a modern word for an important feature of twentieth-century world history. The ending of colonial rule is not, of course, an exclusively twentieth-century phenomenon, the fall of empires has gone on for almost as long as their rise. Even in the context of the modern British Empire in the last 150 years the expansion and contraction of formal imperial control has often run in parallel. Between 1841 and 1871, for example, Great Britain annexed or occupied the Gold Coast, Labuan, the Punjab, Sind, Hong Kong, Berar, Oudh, Lower Burma, Kowloon, Sierra Leone, Basutoland, Griqualand and the Transvaal; in the same period she gave self-government to Upper and Lower Canada, New Brunswick, Nova Scotia, New Zealand, the Australian colonies and Cape Colony. The great period of British imperial expansion in Africa after 1880 was crowned by the grant of self-government to the Transvaal and Orange Free State in 1906–7. Britain's acquisition of mandated territories in Tanganyika, Palestine, Iraq and elsewhere after 1918 was matched by her retreat from direct rule in Egypt and Eire. Only after 1945 has one trend, imperial contraction, not been balanced by its opposite.

Since the growth and shrinkage of the British Empire have, until recently, gone hand in hand, it follows that imperialism and decolonization must be studied as a single, integrated phenomenon and that theoretical explanations based on the analysis of one half of the process must be made applicable to the other. To study the fall of the British Empire, then, we need also to understand its rise. A good starting point is the analysis of the expansion of British power and influence in the nineteenth century provided by R. E. Robinson and J. A. Gallagher in 'The Imperialism of Free Trade':

> Imperialism, perhaps, may be defined as a sufficient political function of . . . [the] process of integrating new regions into the expanding economy; its character is largely decided by the various and changing relationships between the political and

economic elements of expansion in any particular region and time. Two qualifications must be made. First, imperialism may be only indirectly connected with economic integration in that it sometimes extends beyond areas of economic development, but acts for their strategic protection. Secondly, although imperialism is a function of economic expansion, it is not a necessary function. Whether imperialist phenomena show themselves or not is determined not only by factors of economic expansion, but equally by the political and social organisation of the regions brought into the orbit of the expansive society and also by the world situation in general.[1]

This summary suggests what might be the most useful points for investigation in studying any particular episode in the expansion, and also in the maintenance and contraction, of British power in the extra-European world. If the rise of the British Empire was the result of the interplay of a complex set of unique factors – economic, political and strategic – acting both at the imperial centre and at the colonial periphery, and if the implementation of formal control or informal influence was a matter of technique, then to paint a true picture of the decolonization of India we must ask the following questions about Britain's relationship with India in the first half of the twentieth century: – what was the purpose of British rule in India? How did India fit into the Empire/Commonwealth as a whole? What interests were at stake and how were they expressed? How could these interests best be secured? What system of rule was best able to do so? What systems were practicable given conditions in India?

One way to answer these questions is to concentrate on imperial policy, on the official mind of British rule in India in the last decades of the Raj. This is an important approach, and one that is used extensively here. It results in the conclusion that the process of decolonization came about through a series of short-term decisions made by British Governments concerned with a limited number of specific objectives and constraints, and underpinned by the broader theme of India's imperial commitment and the financial and political problems of the Raj. An analysis along these lines can take us a long way, but it needs to be placed in a wider context. If British nineteenth-century imperialism was a sufficient, although not a necessary, function of the process of integrating new regions into an expanding economy, what was British twentieth-century decolonization in these terms? To deal with this we need to investigate the relationship between the Indian, imperial and international economies and the impact that changes in this relationship had upon the official mind of Government in India and Britain. The interaction of economic forces, and their effect on decolonization, cannot be properly understood unless we know a good deal about the institutions that integrated the Indian economy and connected it to the outside world. The most important of these linkages were those provided by foreign, expatriate and indigenous trading and banking firms, and by the departments of the colonial Government that dealt with industry, trade and monetary matters. An analysis of these institutions enables us to appreciate more precisely the problems and purposed of imperial policy and also to show how that policy influenced, and was influenced by, major changes in the Indian, imperial and international monetary and commercial systems.

Our main concern, then, must be to investigate the importance of fluctuating economic conditions in determining changes in the nature and objectives of British rule in India between 1914 and 1947. Chapter 1 provides an analysis of the structure on which India's role in the world economy, and the Government of India's place in the imperial polity, rested before the First World War. The next three chapters describe, thematically, the major changes in this structure that took place up to 1947: chapter 2 deals with India's role in the world economy in the inter-war years, concentrating on the impact of macro-economic change on the behaviour of indigenous, expatriate and foreign business interests; chapter 3 considers the colonial Government's place in Indian economic life and the extent to which it was able to meet the demands put upon it by the difficult economic conditions of the period from 1914 to 1947; chapter 4 focuses directly on the official mind of decolonization and investigates the attempts of successive British Governments to adapt their systems of control over India to changes in economic conditions – parts of this chapter have already appeared in two articles, 'India and the British Empire 1880–1935' and 'India and the British Empire 1935–1947' published in the *Indian Economic and Social History Review* in 1975 and 1976, and I am grateful to the Editor of this journal for permission to use them here. Finally, the concluding chapter places the analysis in a wider context, both in terms of events in other parts of the British Empire and with regard to the political and social problems that developed in parallel to the economic events set out in the body of the text.

The argument is supported at various points by a number of statistical tables. Because of imperfections in the source material on which these are based, and of the crudeness of the techniques used in compiling them, these tables are intended only to be illustrative; they should not be used as the basis of a sophisticated statistical approach. It should be noted that, following Government of India practice, most of the tables deal in financial years, which ran from April to March. Many of the figures are given in lakhs and crores of rupees. One lakh is one hundred thousand (usually written 1,00,000) and one crore is ten million (usually written 1,00,00,000). The rupee was worth 1s 4d (6·7p) from the late 1890s until 1917. After this date the rate rose sharply, reaching 2s 4d (11·7p) in the winter of 1919–20, and then collapsed dramatically to 1s 3d (6·2p) within a year. Over the next three years the ratio slowly revived, reaching 1s 6d (7·5p) in 1924 and being held at that level for the rest of our period. Government revenue and expenditure accounts treated the rupee as worth 1s 4d until 1920, 2s (10p) from 1920 to 1927 and 1s 6d thereafter. Sterling figures are given in pounds, shillings and old pence.

My work has concentrated on the economic history of decolonization in India, rather than on the economic history of India as a whole – even within this compass it is not meant to be definitive. Much of the text deals with monetary history, and discussion of other sectors of the Indian and imperial economies has had to be curtailed to make room for this. This has been done partly because Indian monetary history is an important subject which has been neglected by modern scholars, and partly because a study of it provides a good basis for constructing an analysis of the history of decolonization which can integrate events in many areas, from the imperial capital to the Indian village. Imperial economic history is at present a complex and confusing subject. As Tony Hopkins has recently pointed out in an introduction to a volume of essays on Indian and African economic history:

> From 1947 onwards decolonization, in destroying the political unity of empires, has also dissolved the established framework of academic study. . . . The remaining imperial historians were left in charge of a weakened centre and without a periphery – or at least a periphery which they no longer understood very well. . . . [There has] emerged a generation of specialists whose

detailed knowledge . . . represented a strength in depth never sought after or even envisaged by previous imperial historians, and which at the esoteric boundaries . . . would probably have been incomprehensible to them.[2]

Thematic studies such as the one that is attempted here may prompt the emasculated centre and the over-vigorous periphery to remember that they have some concerns in common and that the economic historiography of the British Empire, and of its constituent parts, would benefit from an attempt to bridge the gulf that now separates them.

The research on which this book is based has been supported by a Senior Rouse Ball Studentship awarded by Trinity College, Cambridge, a project grant made by the UK Social Sciences Research Council and a University Research Fellowship held in the Department of Economic and Social History, University of Birmingham. Generous grants towards research expenses have been made by the Master and Fellows of Trinity College, Cambridge, by the Managers of the Smuts Memorial Fund at Cambridge and by the Trustees of the Houblon-Norman Fund of the Bank of England. I am most grateful to these institutions for their support, and also to the staffs of the several libraries and archives in Britain and India who have helped with this research. I should like to thank also the many friends and colleagues who have contributed much to the quality of my work, in particular Chris Bayly, Ian Brown, Peter Cain, Robi Chatterji, Clive Dewey, Ian Drummond, Tony Hopkins, Sue Howson, Rajat Ray, Eric Stokes, John Toye and David Washbrook. My debts to Jack Gallagher and Anil Seal are heavy; Christopher Baker has endured long conversations that were a great help in tempering the ideas that appear in this book; Leslie Pressnell's encouragement and advice gave me the confidence to tackle the difficult subject of monetary history; Caroline, my wife, has again provided full support despite unprecedented distractions.

University of Birmingham　　　　　　　　　　　　　　B. R. TOMLINSON
March 1978

Abbreviations

A. & F	Accounts and Finance Branch
CAB	Cabinet Office Papers
C.D.	Commerce Department Papers
C.I.G.S.	Chief of the Imperial General Staff
C.L.A.	Central Legislative Assembly
E.H. & L.	Department of Education, Health and Lands Papers
F.C.	Finance Collection
F.D.	Finance Department Papers
G.o.I.	Government of India
G.S.R.	Gold Standard Reserve
I. & L.	Department of Industries and Labour Papers
I.O.	India Office
M.L.A.	Member of Legislative Assembly
PREM	Premier's Office Papers
Procs.	Proceedings
T.	Treasury Papers

1. The Political Economy of the Raj in 1913

The broad outlines of India's role in the imperial economy before the First World War are well known. In common with most other countries in Asia, Africa, Latin America and Australasia she acted as a supplier of raw materials, industrial inputs and foodstuffs to the major industrialised nations, and as a market for their exports of capital and mass-produced consumer and capital goods. Thus India's export trade was based on raw cotton, raw jute, rice, tea, oilseeds, wheat and raw hides sent, in the main, to Britain, Europe and North America, while her imports were dominated by goods coming from these parts of the world, in particular cotton textiles, metal manufactures and engineering products.

This picture is over-simplified, of course. India exported manufactured goods as well as raw materials. Jute cloth and gunny bags, and cotton twist, yarn and piece-goods featured prominently in the list of her exports; in jute manufactures she was the world's most important consumer and producer in 1913, in cotton yarn she was second only to Britain as a supplier of total world trade. Of her imports, gold and silver bullion represented an important percentage – 23 per cent in 1913 – of her trade with the industrialised world. A large segment of India's foreign trade was carried out with other non-European economies, especially those of Southeast Asia. The largest items in this were exports of raw cotton to Japan, of cotton yarn to China and of jute manufactures and rice to the whole area. In return, India imported raw and manufactured silk from China and Hong Kong and sugar from Java and Mauritius.

Even so, a large proportion of India's foreign trade in 1913 took the form of exchanging primary produce for consumer and capital goods with the advanced economies of the West. Britain was the most important trading partner, although she dominated imports far more than exports. Britain bought substantial amounts of Indian tea, raw jute, wheat and dressed hides, but the rest of Europe provided a bigger market for exports of raw jute, raw cotton, rice, oil-seeds and raw hides and skins. From 1900 to 1913 continental Europe as a whole bought more Indian products than did Britain. On the other hand, Britain remained far and away the largest supplier of India's imports, providing over 60 per cent in 1913.[1]

In 1913 India was the largest single market for British exports. She was not equally important to all British exporters, but for several staple industries, notably cotton textiles and certain types of iron and steel and engineering products, India was the best customer. Manufacturing cotton was the most important industry in Britain before the First World War; it was also a business that depended heavily on the export trade. In 1913 cotton manufactures accounted for almost one quarter of the total value of British exports; in that year 75 per cent of yarn and over 85 per cent of piece-good production by volume was exported. India was the third most important market for exports of British yarn in 1913, taking 18 per cent of total exports by volume, and by far the most important market for exports of British piece-goods, taking 43 per cent of total exports by volume. In monetary terms, cotton manufactures represented more than one third of India's total imports and over half her imports from Britain in 1913–14. The year 1913 has been regarded as the great climacteric of British cotton trade with India, the only time that British exports of piece-goods exceeded 3000 million yards. In fact it was clear even at the time that the Indian market was in danger, for Lancashire's sales of coarse quality grey goods were suffering heavily from the competition of domestic producers. Yet India was still of immense importance to British cotton manufacturers, not least because the Indian market had provided an area of expansion in the late nineteenth century, a time when sales to Europe and North America were being severely affected by the growth of domestic protected competition.[2]

The subject of the British cotton trade with India in the late nineteenth and early twentieth centuries has tended to dominate the minds of students of the period to an even greater extent than the figures for Lancashire's exports dominated the trade statistics themselves. It is often forgotten that India was, relatively speaking, an almost equally important market for other British staple exports. In 1907 metal manufactures and engineering products accounted for over 16 per cent of net British production. These industries covered a wide range of products and for many of them the export market, in particular the Indian market, was important. India was the largest customer for British exports of iron and steel manufactures in 1913, taking 17 per cent of them by value. These exports, which represented almost one tenth of India's import bill in that year, consisted mostly of steel girders and rails, galvanised sheets and tinplate. For girders, sheets and plates India was the largest single market and for rails the second largest. Imported goods supplied 96 per cent of total Indian consumption of iron and steel products and Britain was the largest supplier. However, her position in metal manufactures was not so dominant as in cotton. In 1913 Britain supplied only 70 per cent of India's imports of steel, most of the rest being supplied by the Belgian industry, for which India had become the second most important export market for steel sheets and plates. In the less important fields of hardware and non-ferrous metals Britain was less well placed and other European manufacturers, especially the Germans and Austrians, supplied a good proportion of India's needs.

India's importance as a market for British engineering products varied from category to category. Her share of British overseas sales of agricultural machinery, machine tools, motor cars, sewing machines and electrical wires and cables was small, but in 1911–13 she was the largest single customer for British exports of textile machinery, boilers, prime movers, locomotives and miscellaneous machinery, and the third largest purchaser of electrical machinery. The Indian market for textile machinery was especially important as this category, the only one in which British manufacturers retained a world-wide superiority, accounted for nearly a quarter of the value of total British exports of general engineering products in 1913. The British hold on the Indian market for imported engineering products remained almost complete.[3]

In many extra-European economies of the late nineteenth century British exports of goods were closely linked to exports of capital. This capital was invested on a portfolio basis – mainly in government loans, social overhead projects and improved communications – and thus helped to create a direct market for the products of British heavy industry, and by raising incomes in primary producing areas created an increased demand for imported consumer goods as well. A number of estimates of the amount of British and other foreign capital at work in India were made between 1900 and 1913 but none of them is more than informed guess-work. For simplicity's sake we will follow here the best known, and most comprehensive of these – those of Sir George Paish in 1911 and 1914[4] – although there is no way of knowing whether they are the most accurate. According to Paish, India and Ceylon together formed the fifth largest recipient of British capital exports in this period, the amount involved representing just over one-tenth of total British capital at work overseas. In 1910 there was £365 million of British capital in India and Ceylon. Of this, 49 per cent was invested in government loans, 37 per cent in railways, 5 per cent in tea and coffee plantations and one per cent or less in each of loans to municipalities, rubber, oil, tramways, public utilities, mines, banks and financial, commercial and industrial firms. According to official sources, three quarters of the total public debt of the Government of India in 1911 had been raised for railway development, and a further 13 per cent for irrigation works. Using these proportions on Paish's figures we can calculate that just under £271 million of British capital exported to India by 1910 – 75 per cent of the total – had been invested in railways.

Paish's estimates are undoubtably too low, for they are based only on public companies registered in Britain. It is impossible to assess the amount of British capital involved in unregistered firms and partnerships, or the amount of expatriate capital bound up in registered and unregistered companies in India. A few estimates can be cited, for what they are worth. In 1910 J. M. Keynes guessed that the amount of private British capital (capital not invested in public companies or government debt) exported to India in the previous decade was £40–50 million, about the same amount as had been repatriated in dividends from such investments.[5] In the same year H. F. Howard estimated the amount of external capital invested in registered rupee companies to be £20 million.[6] Information scattered through the volumes of evidence to the Indian Industrial Commission, collected in 1915–16, suggests that as much as three-quarters of the capital subscribed to joint-stock companies in India in many sectors of industry had been put up by British residents and expatriates.[7] The total amount of capital invested in such joint-stock companies was £24·8 million in 1901–2 and £42·5 million in 1910–11; over 60 per cent of it was in companies primarily orientated towards the export market.[8] However, this capital represents only a small fraction of the total figure of Indian savings not directly employed in agriculture.

In 1913, then, the pattern of British capital export to India was similar to the norm. British investors and British businessmen who had links with India put their money into generating social overheads, creating transport networks and lubricating the cogs of Indian enterprise that meshed with the world economy. It is hard to say to what extent British investment in India had helped to generate Indian imports of consumer goods from Britain – the amount of extra purchasing power for Lancashire cottons created by that investment cannot be calculated. It is probably true, however, to say that the improved transport that British-subscribed railway lines provided did help the spread of Lancashire goods, although it must be remembered that in 1913 large tracts of India were still virtually unaffected by such railways. For capital goods there is a much clearer correlation. Railways required rails, locomotives and other plant and rolling stock; irrigation schemes required pumps; cotton, jute, flour and sugar mills and presses required machinery and millwork. To the extent that these enterprises had been funded by British capital, or had been enabled to prosper thanks to an environment created by the employment of British capital, such investment created a potential market for British metal manufactures and engineering products. These enterprises did not, of course, generate an automatic market for *British* capital goods exports any more than British capital created a closed market for *British* consumer goods, but there were important structural reasons why British firms were likely to be asked to supply India's import requirements before 1914. The British cotton industry was the only foreign one willing or able to supply suitable goods for the Indian market. The same point applies to some sectors of British industry exporting capital goods to India – textile machinery manufacturers, for example. Other British manufacturers were cushioned by the facts that it was easier for them to make contact with the British export/import firms that dominated India's foreign trade, that the majority of their customers in India bought goods through London agencies, and that most classes of government stores bought outside India were statutorily reserved for British products.

In the context of Britain's place in the world economy of the late nineteenth and early twentieth centuries India's role as a major purchaser of British manufactures, and an important supplier of textile goods and raw materials to other parts of the world, had a special significance. It has been estimated that in 1910–11 India had a visible balance of payments surplus of about £29 million with the rest of the world. This surplus covered a visible deficit of £35 million with Britain and a further deficit of £25 million with Britain on invisibles and capital transactions. Moreover, India was able to maintain a balance of payments surplus with just those areas of the world – notably North America and continental Europe – with which Britain's deficit was increasing. Indian exports to these areas, unlike British ones, were unaffected by the rise of protective and revenue tariffs since she supplied goods essential for the industrialisation of those countries which were now challenging British supremacy even in the United Kingdom market. Thus it has been calculated that Britain's visible and invisible payments surplus with India enabled her to make good between two-fifths and one-third of her deficit with the other industrialised nations, and to continue to perform as an economy with a world-wide balance of payments surplus long after her trading position had declined.[9]

Reconstructing the broad outlines of India's foreign trade, and of her place in the international pattern of settlements, is important if one wishes to understand how the world economy worked before the First World War. But such a reconstruction is of less use as a guide to the motives and perceptions of the various participants in Indian government, trade and finance, or in assessing the impact of external stimuli on the pattern of India's economic and political development in that period. As a short cut to causality in these fields, studying the statistical outline of the world economy can be positively misleading, unless one can provide a complementary analysis of the essential economic linkages between India and the outside world. We must get behind the abstracted analysis of monetary systems and patterns of commodity trade and capital flow to study the individuals, firms and government departments which performed the actions that made up these larger units.

Between 1900 and 1913 the world demand for Indian produce grew and the prices that India's customers were prepared to pay for her exports rose steadily. Certain sectors of the Indian economy must, therefore, have benefited from the increase in trade. The burden of taxation did not increase significantly during this period,[10] and so it cannot be argued that the Government simply expropriated the surplus of the Indian producer. But the problem of identifying the groups whose prosperity increased is a complex one. The marketing of export commodities was bedevilled by the actions of middlemen; many intermediaries stood between the peasant producer and the foreign consumer. Up-country merchants and moneylenders who provided local capital and transport, as well as the export/import firms of the great ports with their Indian agents, all made a profit out of the export trade.[11] However, not all producers were deprived of a fair return for their efforts. Something of the complexity of the rural economy, and of the difficulties of generalising about it, is brought out in the following extract from a report by the Governor of Bihar and Orissa on the grain trade in that province prepared for the 1921 Census of India:

> In general terms . . . it may be said that the cultivator takes no part in and gets none of the profits that are made out of the marketing of the produce of his fields. The risks of the local trade are shouldered by the *beparis* and *goladars* [local and up-country traders] and the profits of it are shared by them; when the grain travels further afield the trade passes into the hands of a set of more substantial middlemen whose resources and whose outlook are larger and whose market is the whole of India. These generalizations of course need qualification to make them fit the facts. . . . The professional middlemen are not the only persons who realize that there is a good thing to be made out of holding up grain for a favourable market, and not infrequently the landlords and more substantial cultivators, who can afford to do so and who have the necessary storage room, do their own marketing: especially in Orissa it is said that the persons who control the local market are not a class apart, but the landlords and tenants themselves.[12]

More recent studies of rural marketing networks in the 1920s, which were much the same as those in operation in 1913, have shown that in the parts of India in which agriculture was the most commercialised and the most orientated towards the export market, credit rates to the cultivator were the lowest and the prices offered for his produce the most competitive in terms of those ruling on world markets.[13] Collusion among international firms was not complete enough in 1913, except, perhaps, in the Bengal jute market, to affect competition for access to Indian raw materials, and hence competition in the prices offered for them.[14] Where large-scale 'exploitation' of the producer occurred it can best be ascribed to the strength of the hold maintained by traditional marketing and credit-supplying agencies and to the inability of the forces of the world economy to break down existing institutional barriers to widespread economic development.

The internal credit network provided the most important set of institutions that mediated between the Indian producer and consumer and the world economy. Here there were major structural dislocations that modified the impact of the export surplus on internal economic development. Very little is known about the way in which the domestic Indian economy was financed during our period. Such information as exists suggests that there was a three-decker system of credit institutions which, while linked together to some extent, were capable of running along distinct, and sometimes diverging, lines.[15]

The overseas shipping of both imported and exported goods was financed, by and large, by a small group of predominantly British exchange banks which had head offices in the major world financial centres. These banks attracted deposits from outside India and, to a lesser extent, from inside the country as well. Their Indian operations were at branch level, and capital was shipped out from London to enable the banks to purchase more Indian exports for rupees than they sold imports for foreign currency. In normal years the banks did not retain much money in India at the end of the trading season, but arranged for their surplus balances to return to the more advanced discount markets of the West.

The next financial sector was made up of the major export/import firms and of the Indian and expatriate joint-stock banks, most notably the Presidency Banks of Bengal, Bombay and Madras. The largest international trading firms financed some overseas trade and, since they too had offices outside India, were able to bring in money when required. The majority of institutions in this sector, however, were dependent on internal sources of finance. The Presidency Banks were statutorily prevented from dealing overseas, and none of the other joint-stock banks had the contacts or the organisation to do so. The Indian banks made advances to industrial concerns and they, as well as the trading firms, financed the purchase and transport of some goods from up-country centres to the ports and vice versa. The Presidency Banks also acted, to a limited extent, as discounters of internal trade bills from other sectors of the money market. The extent to which by 1913 these banks had penetrated into the financing of internal trade, or the movement of goods for export from the producer to the port cities, is still unclear, but their activities were certainly limited enough to

leave room for a substantial and important indigenous banking network.
It has been estimated that, in 1930, 90 per cent of total credit was provided by the indigenous banking sector.[16] What is less certain is the way in which this native money market worked, and its links to both the peasant and the 'Westernised' credit institutions. Local and provincial native bankers certainly loaned money to rural traders, and may well have run the trade in gold bullion (which had become the preferred savings medium of the bulk of the rural population by 1913). These bankers borrowed from the Presidency Banks when they needed money to finance trade, but do not seem to have lent to the Westernised sector even when the rates offered by the exchange and joint-stock banks were appreciably higher than bazaar interest rates. These structural dislocations were clearly explained by an official of the Bank of Bombay in 1898:

> The Shroffs [native bankers], who finance nearly the whole of the internal trade of India, rarely, if ever, discount European Paper and never purchase foreign or sterling bills. Neither do they lend money on Government Paper or similar securities, but confine their advances to the discount of *hoondees* [internal trade bills], to loans to cultivators, and against gold and silver bullion. The *hoondees* they purchase are for the most part those of traders, small and large, at rates of discount ranging from 9 to 25 per cent per annum, but the *hoondees* they buy and sell to each other, which are chiefly the traders' *hoondees* bearing the Shroffs' own endorsements, rule the rates in the native bazaar, and are generally negotiated, during the busy season, at from 5 to 8 per cent discount. They also discount their endorsements pretty largely with the Presidency Banks when rates are low, and discontinue doing so when they rise above 6 per cent. They also speculate largely at times in Government Paper, especially during the off season, but rarely or never hold it or lend on it.[17]

Much of the profits that were made in rural trade and marketing were retained by this indigenous banking sector. Such bankers were a much more attractive source of capital for up-country traders than was the joint-stock banking network. Except in Madras, there was little borrowing from the Westernised banking sector for the local produce trade because of the difficulties that small traders and up-country merchants faced in meeting such banks' requirements about security for their loans. In one town in Bihar and Orissa in the 1920s, for example, the up-country traders preferred to pay 9 per cent on advances from indigenous bankers than pay 7 per cent for advances from joint-stock banks.[18] Conditions were much the same in 1913.

The way in which the various sectors of the money market worked in India before 1914 reveals, in essence, the way in which the impact of a growing international market for Indian produce had helped to strengthen traditional agencies, rather than cause a breakdown of an old system under the impact of the world economy. The stability and self-sufficiency of the unmodernised banking sector prevented the transformation of the Indian money market and domestic economy on Western lines. A large percentage of the profits of internal and external trade was retained by the producers and by the indigenous bankers who financed the first movement of crops. The established view that peasant profits were simply hoarded as bullion, and so were lost to the credit network, is probably mistaken, for holdings of precious metals were regarded as an indication of credit-rating for loans from local moneylenders and bankers for agricultural capital. Some proportion of India's imports of treasure ought to be regarded as imports of capital, for they certainly acted as the basis for credit expansion within the indigenous money market.[19] However, the disjointed structure of the internal money market helped to ensure that such profits were not usually fed back into the non-agricultural and non-trading sectors of the economy. Only in Ahmedabad do native bankers seem to have put capital into large-scale industry extensively before 1930, the purchase and mortgage of property being their favoured type of long-term investment.[20]

Not all the advanced sector of the Indian economy in 1913 was concerned with the export of primary produce and the import of bullion and manufactured goods. Firstly, there was a large internal trade, especially in food-grains. It was estimated in the late 1920s that the export trade consumed only between 9 and 17 per cent of India's total agricultural production, and the proportion was probably no larger in 1913.[21] Secondly, the activities of Indian entrepreneurs had led to the development of large-scale industrial enterprises in some areas, most notably the cotton textile mills of western India and a range of secondary consumer goods industries elsewhere. By 1914 India possessed jute, cotton and coal industries, and a railway network, that were significant in global terms. Her

The Political Economy of the Raj in 1913   11

imports of capital goods ran at around 20 per cent of her total imports – only a little less than in the case of Australia.[22] Yet it must be remembered that, over the field of industry in India as a whole and especially in heavy industry, British capital investments and expatriate entrepreneurs were predominant. Our analysis of the network of financial and commercial institutions that linked India to the world economy in 1913 suggests that one reason for this was the relatively small demand in India for manufactured goods and the problems of the supply of capital for industry from the agrarian and trading sectors of the economy that were run by traditional financial institutions.[23] Given the dislocations in the internal banking structure, the non-monetisation of large sectors of the rural economy and the absence of even a rudimentary stock exchange before 1914, it is hardly surprising that industrial entrepreneurs often found difficulty in raising adequate amounts of capital. As one witness complained to the Indian Industrial Commission of 1916–18:

> There is no flow of capital for industrial enterprises, and if there is any, it is only for petty industrial concerns from the small savings of the middle-class population. The wealthy classes [landowners, traders and indigenous bankers] . . ., look for what they consider safe investments on mortgages of land, houses and jewellery. With the rates of interest that are easily obtainable, money-lending is a favourite occupation.[24]

The Industrial Commission itself chose to stress the underdevelopment of financial institutions, arguing that 'the wealth actually possessed does a very small amount of work owing to its inactivity'[25] because of the lack of an integrated, efficient banking network:

> There is a considerable accumulation of capital in India, and to this new savings are being added every year. Some part of these savings is invested directly in the extension of industry. But we must draw attention to the vast differences in economic conditions which prevail in different parts of India. Banking facilities do not exist at all for a great majority of agriculturalists. . . . Even where branches of banks exist in moffusil towns, they do not unfortunately attract the custom of the small trader or the agriculturalist; nor do these, under existing conditions, possess the confidence of the banks. . . . The larger

> *mahajans* [moneylenders] who finance landowners or regular traders . . . do not consider that organised industries, except a few well-known and well-established ones with the value of which they are fully acquainted, furnish acceptable security, and when they lend to others, they exact heavy interest.
> . . . Thus, except for the branches of presidency and joint-stock banks and a few local banks, such capital as exists in the moffusil is unorganised, and the transfer of money is a personal transaction between the payer and the reciepient. . . . The employment of wealth by those agriculturalists who possess it follows traditional lines. . . . well-to-do agriculturalists are found owning a fair quantity of jewellery which is worn by their womenfolk, and they keep in addition a certain amount of rupees or sovereigns, a part of which is used for the current expenses of their household and of their cultivation. The rest they hoard against anticipated future necessities or lend to their neighbours.
> . . . We may now describe the state of affairs in the presidency towns where a much larger proportion of the exchanges takes place through banks, and there is a greater readiness on the part of the public to invest. . . . [Even here] there is a complaint that the existing banking system is too inelastic, . . . and that, in respect of industries, development is greatly retarded because the banks refuse to advance money for lengthy periods on the security of buildings and plant. . . . [Yet] the attempt in the Punjab to introduce banking on industrial lines failed, owing, among other causes, to the attempts of banks to finance long-term business with short-term deposits, and to the fact that they sank far too great a proportion of their funds in a single industry.[26]

The Commissioners probably underestimated the strength and sophistication of the indigenous trading and banking institutions, but were quite right to stress these firms' reluctance to invest in industry. The chief difference between expatriate and Indian would-be industrialists was simply that the former had access to external sources of finance, which allowed them to operate in a small, and often insecure, way.

In 1913, then, one major constraint on the further development of industry in India was the high equilibrium trap which retained the bulk of Indian internal savings in the non-industrial sector, buttressed by the misshapen development of financial and credit-supply institutions in the subcontinent. Indigenous industrial enterprise using local capital would not grow substantially until one of two things happened. Either the supply of manufactures from overseas had to be disrupted to allow increased demand which would enable the often speculative, under-capitalised Indian factories to survive and develop, or the established institutional pattern for the allocation of savings had to be broken down. This could result from the creation of new surpluses greater than could be handled by the traditional money market, or from the collapse of the profitability of traditional activities and of the institutional structure that supplied them. Protective tariffs for infant industries, the great cry of economic nationalism in this and later periods, would only supply one half of the less important of these two alternative scenarios. Only when the external network for the supply of goods and the internal network for the supply of credit were both disrupted, as was to happen in the 1930s and 1940s, was it likely that Indian industrial production would increase significantly. With hindsight, therefore, we can argue that one powerful reason why India had not been industrialised before the First World War by the activities of Indian entrepreneurs was, again, because the traditional institutions of the internal economy had been able to adapt too well to the new opportunities opened up for them by the expansion of India's role in the world economy.

Of the several institutional networks that linked India to the international economy in 1913 those provided by the colonial Government were among the most important. The policies and actions of the Government of India and the India Office over trade, financial and political questions provide the most accessible area in which to study the way such linkages worked in practice. In considering the attitude of the colonial Government to India's role in the international economy it is important to realise that Government officials had an outlook that was distinctly different from that of foreign, expatriate or native producers or consumers. The monetary, fiscal, commercial and industrial policy of the Government of India and the Secretary of State could have a considerable effect on the devleopment of the Indian economy and polity, but such policies were rarely designed solely with private interests in mind.

Government of India officials of the late nineteenth century were aware that agriculture was overwhelmingly the most important sector of the domestic economy. They also held, by and large, to the conventional wisdom of the day that international trade would be the vehicle for the transmission of economic development throughout the world and that such trade, and hence such development, was the result of the international specialisation. Thus the Indian Government encouraged the development of the agricultural export sector and railway construction in the belief that these would operate as the lead sectors which would bring on private development elsewhere as the economy expanded. The major items of Government capital expenditure – irrigation, agricultural research and assistance and transport, especially railways – were aimed at achieving a significant rate of growth in the agricultural sector[27]

External trade was seen as the key to India's economic development, but internal trade and industrialisation were recognised as being important as well. In this field, as in so many others, Government policy was never consistent for long. The development of the cotton and jute industries, and of coal mining, could also be seen as a vindication of official ideas that free trade and *laissez-faire* policies would promote those industries for which India provided a suitable environment. Nor was the Government of India always in practice as non-interventionist in its encouragement of Indian industry as classical economic theoreticians would have wished. At times, between 1903 and 1910 for example, the colonial Government did have an industrial policy. The purchase of Government stores (goods bought by Government for consumption by departments and official agencies) from the 1880s onwards provides an important example of this. As one student of Government stores policy has concluded:

> The Indian Government endeavoured to pursue a *laissez-faire* policy in India. . . . It seems, however, that *laissez-faire* was a dogma rather than a fact; it was a dogma which very often conflicted with reality. The Indian Government could not ignore reality and could not, therefore, consistently pursue a *laissez-faire* policy. The Government had to participate, in varying degrees, in a variety of undertakings. Government action was found to be necessary to help and accelerate development.[28]

Thus, in the late nineteenth century, the Government established a broad range of public sector industries including engineering workshops, railway workshops and coal mines. Government also gave some encouragement to the development of heavy industry in the private sector by making a small grant to the Bengal Iron and Steel Company and by providing a purchasing guarantee and railway concessions for the Tata Iron and Steel Company.[29]

The chief motive for this official involvement was fiscal, rather than developmental. From 1883 onwards the stores purchase rules had been consistently revised to encourage the purchase of locally manufactured articles. Because of the weakness of the silver standard rupee against sterling in the next decade, buying stores in London added disproportionately to the Government's residual financial and monetary problems. Encouraging Indian manufacture was thus important to the Government of India, but for different reasons than those which motivated British and Indian industrialists.

The fact that the colonial Government had its own reasons for taking actions that affected the economic relations between India and Britain is especially important in analysing tariff policy. Critics of Government policy before 1914 seized on tariff policy as the clearest example of the Government of India's willingness to favour British businessmen at the expense of potential Indian rivals. The failure of the Government of India to impose preferential tariffs to protect infant Indian industries against competition from British imports has been seen as one of the most important devices by which the exploitation of India under British rule was carried out.

It is undeniable that powerful British interests felt very strongly about Indian tariffs, and especially about any arrangements that might give a *de facto* preference to Indian industries competing with British ones. The most important of these interests, the Lancashire cotton manufacturers, were able to persuade the Secretary of State to force the Government of India to impose a countervailing excise on Indian cotton manufactures when a general tariff of 5 per cent was imposed in 1894. But the Lancashire cotton industry was a special case, being uniquely powerful among British pressure groups on the parliamentary scene in the late nineteenth century. The interests of Lancashire were hardly synonymous with those of British capitalism as a whole; they contradicted, for example, the interests of British manufacturers of textile machinery who relied on the Indian market as well as the interests of British expatriates who had invested in the Bombay industry. It has, indeed, been argued that Lancashire's campaign against the cotton tariff was only so successful because it became part of a larger political issue within

Parliament and within the internal workings of the India Office and the Government of India.[30]

Government of India officials tried hard to ensure that their fiscal policies did not do Indian industries any extra harm. A serious attempt was made to exempt from tariffs goods which were classed as industrial inputs. Using tariff policy to encourage industrial development directly was not thought advisable or practical on the whole, not least because it was feared that any protected sector of Indian industry would be dominated by fresh imports of British capital. In any case, the colonial Government needed to encourage imports, or at least not to discourage them actively, because imports brought in the customs duties which were a much more popular source of revenue than was direct taxation.

In its commercial and industrial policy up to 1913 the Government of India did not feel itself to be the protector of private British economic interests, and it was rarely forced by circumstances to act as if it were. On the other hand, commercial and industrial policies were not really central to the concerns of the Government of India in this period and Government policy in these fields did not provide an important part of the mechanisms or linkages through which India's external and internal economic life was carried on. The role of Government was, in practice, much more important in financial and monetary matters, for it was in this field that the day-to-day concerns of the Government of India and of British and Indian businessmen came together most closely.

The most striking feature of India's external economy from 1900 to 1913 was her steadily increasing balance of payments surplus on commodity account and the large amounts of British capital exported for use in India. The most reliable figures available show that India's commodity trade surplus in the period (including trade in precious metals) was over Rs. 5483 million, while her deficit on account of service transactions and interest payments was about Rs. 7019 million. The balance was met by the import of foreign capital, almost exclusively British. If India's imports of treasure are treated as a capital rather than as a commodity item, her commodity trade surplus in this period works out at Rs. 9328 million, with an additional gross capital inflow of Rs. 3845 million worth of treasure and Rs. 1471 million worth of British investment.[31]

India's commodity surplus and capital imports meant that, in a normal year, export/import trading firms and the exchange banks needed to buy rupees for foreign currency.[32] Until the 1890s the most usual way of doing this was by exporting silver bullion to India, which could then be presented to the Indian mints and coined into rupees. However, during the 1870s and 1880s the stability of the rupee exchange became jeopardised as the world price of silver fell in relation to gold. As the gold price of silver fell, so did the exchange rate of the rupee in relation to the currencies of India's major non-Asian trading partners and creditors. In 1893 the Government of India closed the Indian mints, thus taking India off the silver standard and, by reducing the issue of new rupees, raising their value as coin against sterling and other gold-based currencies.

The instability of the rupee exchange had had a depressing effect on India's export trade in the 1880s but powerful interests, notably the British-dominated tea industry, were still strongly in favour of keeping to a declining silver standard. The Government of India's action in abandoning silver and forcing up the exchange rate in the 1890s was based on a perception of its own requirements. The Indian Government had a number of obligations in London which had to be met by money raised in India, then converted into sterling and remitted to the Secretary of State at the India Office. These obligations, chiefly the interest payments on Government sterling debt plus the 'Home Charges' (the cost of the upkeep of the India Office and the pay and pensions, leave allowances and training costs of military and civilian personnel destined for India), ran at around £17 million per annum in the late nineteenth and early twentieth centuries, although they represented less than 2 per cent of the value of India's exports of commodities in that period.[33] A breakdown of the Government of India's expenditure in London in 1913–14 is given in Table 1.1.

To transfer this money from rupees in India to sterling in London the Secretary of State sold Council Bills each week to purchasers of Indian goods who needed rupees to pay for them. Council Bills were drafts sold in London for sterling which could be cashed at Government treasuries in India for rupees. The instability and decline of the rupee exchange rate was causing severe problems for Government finance by the 1890s; the fall in the exchange between 1873 and 1892 meant that the Government had to spend one third more rupees to buy the same amount of sterling. Forcing up the exchange rate and finding a stable currency system was now essential. It was for this reason that the mints were closed.

The making of Indian currency policy in the 1890s was

TABLE 1.1. Government of India's Expenditure in England 1913–14 (in £'000s)

Interest on debt:	
Railways	9000
Irrigation and public works	198
Other	2149
TOTAL	11347
Expenditure by departments	174
Military charges	4512
Civil charges and furlough	698
Pensions and allowances	2066
Stores for India	1503
Miscellaneous	12
TOTAL GROSS EXPENDITURE IN ENGLAND	20312
Gross expenditure in India	63440

Note: £1 = Rs. 15

Source: *Statistical Abstract for British India 1911–12 to 1921–2*, pp. 126 and 191–3.

dominated by two special currency commissions – the Herschell Committee of 1893 and the Fowler Committee of 1898–9. Both these bodies were appointed by the Secretary of State to devise a solution to the currency problem, and both produced substantially the same recommendations – a gold standard for India. Under this system it was supposed that India's international settlements would be met by the import and export of gold coin and bullion. Imported gold would swell the currency in circulation (open mints would coin bullion into sovereigns) and exported gold would contract it. If India had a large balance of payments surplus under this system the inflow of gold would increase the level of circulating currency and would raise the price of Indian produce while lowering the prices of Indian imports and those ruling in the markets for her exports. Thus the demand for Indian exports would fall, the balance of payments would turn against her and she would have to export gold to meet her new international indebtedness. Reducing India's stock of gold would reduce the circulating currency, bring down Indian prices, raise external prices and so start the cycle of adjustment moving round again.

Placing the rupee on the international gold standard meant

providing a gold coinage for India, so that imports and exports of gold would have a direct effect on the level of internal prices. Both the Herschell and the Fowler Committees recommended that such a coinage be introduced, based on the sovereign being minted in India and circulating at the rate of Rs. 15 = £1. Unfortunately, the initial attempts to push sovereigns into circulation were frustrated by the unwillingness of the Indian public to accept a gold coinage, while the British Treasury was consistently hostile to the idea of minting sovereigns in India. A gold coinage and a full gold standard remained the official aim of the Government of India's currency policy from 1898 to 1913, but officials had little idea of how to bring this about.

In practice, India was on a gold-exchange standard, not a gold standard, from 1898 onwards. Although the free import and export of gold was allowed the mints were not reopened and the rupee was linked to the international monetary system through the sterling exchange. India's balance of trade surplus could still be settled by the import of gold or silver bullion, or of sovereigns, but a more important mechanism was now provided by an expansion of the Council Bill policy of the Secretary of State. Until the late 1890s the Secretary of State had limited his weekly offer of Council Bills to the amounts of sterling exchange needed to meet the Government of India's commitments in London but, once the failure to establish an effective gold coinage in India became clear, he assumed a more complex and sophisticated role. The architects of the new system, Sir Lionel Abrahams at the India Office and Sir Edward Law in the Government of India, argued that, since the rupee was a token coin exchangeable for gold, the only useful function for India's gold reserves was as a support for the exchange rate in time of weakness. To do this with maximum efficiency and at minimum cost these reserves had to be lodged in London so that the authorities could support the exchange by buying rupees in India and paying out gold for them in Britain.

The absence of a gold coinage in India meant that sovereigns and gold bullion sent to India to pay for produce, or as new investment, could not be passed straight into circulation but had to be sold to the Government to obtain silver rupees. This expansion of currency could only be effected by coining new rupees (paper currency being a new and relatively untried device which had to be backed by silver coinage to meet a possible run on it) and the silver bullion needed for this could be bought most cheaply in London. Shipping gold from India to buy such bullion was seen as needlessly expensive. It was therefore thought better in all ways for the India Office to purchase the gold needed to meet India's obligations in London by offering sterling bills on India. The surplus of the proceeds of these sales was then used to buy silver which was shipped to India to be coined and used to meet the Council Bills as they were presented.[34] It was estimated that, between 1904–5 and 1910–11, half of India's visible balance of trade surplus in goods was financed by the sales of Council Bills. The new policy of the Secretary of State did not prevent private interests shipping gold bullion and coin to India, however, and between 1904–5 and 1910–11 another third of India's visible trade surplus was met in this way.[35] These bullion imports are an important, but often neglected, feature of India's commodity trade. In 1913, for example, net imports of gold and silver from the United Kingdom made up over 20 per cent of the value of total British exports to India and nearly 40 per cent of Britain's visible balance of payments surplus with her.[36]

The gold exchange standard was not the result of any long-term, planned policy. Indeed both the currency committees of the 1890s, to which the Indian authorities remained technically bound, had specifically rejected the scheme as too audacious. Yet, although it was not based on a widely accepted grand theory, and although it became apparent that neither the India Office nor the Government of India were always sure how it should be run, the system was successful. Only in 1906–8 was the smooth running interrupted when the authorities first coined too many rupees to meet an imagined trade boom and were then confused and tardy about contracting the currency and defending the exchange by selling Reverse Councils (buying up rupees in India in exchange for bills cashable in gold in London). In 1913 the Royal Commission on Indian Finance and Currency was appointed to review the situation and this body approved the gold exchange standard as a *fait accompli*. Even the long-term goal of a gold coinage was now thought to be unnecessary, although the Commission conceded that there was still no objection in principle to coining sovereigns in India should Indian opinion strongly demand it.[37]

To those critical of the Government of India's intentions, both at the time and more recently, the gold exchange standard has looked suspiciously like a managed currency system, and one that was being managed by people who did not necessarily have India's interest at heart.[38] The basis of these attacks has been, as Keynes pointed out, the belief that 'the amount of gold a country holds at home, rather than the degree of promptness and certainty with which at all times it can meet its international engagements, is the measure of financial strength'.[39] Most of the attacks were ill-founded: the gold exchange standard did not lead to a managed currency in India, for selling Council Bills did not create a demand for rupees, such sales being simply a way of providing rupees to satisfy the demand for Indian goods. Yet the involvement of Government agencies in providing the mechanisms by which Indian trade was financed, and the dislocation in the internal and external credit networks of the country, did make the India Office and the Government of India accessible to criticisms that would not have been made had there been an 'automatic' currency system, or an independent central bank and an integrated national money market in India.

From 1898 to 1913 there was a tendency for the Secretary of State to accumulate capital in London. The profit on rupee coinage (since the rupee was worth more as coin than as bullion, a given amount of silver would produce more rupees than its bullion value) was set aside in the London-based Gold Standard Reserve to meet a future run on the exchange. A proportion of the Paper Currency Reserve and of the Indian Government's treasury balances were also held in London. Some of these reserves, which for part of each year included the amounts raised by the sales of Council Bills which had not yet been spent on silver to be shipped to India for coinage, were invested in British Government securities and a small amount of them was loaned, for interest, to the Bank of England and other City institutions. When this was discovered in India a cry went up that India's resources were being used to subsidise the British economy at a time when interest rates in India were so high as to impede the normal flow of trade.

British businessmen in India, especially Montagu Webb of the Karachi Chamber of Commerce, were especially outspoken about the failure, as they saw it, of the Government of India to encourage Indian interests by holding all their reserves in India and by investing them on the Indian credit market. Webb's campaign, carried on in *The Times* in November 1912, provided useful ammunition for the parliamentary attack on the India Office for its handling of Indian monetary affairs which resulted in the appointment of the Royal Commission in 1913.[40] These views have also been used extensively by a modern economist in an attempt to show that Britain was only able to run the international gold standard before 1914 by ruthlessly exploiting the strength of the rupee to prop up sterling.[41]

These accusations do not stand up to close scrutiny. While it is true that the Secretary of State invested a part of the Indian reserves in British Government securities, and that he lent money from them to the Bank of England and other City institutions, the amounts involved were tiny. By 1912, £16 million had been invested from the Gold Standard Reserve in British Government securities, while the total British Government debt was over £600 million.[42] The sums which the Secretary of State lent out to the City fluctuated from just over £1 million in 1908, to £3 million in 1910, to £1·5 million from 1911 to 1913.[43] The India Office's dealings with the Bank of England, which were done to keep interest rates in London up, not down, took place only in 1890, 1893 and 1896–9 and never amounted to more than £3 million in a single year.[44]

Between 1900 and 1913 the Secretary of State had concentrated on building up the Gold Standard Reserve in London. Selling Council Bills in London to finance Indian trade helped this process, for such bills were met in India by silver rupees, the coinage of which provided profits that were set aside in the Reserve. The build-up of the Reserve was rapid – in December 1901 it contained £3·4 million, two thirds of it in India; by December 1912 the figure stood at £20·9 million, over £17 million of it in London. Many critics of the gold exchange standard have held that the G.S.R. was too large and that the profits on coinage could have been better employed as loans in India to boost capital works and industrial development. Almost as soon as the G.S.R. was set up, officials in India began to announce their views on its optimum size. The estimates of this figure rose over the years, from £10 million in 1904 to £25 million in 1912. Once these totals were reached it was suggested that the profits on coinage be used for capital programmes in India, as had been done in a small way in 1907 when just over £1 million of these profits had been diverted to railway capital schemes.[45]

In 1913 the Royal Commission on Indian Finance and Currency broke with tradition by laying down that no limit should be set to the size of the G.S.R.[46] It seems fanciful, however, to view this recommendation, which went against the advice of the India Office, as a deliberate attempt to benefit the London capital market at the expense of the Indian one. The Commission's decision had much more to do with the problems of estimating the extent of a possible future run on the exchange, given that India's one year of adverse trading on the gold exchange standard (in 1907–8) had cost the reserves £25 million, and had cut the gold and sterling balances of the G.S.R. by half.[47] To ease Indian credit rates the Royal Commission suggested that a portion of Government cash balances and currency reserves held in India be loaned out to the local money market at times of stringency.[48]

It is neither accurate nor useful to regard the gold exchange standard as a device conceived by British financial interests to appropriate India's gold or to hamper her economic development. It must be remembered that the world economy in 1913 was based on an international network and that had India received payment for all her exports in gold, for which there was no established banking system, rather than taking much of it in sterling, for which such a system existed, it is possible that the outflow of gold from Europe and North America would have impeded the expansion of the economies of India's customers and so reduced her own export-led development in this period. In any case, even with a full gold standard, it would have been impossible to prevent the British economy from acquiring gold from India should it have wished to. Britain was India's creditor during the life of the gold exchange standard; her balance of payments surplus on current account was settled by the flow of British capital for investment in India and by the short-term credits represented by Council Bills and the transfer of funds by the exchange banks. Were the London money market to be short of funds, high interest rates would have prevented this balancing process from taking place and India would then only have been able to pay for British goods, services and past capital by exporting gold to London.

All this is not to deny, of course, that there were major structural imperfections in the Indian currency and financial systems of the early twentieth century, but the external currency system must be seen as an adaptation to a larger set of circumstances, rather than as the sole, or as a major, cause of internal disruption. Viewed from outside, the Indian currency system worked smoothly enough between 1900 and 1913, with only one turbulent period (1907–8). Viewed from inside India, on the other hand, the currency system was much less stable. Each year the level of activity in India fell into two distinct parts – a 'busy' season when Government revenue was collected and crops sold and shipped abroad, and a 'slack' season when demand for finance and credit was slight. Whenever agrarian output was normal, interest rates soared in the busy season, as cultivators sold their produce to pay rent and revenue, traders demanded funds to buy and move the crops, and export/import firms did the bulk of their business. The problem of credit supply in the busy season was exacerbated by the inability of Indian banking institutions to attract funds from abroad, and by the habit of the indigenous bankers of borrowing from the Westernised banking sector when money was tight, but of not lending to it at any time. It was this demand for extra funds which led to agitation for Government reserves to be put at the disposal of the Indian money market.

The structural imperfections of the Indian credit network and of the institutions that connected its various parts made the domestic economy sensitive to outside influences. Many transactions of the three sectors of the Indian money market were linked, to the extent that each dealt with goods that had been imported or that were to be exported. The exchange banks and large export/import firms that had access to money markets outside India were able to supply extra credit for the financing of foreign trade. Some of these firms dealt directly with up-country merchants, while many more did business with the Presidency Banks. Since native bankers and Indian joint-stock banks also discounted some bills with the Presidency Banks, foreign funds could move up-country to attract trade for the foreign trade sector and were also used by the rest of the money market to provide liquidity for transactions within the domestic economy. Funds for the marketing and movement of agrarian produce were also supplied by the indigenous banking network from its own reserves. But since these were often held in bullion, and because there was no central bank and the use of modern banking instruments such as cheques was limited, the domestically-supplied internal credit market was somewhat inelastic and unresponsive. The import of funds through the Council Bill system was not, as Keynes and later commentators have asserted,[49] the only way in which the money supply in India could be increased once the mints had been closed, for the indigenous banking system was sophisticated and some of the holdings of treasure of both native bankers and substantial cultivators acted as a basis for credit expansion. Yet it remains true that, just as the production of crops for export was the sector of agriculture in which there was most potential for profit in this period, so the importing of funds from abroad to pay for such crops was qualitatively the most

The Political Economy of the Raj in 1913

important way in which the money supply was augmented each year. For this reason world demand for Indian currency, either to buy goods or to make investments, and the marginal fluctuations in rates of interest in financial centres outside India, had a disproportionately large impact on the working of the entire monetised economy.

The way that Government monetary policy linked the internal and external financial systems made this impact even greater. The sectors of the Indian credit network that did not deal in foreign trade – especially those concerned with the financing of local industry and of its supply of raw materials, and with the trade in food grains – were liable to suffer stringencies of credit. When India's established foreign commodity trade surplus, or her imports of capital, were disrupted, the Indian authorities would find it difficult to obtain remittances to meet their obligations in London and would be forced to contract the currency and draw funds off the market to reduce the domestic resources available for financing exports, and thus to force foreigners who required rupees to obtain them by importing currency rather than by borrowing locally. Since the domestic resources used for financing exports were the same as those used in the financing of internal trade, such action would have a markedly disruptive effect on the level of activity throughout the domestic economy, given the lack of flexibility of the internal money market. It was in this way that, in the years after 1913, fluctuations in the world demand for Indian goods and in the degree of foreign confidence in the rupee were to have their biggest impact on the Indian economy as a whole.

The commercial and monetary policy of the Government of India was important in determining the relationship of India to the world economy. But Government action was not the only factor which affected this relationship and its impact was probably not critical, although it did provide the set of institutional linkages that were the most obvious and were the easiest to change. If the particular interests of Government are properly understood, we do not need a conspiracy theory of imperialism to explain why the Government of India took the action it did to influence the working of the internal economy before 1914. The Indian administration was mainly concerned with the day-to-day running of its own business. In financial terms this meant two things only – obtaining adequate revenue to meet its commitments in India and Britain, and securing enough remittance to pay its sterling debts. The management of the other sets of relationships between the Government and its subjects was determined to a large extent by these imperatives. This can be seen clearly in the way in which the Government attempted to influence Indian political development in the late nineteenth and early twentieth centuries.

In 1913 the structure of government in India was still extremely centralised. Nowhere was this more important than in the administration of public finance. The bulk of Indian revenue, including the staple land revenue, was collected in the provinces, but a large proportion of it was sent up to the centre. The history of Indian administration in the late nineteenth century is of a continuing and deepening financial crisis, mainly caused by the instability and decline of the rupee exchange. To meet this crisis the Indian Government had realised in the 1870s that new forms of taxation were required, but the Government of India did not know enough about its subjects to be able to devise and administer effective and safe new taxes. Devolution was the only answer.[50]

This devolution took two forms. Firstly, provincial and local administrations, in the form of provincial governments and district and municipal councils, were encouraged to find new revenue sources and to exercise economy in the spending of these by being granted some autonomy of administration. Secondly, representative Indians, nominated at first and then elected, were associated with these local and provincial administrations. It was thought that Indian members of municipalities and district boards would be more efficient in raising, and more careful in spending, local taxes if they were responsible to an electorate. Thus in the United Provinces each successive financial crisis since the 1860s had resulted in municipal government becoming more representative. Baring and Colvin, the Finance Members of the Government of India in the early 1880s, were the main supporters of Lord Ripon's attempts to make the structure of local government democratic.[51]

The administrative changes of the late nineteenth century never completely solved the financial problems of the Raj. Limited devolution was not enough. Even in 1913, when the provincial administrations retained all receipts from law and justice, education and public works and the provincial rates, plus half the proceeds of the forests, excise, stamp duty, registration fees and licence tax, they had not sufficient funds to release the whole of the land revenue for the use of central Government. Granting administrative responsibility encouraged more, not less, expenditure. Nor could Indians be given political power only as it suited the fiscal needs of the Raj. As Evelyn Baring had pointed out in 1883, 'when once the ball of political reform is set rolling, it is apt to gather speed as it goes on'.[52] By 1913 administrative, financial and political pressures for further devolution were growing apace. While there was not complete financial autonomy in the provinces, the central Government was able to enjoy a share in the land revenue and, in time of crisis, could eat up provincial surpluses to meet its own commitments. This system helped the Government of India to survive the exchange difficulties of the 1890s but, as the Royal Commission upon Decentralisation in India discovered in 1908, the days of 'divided' revenue heads (collected by the provinces and spent by the centre) were numbered.[53]

Perhaps the best way of understanding the particular purposes of the colonial Government in India is to analyse these in terms of an 'imperial factor' that imposed an 'imperial commitment' on the Government of India. We have seen that the Indian Raj was a major asset to the imperial system, but to elucidate British commercial and financial interests in India is not to imagine that these determined British policy directly. British policy in India was not governed by a long-term strategy, but by a series of short-term expedients. Imperial policy-makers were not concerned with India's role in the empire as such, but only with those aspects of it that impinged on the limited obligations of government. The imperial commitment was not cut and dried; it should be thought of more as a series of mental reflex actions in the official mind than as the underlying principle of a coherent policy.

In the years before 1914 India's imperial commitment meant three things in practice: that India should be retained as a market for British exports, which meant that the Government of India should not impose insurmountable barriers, especially tariffs, to the flow of British merchandise to India; that the Indian army be kept available for the imperial cause; and that the Indian administration should ensure that repayment of interest on guaranteed debt bonds was made smoothly and that adequate revenue and remittance was available for the Home Charges. Isolating the imperial factor in India policy allows us to pin-point the fundamental dichotomy of British rule in India. Each prong of its triple commitment cost the Government of India money. The requirements of British exporters obstructed attempts to impose revenue tariffs; the Home Charges and debt repayments were always a strain on revenues, and could be crippling when the rupee exchange was low; the army, with its high percentage of British troops whose pay, pensions and training costs were a great deal higher than those of native sepoys, was another drain on resources, especially when it was overseas playing an imperial role. The Government of India's revenues were limited and the secret of successful Indian government was thought to be low taxation. To keep itself solvent and secure the colonial Government had to balance imperial commitments against the demands of its subjects. Keeping this equilibrium lay at the heart of the problems of the Raj.

Even in 1913 the Government of India's ability to maintain its imperial commitment in full was less securely based than it appeared to be. Bad harvests in India or a depression in world trade which would jeopardise the export surplus, a change in the balance of power in Asia which would place new demands upon the Indian army, a decline in the competitiveness of British exports or the emergence of new rivals for the Indian market, a serious disturbance in the world monetary system or in the exchange rate of the rupee, the need to devote more revenue to buying off the demands of Indian politicians for a share in the resources of Government – all these could upset the delicate balance that the Government of India had struck between maintaining imperial and domestic commitments.

This analysis can be put in another, more direct, way by isolating the pressures that could be put upon the Indian administration by its domestic and imperial partners in colonial government. In 1913 the bulk of revenue was still extracted from the undifferentiated mass of the Indian population in the form of the land revenue, salt tax and various excises. The ability of domestic opinion to force increased expenditure on education, public works, irrigation and so on was small compared to the pressure that London could exert for spending on debt repayment and the army. Only a fundamental change in the administrative and political structure could increase the power of the domestic, and decrease the power of the imperial, pressures on the Government of India's scarce resources. The problems of public finance always involved the Indian Government in a close dialogue with certain groups among its subjects and its masters. Before the First World War the latter were much more clearly articulated than the former, and so tended to dominate the policy-making process.

The Political Economy of the Raj in 1913

The impact that the world economy had had on India in the late nineteenth and early twentieth centuries meant that there were no real pressures on the Indian Government to rethink its relationship to the colonial society. The ability of the indigenous economic and financial institutions to absorb the new pressures, and to take advantage of the new opportunities, produced by the steadily increasing world demand for Indian goods, meant that the concerns of Government could remain limited and non-interventionary. The low profile of Government helped to ensure that formal political development was also limited, and that the attention of politicians was focused on subjects which had little relevance to the bulk of the native population.

This tranquillity was the result of the success with which the Indian economy had adapted itself to external demands, although the advantages that India had gained from this may not have been as great as they could have been in an ideal world. The major political and economic problems that were to bedevil the Government of India's relations with its subjects for the next thirty years were to grow out of the breakdown of the international economic system that had been established by 1913. The new traumas of the inter-war period were to be the result of dramatic further changes in the nature of the world economy and of the failure of the established institutions of political control and economic linkage to re-adapt satisfactorily to new circumstances.

2. India and the World Economy, 1919–1939

The period from the end of the First World War to the outbreak of the Second was one of disturbance for the international economy. These years saw the collapse of the pattern of world trade, investment and multilateral settlement that had become established in the second half of the nineteenth century. The war years of 1914–18 disrupted international trade; the inter-war period saw one major boom (1919–20), one major slump (1920–2) and one of the deepest depressions that the world has known in modern times (1929–33). These traumas hit India along with other countries and helped to alter significantly her relationship with the international economy.

The most striking changes in this period concerned India's participation in international trade. Her percentage share of the value of world trade (in gold dollars) fell from 3·75 in 1913 to 3·5 in 1924, to 3·2 in 1928, to 2·6 in 1932 and to 2·5 in 1937.[1] Equally important were changes in the composition of her trade. Here exports remained remarkably consistent, raw cotton, raw jute, jute bags and cloth and tea dominating throughout the period. Groundnuts were the only new commodity to emerge as an important export while lac and cotton piece-goods both declined considerably. By the mid-1920s the quantities of India's staple exports sold abroad had passed their 1913 levels and, with the exceptions of linseed and cotton piece-goods, this state of affairs continued for the rest of the decade. The depression of the early 1930s hit the whole export trade yet, by 1936, only tea and hides and skins had failed to make up the ground lost since 1928, while mica, linseed, jute bags and cloth and raw cotton had staged notable recoveries. In imports there was a much more striking real and relative decline in major commodities. Cotton piece-goods, which still contributed almost a quarter of the value of total imports in 1920, had declined to only 10 per cent in 1936 and had been overtaken by machinery and millwork as the country's largest single class of imports. Despite the fall of prices, the value of imports of raw cotton and machinery increased between the early 1920s and the late 1930s, while that of cotton piece-goods, sugar, matches and soap shrank significantly. During the 1920s the pattern of Indian imports remained similar to the one which had been established by 1913, while the poor years of the early 1930s depressed the quantities of all imports. By the late 1930s the amounts of imported cotton piece-goods, sugar, soap and cement had fallen still further, while iron and steel, matches and kerosene had stagnated. Only paper and raw cotton were now above their 1928 levels and only paper, machinery, dyes and motor cars had recovered from their depressed state.[2]

The causes of the changes in the quantity, value and composition of India's import trade in the inter-war period were complex, but a simple analysis of the breakdown of classes of goods suggests one promising line of approach. In 1925–6, 54 per cent of India's imports were consumer goods (food, drink, tobacco, apparel, cutlery, certain instruments and apparatus, paper, textiles and some vehicles), 15·6 per cent were raw materials (hides and skins, rubber, cotton, silk, wool, hemp, timber, gums, resin, oils, dyes and textile yarns) and 23·2 per cent were capital goods (electrical instruments, machinery and millwork, printing machinery, railway plant and rolling stock, certain vehicles, metal manufactures and some hardware) with the rest unclassified. In 1931–2 these percentages were 51·6, 23·4 and 21·7; in 1935–6 they were 48·9, 23·8 and 26·1 and in 1938–9 they were 33·0, 28·4 and 25·9.[3] These figures give some indication that by the 1930s, in common with a number of other countries, India was transforming her relationship with the international economy by import-substitution in consumer goods, drawing more heavily instead on outside supplies of raw materials and capital goods.[4] Other evidence supports this conclusion. Table 2.1 gives an idea of crude changes in indigenous production based on figures for Indian output and total imports in six important commodities. Indian industries as a whole, although stagnant for much of the 1920s, suffered relatively little during the depression and made striking advances after 1934. The available statistics of comparative industrial production are not very reliable but, as Table 2.2 shows, they indicate considerable development in India during the 1930s. By 1945 India was the tenth largest producer of manufactured goods in the world. This is not to say that she had

TABLE 2.1. India's Industrial Progress in Import-Substitution 1919–1936

	1919 % Indian produced	1936 % Indian produced
Cotton goods		
grey and white	57·6	85·3
coloured	69·6	74·1
Sugar	12·0	96·0
Steel	14·0[a]	70·0
Paper	54·0[b]	78·0
Cement	51·0	95·4
Tinplate	24·5[c]	71·4[d]

[a] 1920; [b] 1924; [c] 1923; [d] 1937

Source: N. S. R. Sastry, *A Statistical Survey of India's Industrial Development* (Bombay, 1947); Sir Harry Townend, *A History of Shaw Wallace & Co.* (Calcutta, 1965); W. A. Johnson, *The Steel Industry of India* (Cambridge, Mass., 1966).

TABLE 2.2. Indices of Industrial Production, India and World 1920–1938
(1925–9 = 100)

	India	World		India	World
1920	82·4	68·9	1930	100·7	101·6
1921	78·4	59·9	1931	108·1	90·5
1922	81·1	73·5	1932	108·1	80·1
1923	81·1	77·2	1933	116·7	89·9
1924	92·6	82·0	1934	132·4	100·8
1925	91·9	89·2	1935	143·0	114·2
1926	100·7	93·5	1936	150·7	131·6
1927	105·4	99·4	1937	163·5	144·7
1928	92·6	104·8	1938	166·8	135·0
1929	109·5	113·3			

Source: League of Nations, *Industrialization and Foreign Trade* (1945), pp. 140–1.

achieved her full potential in terms of her vast population and raw material resources: even by 1947 the value of average per capita output of manufactured goods was a quarter that of Egypt and one tenth that of Mexico.[5] The average annual growth of the workforce in industrial establishments was only 1 per cent from 1921 to 1931, although this figure rose to 4 to 5 per cent for 1932 to 1937.[6] The 1930s were not a boom period for all sectors of Indian industry. Estimates of the real value of imports of machinery and millwork suggest that investment in new plant for the cotton textile industry was never as high in this decade as it had been during the restocking booms of the early and late 1920s,[7] while iron and steel and other capital goods industries suffered from the cutback in Government expenditure on capital account during and after the Great Depression. The variations in industrial production in major industries are given in Table 2.3. No figures for the value of Indian industrial output are available for the inter-war period, but in 1946, the first year for which there are such figures, Indian production was heavily biased towards consumer goods – the cotton, sugar and vegetable oil industries supplying 62 per cent of output and the iron and steel and engineering industries supplying only 10·5 per cent.[8] It seems likely that the production of consumer goods was even more important before 1939 – in 1948, 58 per cent of industrial workers were employed in making finished consumer goods, 16 per cent in making capital goods and 26 per cent in intermediates, while in 1936 these percentages had been 67, 15 and 18.[9]

TABLE 2.3. Indices of Indian Industrial Production 1925–1937 (1925 = 100)

	1931	1937
Cotton	111	152
Jute	81	90
Sugar	128	584
Iron and steel	84	133
Paper	119	168
Cement	121	222
Coal	92	103

Source: V. Anstey, *The Economic Development of India* (London, 1952), p. 519.

Industrial development in India was helped by the disruption of the supply of overseas manufactured goods which resulted partly from war conditions and partly from the fiscal difficulties and political pressures of the inter-war years. During the First World War the export-orientated jute and tanning industries suffered a check, while the cotton industry began to produce more for the home market and the iron and steel, cement, engineering and chemical industries expanded somewhat. In the inter-war period there was an increasing reliance by central Government on revenue raised from customs, while the official response to pressures for tariff protection and changes in Government stores policy to favour Indian manufacturers also gave a significant boost to industrialisation by altering the comparative prices of indigenous and imported goods.[10] The expansion of industrial enterprises was not entirely due to this, however. It was also linked to important structural changes within the domestic economy. To understand these we must now consider the impact of the decline of India's international trade on other sectors of the economy.

By contrast with the industrial sector, the period was a consistently difficult one for Indian agriculture. Since production remained fairly constant while the prices of food and raw materials fell more than those of manufactured goods, the external terms of trade moved against India and the internal terms of trade moved against the agrarian sector. Yet, although the rural economy ran into difficulties, it is hard to make broad generalisations about changes in the level of purchasing power within the internal economy. The profitability of Indian agriculture was not determined by a single factor; there was considerable variation in the impact of the depression of the early 1930s on different regions, and on different producers within the same region. As Table 2.4 shows, it is not easy to find a simple correlation between the fall in prices and other indicators of internal economic activity. Disruptions in external and internal markets seem to have had only a limited effect on the pattern of crop sowing and production which, for major crops at least, remained remarkably constant throughout the period.[11] Even the cultivators of linseed, sesame seed, cotton seed and mustard seed, the commodities that suffered the greatest decline in external demand in the 1920s and early 1930s, appear to have found satisfactory alternative markets, while the decline in groundnut exports in the late 1930s was balanced by an increase in the exports of manufactured groundnut oil.[12] In Bengal a degree of substitution of rice for jute cultivation was noted at times when the jute industry was heavily depressed;[13] elsewhere some switching between cotton and groundnut cultivation took place following changes in price levels[14] and the production of sugar increased, especially in the 1930s. Yet, overall, the picture is one of remarkable stability, not

TABLE 2.4 Indices of Internal Economic Activity 1920–1939
(1928–9 = 100)

	1920–1	1923–4	1926–7	1929–30	1932–3	1935–6	1938–9
Wholesale prices:[a]							
Calcutta	123[b]	118	102	97	63	63	65
Bombay	136[b]	124	102	99	75	68	69
Retail price of food	128[b]	88	103	106	54	54	55
Railway traffic[c]	80	88	99	98	75	93	101
Per capita consumption:							
Cotton[d]	92	88	111	117	121	119	121
Kerosene	78	98	97	115	94	86	91
Sugar	na	56	79	101	76	78	78
Tea	82	82	82	112	100	129	159

[a] in calendar years (viz. 1920–1 is 1920); 1928 = 100.
[b] 1921.
[c] quantity of goods carried per mile of track open.
[d] piece-goods only.

Note: 1928–9 has been selected as base as the last pre-depression year.

Source: Calculated from figures in *Statistical Abstracts for British India* and *Recent Social and Economic Trends in India* (1946).

least in the proportion of Indian production of staple crops that was exported.[15] The only major crops which commanded significantly increased acreage in the 1930s, as compared to the 1920s, were those – sugarcane and groundnuts – which came to enjoy a new domestic demand as inputs to expanding local industries.[16]

Fluctuations in the performance of the world economy made their deepest impact on the trading and credit-supply networks that had linked India to the international economy in 1913. Before the First World War the supply of capital and credit for agriculture, trade and industry was provided by a money market which fell into three imperfectly integrated sectors. Funds accumulated by the external trading sector, and by the indigenous bankers and moneylenders, were often removed from circulation at the end of the trading season. In bad years, decreased world demand for Indian currency could have a disproportionately large impact on credit rates throughout the economy because the monetary policy of Government, and its readiness to expand or contract the money supply, was largely determined by the Secretary of State's foreign currency requirements.

As the world economy faltered towards depression in the late 1920s pressure on the marketing and credit networks in India became increasingly severe. The decline in India's terms of trade sapped her visible export surplus, while uncertainties about the future exchange rate of the rupee discouraged foreign investors, large export/import firms and the exchange banks from holding surplus funds in rupees. This diminution of commodity exports and capital imports put the funding of the Government of India's commitments in London at risk. To transfer money to London the Indian authorities now had to remit through the currency reserves, sell sterling exchange to restore confidence in the exchange rate and raise interest rates to discourage the withdrawal of investment and to encourage the export of fresh funds to India.[17] Remitting through the reserves meant withdrawing currency notes from circulation in India and using as revenue the bullion and securities held in London to back these notes, while selling sterling for rupees also contracted the circulating currency in India. The result of these measures was a fall in the money supply of about 6 per cent in each of the years 1929–30 and 1930–1.[18] Their impact on internal credit networks and on business activity in general was probably more intense than these figures would suggest. Any crisis of external finance affected the internal economy by reducing the seasonal inflow of money and credit that normally took place through the sale of sterling for rupee drafts, while official measures to discourage currency speculation and disinvestment further decreased the finance available to the Westernised and, to a lesser extent, the indigenous sectors for use in internal trade. In addition, monetary stringency had a direct effect on local industry. One of the residual problems of Indian manufacturers before 1914, and in the 1920s as well, had been that of obtaining working capital. The rates at which such short-term funds were advanced was dependent on other money rates and, during the trading season each year (which was also the time at which many factories needed extra capital to purchase raw materials), interest rates rose sharply.[19] As the world economy became depressed Indian industry was hit by the tightening of credit as well as by the loss of the purchasing power of its internal and external customers.

The contraction of credit that accompanied the depression everywhere was more short-lived in India than in many other countries. In December 1931 the Imperial Bank Of India bank rate reached a peak of 8 per cent; by July 1932 it was down to 4 per cent, its lowest level for five years, and from February 1933 until the end of our period it was never over 3·5 per cent. The central

Government Three-Month Treasury Bill rate behaved in the same way, falling from over 7 per cent in December 1931 to less than 3 per cent by July 1932 and not exceeding this level for the rest of the decade.[20] The explanation for this lies in the differing reactions of the various sectors of the internal economy to the impact of worldwide depression. The most striking development of the period was the export of substantial amounts of privately-owned gold from September 1931 onwards, which turned India into a net exporter of precious metals for the rest of the 1930s. The flow of imported gold which had been such a feature of the Indian economy before the depression was now reversed; between 1931 and 1939 net exports of treasure were worth Rs. 349·41 crores.

These gold exports have often been regarded simply as enforced disinvestment by the agrarian population, straightforward proof of the fact that the depression was forcing the rural economy to draw on all its accumulated resources to make ends meet. Clearly there is some truth in this. A part at least of the gold exports (although it is impossible to know how large a part) was the result of 'distress' selling by landlords and tenants to meet fixed demands for rent and land revenue at a time when the market for their produce was disrupted. Yet it is also true that there were substantial profits to be made from the gold trade. Once the rupee and sterling had been devalued against gold in September 1931 Indian gold could be sold abroad for considerably more than had been paid for it even one year before. The fall in internal prices increased these returns in real terms. Thus a number of observers, many of them in the Government of India, saw the gold exports as the result of speculation, or of a rational desire to maximise profits from this new source.

Estimating the proportion of distress to speculative sales of gold is not germane to our purpose here. The more important point is simply that bullion exports did not represent a gift from India to the world economy, but were paid for in rupees and, ultimately, in foreign currency. To the extent that gold holdings had been used as security (implicit or explicit) for agrarian and trading credit, bullion exports can be said to represent a disinvestment in agriculture and in trade; but such sales did not diminish, and may well have increased, the total available purchasing power in India. Some of the returns from gold sales were simply used to pay land revenue, or the interest on rural indebtedness, and to maintain consumption of staple items. On the other hand, some also seem to have been reinvested in the non-agricultural economy or held as cash, mostly in the form of bank deposits. The available information on the direction of savings in the period is too sketchy to produce a comprehensive statistical estimate of any change but, as Table 2.5 indicates, substantial increases can be seen in the level of deposits in Indian joint-stock banks and co-operative banks, and in small savings in post office savings banks and cash certificates. It is also interesting that the bank deposit element of money supply increased consistently after 1931.[21] Bank deposits were held by manufacturing and trading firms as well as by individuals, but the impression remains that the post-depression period saw a significant rise in small savings and in the supply of short-term, liquid funds within the Westernised banking system.

TABLE 2.5. Partial Estimate of Allocation of Internal Savings in India 1930–39 (in Rs. lakhs)

	1930	1933	1936	1939	% rise 1930–9
Total private cash deposited with banks:					
Imperial bank[a]	76,60	74,13	78,80	87,84	14.7
Joint-stock banks	63,25	71,67	98,14	100,73	59.3
Exchange banks	68,11	70,78	75,23	74,08	8.8
Co-operative banks	12,57	17,12	20,57	22,94	82.5
Paid-up capital of joint-stock companies	286,34	286,47	302,63	290,39	1.4
Post Office savings bank balances and cash certificates	72,13	99,04	133,23	141,43	96.1
Premium income of life insurance companies	7,96	9,63	13,02	14,26	79.1
Government of India funded rupee debt	405,11	446,89	426,18	438,53	8.2
Net private imports of treasure	24,43	−57,23	−14,50	−30,28	—

[a] private deposits only.

Source: Calculated from figures in *Statistical Abstract for British India 1930–1 to 1939–40* (Cmd. 6441 of 1943), Tables 165, 264 and *Banking and Monetary Statistics of India*, pp. 369, 378, 784, 881 and 922.

The most important effect of the new liquidity brought about by the gold sales was on the financing of foreign trade, with the implications that this had for credit supply within the internal money market. After 1931 gold bullion became India's most important export commodity, contributing about 30 per cent of the total value of exports from 1931–2 to 1934–5 and between 8 and 19 per cent thereafter. The flow of funds to India to pay for these exports enabled the Government to meet its commitments in London without difficulty and provided the exchange stability necessary for a cheap money policy. The abundance of funds, and the ease with which credit could now be supplied and obtained in the Westernised banking sector also helped to meet the requirements of Indian industry for working capital, and probably for block capital as well. No quantitative estimates of the extent of this change can be made, but it is striking that, in contrast to the many complaints about the reluctance of joint-stock banks to lend to industry in the late 1920s,[22] by 1952 over one-third of all such banks' deposits were being loaned to industrial concerns.[23] Much had happened to the Indian economy between the 1930s and the 1950s but it seems possible that this new trend began before the Second World War.

In contrast to the Westernised sector, the indigenous bankers suffered a decline during and after the depression. Quantitative estimates are again impossible, but the qualitative evidence is suggestive. One authority has asserted that, in 1930, indigenous bankers financed 90 per cent of India's internal trade.[24] A contemporary expert, V. Ramadas Pantalu, claimed in a minute of dissent to the report of the Indian Central Banking Enquiry Committee of 1931:

> The real banking agency of the people still lies outside the modern banking organisation of the country. Agriculture, rural trade and rural industry derive their finance almost exclusively from the indigenous agency. So do small traders and handicraft industrialists in urban areas. The finance thus derived is considerable and enters very largely into the economic life of the vast rural and urban population who depend solely on it.[25]

The majority report of the same committee reached much the same conclusion:

> We are impressed by the fact that out of 2500 towns in India, joint-stock banks and their branches exist in less than 400 places, and for banking facilities elsewhere, agriculturalists, traders, merchants and small industrialists have to depend largely on

indigenous bankers and local money-lenders. In many provinces, even in localities where a joint-stock bank or its branch exists, the indigenous local bankers continue to render valuable service in connection with the financing of internal trade and middle-sized and small industries and remittance work. A large section of the community is thus still dependent on the indigenous bankers for the financial facilities it requires.[26]

The Central Banking Enquiry Committee had collected its evidence in the late 1920s, and no new survey of the financing of internal trade was carried out until the All-India Rural Credit Survey reported in 1954. By this time a significant change had taken place. As the authors of the Survey pointed out:

> We have seen that, as part of the superstructure of private credit for trade in commodities, commercial banks have assumed a role which is now far ahead of that of indigenous bankers[27] . . . it would appear that the prominence of moneylenders as a major source of credit for trade in agricultural commodities is confined to the largely non-commercialised areas where commercial banking activity has not made much advance.[28]

Of over three thousand cases of borrowing by traders in agrarian produce recorded by the Survey, 48 per cent were made from commercial banks, 45 per cent from moneylenders and 7 per cent from indigenous bankers.[29] Of nearly one thousand urban moneylenders who reported using borrowed funds, one-third had obtained them from commercial banks and only one-ninth from indigenous bankers.[30] This evidence calls severely into question the conclusion of such scholars as J. S. G. Wilson that indigenous bankers and moneylenders still financed 75 to 90 per cent of the total internal trade of India in the mid-1950s.[31]

It is impossible to estimate how much of this important structural change in the Indian money market had taken place by 1939. In so far as the decline of indigenous bankers can be mapped by the advance of joint-stock banking institutions, some indications of developments in the 1930s can be obtained from Table 2.6, which shows that although by 1939 joint-stock banks had not developed as far as they were to do by the time of the Rural Credit Survey, they had advanced significantly over their spread in 1929, the year that the Banking Enquiry Committee had taken its evidence. The

TABLE 2.6. Branches of Commercial Banks in India 1929–1952

	Imperial Bank of India	Large joint-stock banks		Small joint-stock banks	
	Branches	Number	Branches	Number	Branches
1929	187	26	399	25	122
1930	189	24	340	30	145
1931	189	26	346	26	125
1932	191	27	368	29	136
1933	194	28	404	29	167
1934	204	31	460	34	168
1935	212	32	520	30	160
1936	249	35	674	35	215
1937	305	35	708	57	361
1938	348	35	660	61	415
1939	372	49[a]	949[a]	105[a]	545[a]
1952	410	132	2607	131	615

[a] 1940.

Source: *Banking and Monetary Statistics of India*, p. 282.

increase in the number and capital of banking and loan companies was a feature of company development in the 1930s[32] and, as we have seen, the amounts of savings that were deposited in such banks also rose during the decade.

It is likely that some of the new commercial bankers of the 1930s were the indigenous bankers of the 1920s who had adapted to new circumstances. This process had begun even before the depression; in 1928 the Chettiar banking community of South India converted part of their indigenous banking, trading and moneylending business into the Bank of Chettinad Ltd., a joint-stock bank with a paid-up capital of a crore of rupees.[33] Evidence of such continuities of personnel does not contradict our conclusion that a major change was taking place in the Indian money market during the 1930s, for the importance of that change was in the institutions that composed the market, not in the individuals who participated in them. Two general conclusions can be drawn about this process: that because of the impact of a depressed world demand for Indian produce on the internal credit networks the money market in India became much better integrated than it had been before, and that there was a definite switch of internal investment out of agriculture and trade and into industry.

The picture of the dislocation of the Indian money markets presented in the Central Banking Enquiry Committee report is similar to the one that we have already painted for the period before 1914. The committee found the money market of the late 1920s to be 'loosely organized'[34] and commented that:

> The ultimate ideal must be the mobilisation of the whole of the floating resources of the country into one large pool into which bills can find their way with as little delay and with the intervention of as few intermediaries as possible. At present the resources more closely resemble a stream which is constantly being blocked by obstacles preventing a free flow of bills.[35]

The principal blockages were the independence of the Westernised and indigenous banking sectors, the lack of control by any central institution over the activities of either the joint-stock banks or the native bankers and the division of control over the supply of currency and credit between the Imperial Bank and the Government of India.[36] The solution was thought to lie in the establishment of a central bank, expansion of the activities of the joint-stock banks and a strengthening of the 'natural link' between the two money markets:

> ... a steady stream of trade bills endorsed by reliable firms or discount houses which are in touch with both markets, and are able to meet the needs at one end of the merchant who prefers the elastic methods of bazaar finance, and to take advantage at the other end of entry into the central finance and money markets.[37]

The structural problems of the Indian money market had not been completely overcome by the 1950s, much less by 1939. Although the Reserve Bank of India was set up in 1935 the activities of indigenous bankers were effectively outside its control, while even joint-stock banks were reluctant to take advantage of its re-discounting facilities.[38] Yet, by 1939, some of the conditions that the Central Banking Enquiry Committee had prescribed as beneficial to the integration of the internal economy had been met, by accident as much as by design. The establishment of a central bank, and the healthiness of India's balance of payments surplus in commodities (thanks to the gold exports), meant that internal credit policy could be orientated towards meeting the needs of the internal economy, rather than those of external finance. The expansion of the activities of the joint-stock banks, and the contraction of those of indigenous bankers organised along traditional lines, gave a greater institutional uniformity to the internal money market. The profits of agriculture past (in the form of money realised from gold sales) and present were increasingly lodged with the Westernised banking institutions which now formed a fairly coherent whole and which were more prepared than had been the peasant, the landlord, the trader or the indigenous banker to invest them in other sectors of the economy.

In addition to these changes in the structure of the money market and in the relative importance of the various institutions that composed it, there is other evidence of a switch from investment in the agrarian to the industrial sector in the 1930s. Before the depression the profits of agriculture tended to remain in the rural economy. Some expansion of small-scale industry for processing agrarian produce had taken place but, in general, the agrarian surplus was ploughed back into agriculture and rural moneylending. As one observer of the rural economy in the late 1920s wrote, 'if they [rich landlords] are not too avaricious and pay only an ordinary amount of care in choosing their customers, they can make higher profits in this rural banking than in any other business'.[39] The decline in the profitability of agriculture and the disruption of established marketing networks that resulted from the depression provided an incentive to diversify investment. Land, as investment or security, ceased to be attractive since much of the produce of such land could not easily be sold at a profit. From the mid-1930s onwards in Madras, for example, landlords and others began to invest increasingly in industry, especially in sugar and cotton, the Chettiars and Naidus diversifying from trading and indigenous banking into cotton mills; company flotations boomed and a stock exchange was established. In the United Provinces and Bihar a number of the rural elite joined forces with urban interests to establish sugar mills and other industries.[40] In the country as a whole between 1931 and 1937 the paid-up capital of joint-stock companies increased by over 10 per cent, while the number of registered companies at work went up by more than one third.

In comparing India's relationship to the international economy in 1939 with that which had existed in 1913 we can see that a definite qualitative change had taken place in the inter-war period.

By the eve of the Second World War the Indian economy was a great deal less 'colonial' than it had been twenty years before, using the classic definition of a colonial economy as one which has no manufacturing industry of its own but which exchanges national primary produce against foreign manufactures through international trade.[41] This change came about not simply because India achieved some isolation from the world economy thanks to the breakdown of international trade during the Great Depression,[42] but rather because a decline in the level of world demand for India's commodity exports (other than gold) damaged the traditional trading and banking institutions that had been able to adapt so well before 1914 to the increasing integration of the Indian and international economies. International economic forces were still as potent agents of economic change as they had been in the late nineteenth and early twentieth centuries, but they now acted as destroyers of those institutional networks that linked the Indian and world economies that they had helped to build up in the earlier period. India's relative disengagement from the international economy in the 1930s was one result of this destruction.

These changes had a profound effect on Indian and imperial politics and government. Their impact on the relationship between the imperial government in London and the Indian Government in New Delhi and between the Government of India and its subjects are dealt with in the next two chapters. The remainder of this chapter will consider a series of ancillary points – the ways in which the economic changes of the inter-war period affected India's role in the multilateral pattern of settlements, the compatibility of the Indian and British economies and the paths followed by expatriate and foreign capital.

Before 1914 India had played an important role in the international pattern of settlements, providing a market for commodity exports and a source of invisible earnings that enabled Britain to meet a large proportion of her balance of payments deficit with the rest of the world, while herself enjoying a considerable visible surplus, and no significant invisible deficit, with other areas. Overall, between 1900 and 1913 at least, India ran a small current balance of payments deficit (visibles minus invisibles) which was made good by the export of capital from Britain. The broad outline of India's pattern of settlements remained much the same in the 1920s, but changed radically during the 1930s. Between 1921–2 and 1929–30

India had an overall current balance of payments deficit of Rs. 224·35 crores, but from 1930–1 to 1938–9 she had a current surplus of Rs. 7·32 crores. Her balance of commodity transactions surplus rose slightly during the latter period, while her balance of service transactions deficit fell. Breakdowns of these figures reveal that the value of India's commodity surplus in the 1930s was based on a fall in the value of her imports more than on a rise in the value of her exports (including treasure), while the amount of her invisible imports of freight and insurance charges and interest payments all declined significantly.[43]

These changes also affected India's balance of payments with Britain. Assuming that the proportion of service and non-commercial transactions remained constant throughout the period, the decline in freight charges and interest payments must have affected Britain's current invisible exports to India during the 1930s. A more obvious change occurred in commodity trade. The decline in the value of India's imports especially affected goods sent from Britain, which was also the main market for gold bullion, India's major export of the 1930s, although much of this was then re-exported either through private trade or official channels. In each year from 1919 to 1930 Britain had a visible surplus with India totalling £219·4 million for the twelve years. In 1931, for the first time since the 1880s, Britain imported more from India than she exported to her and, between 1931 and 1938, ran up a total commodity trade deficit of £79·5 million.[44] This new development was the result both of the decreasing importance of Britain as a supplier of Indian imports and of the increasing importance of Britain as a market for Indian exports, despite the attempts of the British Government, at the 1932 Imperial Economic Conference and elsewhere, to increase the share of British goods in the imports of other imperial countries.[45]

During the 1920s India continued to play her traditional role in the international pattern of settlements, running up visible trade surpluses with most areas of the world to meet a visible and invisible deficit with Britain. By the late 1930s, however, the situation had changed considerably and India was using visible surpluses with Britain and the rest of the industrialised world to meet a visible deficit with her suppliers of industrial raw materials in Asia, Africa and the Middle East as well as to meet a reduced invisible deficit with Britain.[46] The only two industrialised nations with which India now had regular visible deficits were Germany and Japan, the former an important supplier of capital goods as well as of consumer goods. Even before the depression India's capacity to help Britain to meet her visible deficit with the rest of the world had declined from its pre-war level. Although India continued to be one of the few countries with which Britain maintained a visible surplus in the 1920s, the proportion of her overall visible deficit made good by exports to India, and the proportion of her invisible surplus which was supplied by India, diminished considerably.[47]

As important as the decline of India's role in Britain's multilateral pattern of settlements with the rest of the world was the decreased marketability of staple British exports in India. In 1913 India had provided the largest single market for British exports of cotton piece-goods, iron and steel manufactures and general and electrical machinery. In 1936–8 India was still the largest single market for British exports of cotton piece-goods, but the percentage she consumed had fallen from nearly 50 to under 14 per cent. For general machinery the picture was similar – India remained the largest single market, but her consumption had dropped from over 20 per cent to under 15 per cent; for electrical goods and apparatus India was now the second largest market with a percentage consumption falling from 13·4 to 11·5 per cent of total British exports; for iron and steel manufactures she was now the third largest market, the percentage falling from 17 to 8 per cent. Only in chemicals had the trend been reversed, India taking 12·4 per cent of total British exports in 1936–8, and representing the largest single market for such goods, as against only 3 per cent in 1913.[48]

The decline of British exports to India during the inter-war period was the result of a number of changes in the British, Indian and international economies. The most obvious developments were the growth of protected import-substitution in India and the decreasing competitiveness of British goods against both indigenous manufacturers and foreign competitors. As Table 2.7 illustrates, British goods were losing ground in the 1920s as well as in the 1930s. In Britain, as in India, the inter-war years saw a definite shift in the pattern of economic activity and in the relation of production for the internal market to that for the external one. Britain's share of world trade in exports fell from 13·9 per cent in 1913 to 10·8 per cent in 1929 to 10·2 per cent in 1938, while her share of world trade in manufacturing fell from 25·4 per cent to 20·1 to 19·1 in the same period. Foreign trade represented 58·8 per cent of British national income in 1911–13, while new overseas investment represented 9·5

India and the World Economy, 1919–1939

TABLE 2.7. Percentage Share of British Goods in India's Imports 1913–1938

	1913–14	1928–9	1938–9
Cotton piece-goods	94	79	32
Iron and steel	78	56	50
Other metal manufacturers	46	34	34
Hardware and cutlery	56	26	29
Electrical machinery	79	66	57
General machinery	92	76	57
Railway locomotives and carriages	95	88	61
Motor vehicles	66	15	30
Chemicals	75	59	57

Source: Calculated from figures in *Statistical Abstract for the British Empire, Statistical Abstract for British India*.

per cent of gross national product; in the 1920s these percentages were 49·3 and 2·4 respectively, while for 1930–8 they were 33·9 and −1 (representing net disinvestment overseas).[49]

Much has been written on the decline of Britain's staple, export-orientated industries in the inter-war years and of the rise of 'new' industries which relied far less on overseas markets.[50] Some of these industries – vehicles, chemicals and electrical appliances and apparatus for example – were important to Britain's overall export performance in the late 1920s and the 1930s, and some of these industries did, as we have seen, find an important market for their goods in India. However, it would be wrong to conclude that the British economy in the late 1930s was the same staple-based, export-orientated structure that it had been in 1913, with only the nature of the staples having changed. Even granted the export performance of the new industries in the Indian market, the growth sectors of British manufacturing industry in the inter-war period were significantly less dependent on production for the less developed imperial economies than they had been in 1913. Table 2.8 is an attempt to show, in simplified form, the declining importance of the export trade in manufacturers in general, and of such exports to India in particular, to British economic activity in the inter-war period.

Changes in the amount and composition of British exports of long-term capital to India mirrored those in the export of commodities,

TABLE 2.8. British Production, Total Exports and Exports to India by Major Heads 1924 and 1935 (by current value in £ million)

	UK production Value	Total exports Value	% of production	Exports to India Value	% of production
1924					
Chemicals	220	25	11.4	0.9	0.4
Metal manufactures	280	96	34.3	17	6.1
Engineering[a]	285	64	22.5	12	4.2
Cotton goods[b]	367	199	54.2	50	13.6
Other	2595	417	16.1	11.1	0.4
TOTAL	3747	801	21.4	91	2.4
1935					
Chemicals	206	21	10.2	1.3	0.6
Metal manufactures	245	56	22.9	4	1.6
Engineering[a]	343	54	15.7	7	2.0
Cotton goods[b]	144	60	41.7	8	5.6
Other	2605	235	9.0	17.7	0.7
TOTAL	3543	426	12.0	38	1.1

[a] electrical and mechanical engineering products plus railway plant and ships.
[b] woven goods and yarn; figure for cotton exports to India includes yarn made from all types of material.
Source: Calculated from figures in *U.K. Censuses of Production; Statistical Abstract for British India; Statistical Abstract for the British Empire*; B. R. Mitchell and P. Deane, *Abstract of British Historical Statistics* (Cambridge, 1962).

although the information available is a good deal less reliable. A number of estimates were made at the time of the extent of foreign private investment in India in the 1920s and 1930s, but none of them is better than informed guess-work and their variations in scope and interpretation mean that no two can be used for comparative purposes.[51] The only useful figures that show changes in British overseas and expatriate public and private investment in India between the wars are those compiled by Dr A. K. Banerji, as given in Table 2.9. It should be noted that the figures for public investment in this table are somewhat misleading. The total amount of Government of India sterling debt did not rise smoothly throughout the period, such investment being concentrated in the early 1920s and the early 1930s. A small amount of sterling public debt – £35.7 million net – was, in fact, repaid between 1934–5 and 1938–9.[52]

The figures for private British overseas and expatriate investment show this to have been virtually stagnant over our period. It is

India and the World Economy, 1919–1939

TABLE 2.9. Nominal British and Expatriate Investment in India 1921 and 1938 (in £ million)

	1921	1938
Public		
Government sterling debt[a]	169·8	262·5
Railway annuities etc.[a]	109·7	72·3
Local government loans	26·2	37·4
Indian government loans[b]	6·3	6·4
Total	312·0	378·6
Private		
Plantations	21·2	32·5
Oil	10·9	22·3
Railways	31·4	19·8
Public utilities	9·8	17·9
Mines	20·6	16·9
Inland shipping	3·8	5·3
Jute	8·3	7·4
Cotton	5·9	4·8
Engineering	3·8	5·1
Sugar	0·9	1·6
Managing agencies	30·0	37·5
Miscellaneous	13·4	13·6
Total[c]	185·0	218·3
GRAND TOTAL	497·0	596·9

[a] assuming all of this to be British-owned.
[b] excluding expatriate holdings of government rupee debt.
[c] including an allowance for unlisted investment. Sterling converted into rupees at £1 = Rs. 13·33.

Source: A. K. Banerji, *India's Balance of Payments 1921–2 to 1938–9* (London, 1963), pp. 81, 171, 175.

interesting to compare maximum figures for industrial investment (plantations, oil, mines, jute, cotton, engineering, sugar and miscellaneous), which showed a rise of only £17 million between 1921 and 1938, with an estimated £144 million new investment in Indian industry (calculated on the basis of the value of imported machinery and millwork) in the same period.[53] Although by 1930 India and Ceylon had become the second largest repository of British overseas investment, only when substantial government loans were floated in London did new capital issues for India represent a significant proportion of the money raised on the London market in any year of this period.[54] The calculation of private investment given in Table 2.9 is based on a number of assumptions which lead to an over-emphasis on investment in a traditional manner (through Managing Agencies) in traditional sectors (jute, coal, plantations, etc.). It is important to appreciate the extent to which such enterprises were, in fact, failing to attract new foreign investment in the inter-war period, but such enterprises were not the only ones in which British capital was employed by the 1930s. As a recent survey has shown,[55] an important qualitative feature of Indian industrial development on the eve of the Second World War was the extent of direct investment by British manufacturing firms in Indian subsidiaries, largely in new sectors of industry such as chemicals, paints and electrical apparatus. By 1939 a number of major British firms, which had previously had no factories in India, had established manufacturing subsidiaries, among them Associated Electrical Industries, British Oxygen, Dunlop, Guest, Keen and Nettlefolds, Imperial Chemical Industries, Metal Box, Philips, Turner Newall and Unilever. The extent of such investment cannot be accurately assessed, although it does not seem to have been very large, nor is it clear how important each of these companies thought their involvement in India to be. What these developments do show is that the loosening of economic ties between Britain and India represented by the decline of traditional outlets for British investment was balanced to some extent by the increased involvement of new types of British investors operating through new forms and in new fields of enterprise.

Between 1919 and 1939 the performance of established British-based companies dealing with India was mixed. There is some evidence to suggest that several of the major firms that had dominated India's foreign trade before the First World War began to restrict their operations in the 1920s. In 1919 the British Trade Commissioner was already expressing disquiet at the lack of enterprise being shown by British expatriate entrepreneurs and the implications of this for the successful marketing of British exports:

> The attitude of the old-established conservative and yet powerful British merchant houses in Calcutta and Bombay, through whose hands in the past both the export and the import trade of the country was transacted, has undergone a gradual change of

recent years. During the war . . . they have amassed considerable fortunes without any particular effort, and are consequently now inclined to confine their attentions to the most lucrative and least troublesome branches of trade. This is especially true of Calcutta, where the activities of the large Clive Street merchants are almost exclusively devoted to the management of jute mills and other industrial works, to the handling of shipping and insurance agencies, and to the shipment of Indian produce and manufactures. . . . The large engineering firms are also now so interested in managing local engineering works that they cannot be expected to pay the same attention to the interests of those United Kingdom engineers whom they represent, and in certain cases their manufacturing and their distributing interests clash.[56]

Even by this early date the defects in the marketing networks of British manufacturers were providing opportunities for their rivals. Before 1914 German export firms had used their assured profits in the hides and skins trade, brought about by a successful ring in this commodity, to extend favourable credit terms to purchasers of German imports; during the First World War the Japanese used the network of contacts built up in exporting raw cotton as the basis for the supply of manufactured cotton imports, while American engineering firms, prospering as a result of technical collaboration agreements with the Tata Iron and Steel Company, dominated the market for public utility enterprises.[57]

The fluctuations in commodity prices and the general commercial uncertainty of the inter-war period encouraged a further disengagement by the major foreign trading firms from the Indian internal economy. Although these firms remained the main linkages between the Indian producer and the foreign consumer for many of India's staple exports, their position was being challenged in some commodities – jute, for example – by Indian rivals. In addition there was a noticeable trend for foreign firms, even those continental European ones which had developed extensive direct purchasing networks in the interior before 1914, to retreat to the port cities and major centres, leaving the increasingly speculative business of buying and moving crops up-country to Indian agents and associates.[58] On the other hand, there is some evidence that foreign banking firms were becoming involved more closely with the internal economy at the same time as the trading firms were disengaging themselves. During the 1920s, for example, the Chartered Bank (an exchange bank) bought a controlling interest in the Allahabad Bank (a joint-stock bank) and used this to expand its business in domestic banking.[59] By the late 1930s the exchange banks were an important source of loan and debenture capital for the manufacturing subsidiaries of British companies set up in new sectors of industry.[60]

The fortunes of the large British expatriate firms at work in India in 1913 were also mixed during the inter-war period. Some of the major Calcutta business houses took advantage of the new opportunities for industrial expansion in the 1930s, especially in civil engineering and steel manufacture, and also set up insurance firms and investment companies. The period as a whole witnessed a number of mergers as large companies took control over smaller concerns. Yet what is more striking is the conservatism of expatriate enterprise. Very few established managing agency houses made any attempt to expand their operations into the 'new' industries being developed in the 1930s, and those that did acted only in collaboration with British-based corporations.[61] In the main it was the Indian entrepreneur who moved into these fields – particularly into cement, sugar and paper, but also into chemicals, paints and electrical goods.

Thanks to the increased integration of financial institutions that took place after the Great Depression, the large Indian corporations that developed in the 1930s were very similar in structure to the expatriate enterprises they were rivalling and supplanting. Many Indian business and industrial houses now had wide interests and owned banks and insurance and investment companies to help finance trading and industrial activities.[62] Changes in the relative strengths of British, expatriate and Indian groups across the country are hard to assess, not least because of problems of definition, but it is clear that, in terms of concentration in industry, Indian groups were expanding faster than their expatriate rivals. In 1931 five of the top twenty industrial groups at work were Indian, in 1939 the figure had increased to six while Tata's remained far and away the largest concern throughout the decade. In 1930–1, 46 per cent of the paid-up capital of rupee companies was in Indian-controlled concerns (those run by Indian managing agents or by groups with a majority of Indian directors); by 1938–9 this figure had reached 55 per cent.[63]

Changes in the working relationship between Indian and British capitalists were complex. Outside Calcutta, and especially in

Bombay, there had always been a measure of co-operation between expatriate and indigenous entrepreneurs. By the 1920s many sectors of the expatriate business community were beginning to realise that, under certain conditions, they could have more in common with their Indian counterparts than they had with the British bureaucracy in the Government of India. Thus the British millowners in Bombay joined their Indian colleagues in pressing for a lower ratio for the rupee in the mid-1920s,[64] while most expatriate businessmen, including the Managing Governors of the Imperial Bank, advocated devaluation in the early 1930s.[65] Officials were well aware of this, although they were not always very happy about it. As Sir James Grigg, Finance Member of the Government of India, complained in 1939, the attitude of expatriate businessmen

> . . . is now frankly that of making friends with the mammon of unrighteousness e.g. Birla and Benthall hunt together for quick profits and the latter does not see that he is thereby weakening his own ultimate safeguard (viz British power) and that he, or rather his competitors and successors, will be swallowed up completely. But perhaps he does see this and doesn't care so long as he himself has got out with his swag. Personally I wouldn't mind if every British businessman in India disappeared tomorrow. . . .[66]

Even outside Bombay expatriate firms came to rely increasingly on Indian investors for share capital in this period. From the First World War onwards British-controlled firms, starved of capital from London, were forming alliances with Indian businessmen. During the war, for example, Sir Rajendra Mookerjee of Calcutta bought his way into Martin Burn, one of the three largest expatriate managing agency houses in India.[67] By 1922 majority ownership (although not control) of the Bengal jute industry had passed into Indian hands.[68] In the 1930s it became common for expatriate firms to have at least a minority of Indian directors on their company boards, as Table 2.10 indicates. The traditional boundaries between Indian and expatriate capital were becoming blurred. As the Associated Chambers of Commerce reported to the Indian Statutory Commission in 1927:

> It is almost impossible to draw any line of demarcation between British and Indian interests in regard to invested capital, for companies floated and managed by British managing agents were

frequently owned to a very large extent by Indians. Similarly, in many companies regarded as Indian, a considerable number of shareholders may be British.[69]

TABLE 2.10. Racial Composition of Rupee Company Boards listed in *Indian Investors' Year-Book* 1925–6 and 1938–9

	1925–6			1938–9		
	British	Indian	Mixed	British	Indian	Mixed
Cotton mills	4	22	44	0	21	36
Jute mills[a]	21	0	25	18	10	32
Sugar mills		not listed		2	13	12
Other[bc]	71	14	50	159	35	192

[a] two unknown in 1925–6.
[b] utilities, transport, plantations, trading and other manufacturing (including sugar mills in 1925–6).
[c] six unknown in 1925–6.

The structure of the managing agency system, which was prevalent in all sectors of expatriate and indigenous business enterprise, meant that a majority Indian shareholding in any company did not necessarily give Indian interests control of company policy. Under agreements signed with the directors, managing agents had a significant amount of, and often complete, control over company finance, management and the personnel of the board. Several of the larger managing agencies cemented this control by buying substantial holdings in the companies they managed, either directly or through subordinate companies. It is probably false to assume that every managing agency could afford to ignore the wishes of company shareholders in every particular, or that all boards of directors of managed companies were simply packed with the holders of multiple directorships who were also partners in the agency itself. The effective power of the managing agency may have rested more on its own shareholding, or that of the group of which it formed a part, in the managed company.[70] However, to the extent that it gave control over company management without extensive share ownership, the managing agency system represented an important bastion of expatriate capital in India.[71]

While expatriate businessmen were prepared to co-operate with Indians to their mutual advantage, they were much less willing to share the sort of control secured by the managing agency system. Several of the old-established agency houses acquired an Indian partner or associate in the 1920s and 1930s, but none had an equality or majority of Indian participation (except, perhaps, Martin Burn). The only example of a new major industrial corporation based on a significant measure of joint control was the Associated Cement Company, founded in 1936. The largest shareholder in this company was the expatriate firm of Killick Nixon, but Indian firms owned 70 per cent of the total shares; the board of directors was made up of nominees of the shareholders in proportion to their holdings.[72] Interestingly enough, the British companies investing in subsidiary manufacturing firms in India also seem to have had little interest in attracting Indian capital or initiating joint control. The only major subsidiary in which there was significant Indian participation was the Asbestos Cement Company, which was 87 per cent owned by Turner Newall and 13 per cent by Associated Cement.[73]

The presence of a minority of Indian directors on the boards of expatriate-controlled companies may have resulted in some changes in corporate policy towards the export of profits, the extent of new investment and so on. In the absence of any detailed studies of major firms all such generalisations must remain speculative. Yet the overall impression remains that, in the inter-war period, no new sense of partnership of control emerged in the relations of foreign, expatriate and indigenous businessmen. The years from 1919 to 1939 saw, rather, the slow decline of expatriate enterprise, a failing, by and large, to adapt to new circumstances, to take advantage of new opportunities, or to meet the challenge of the rising Indian groups on the one hand and of the new subsidiary manufacturing companies on the other.

The changes that took place in India's relations with the world economy between 1919 and 1939 did not necessarily mean the end of her links with Britain. What it did mean was that the firms and individuals who created and exploited such links had to adapt their activities. The traditional sectors of the British metropolitan and expatriate communities seem to have been unable, or unwilling, to do so. The strengthening of the new links that had been forged in this period – the export of new types of goods from Britain, the investment of new forms of capital in new fields of enterprise – depended on a quite different structure of Indian administration and economic development than that which was possible within the established imperial framework. To some extent the sectors of the British economy interested in India in 1913 had benefited from the fact that India was a part of the Empire and that her Government was, in some aspects, under London's ultimate control. By 1939 this tie between entrepreneurial and administrative interests had weakened considerably, at least for the expanding sectors of British enterprise in India which required Government to develop the Indian economy in ways that no colonial administration dare risk. By 1939 the Indian economy was a good deal less complementary to the British one than had been the case in 1913, for the destructive impact of the decline of world demand for Indian produce had severely affected India's place in the imperial economic system. But we cannot assume that these changes, important though they were, necessarily had a direct bearing on the process of decolonization. To establish that such an impact did exist, and to find out how it made itself felt, we must consider the effect of economic change on the official institutions that bound Britain and India together. The next two chapters will attempt to do this by analysing the changing objectives and actions of the Government of India and the British Government in the period from 1914 to 1947.

3. The Colonial Government and the Indian Economy: Central Government Economic Policy, 1914–1947

To compare the role that central Government played in regulating and controlling the Indian economy in 1947 with the position that it held in 1913 is to be struck by an almost complete reversal of attitudes and actions. In 1913 *laissez-faire* held the field; by 1947 Government policy had become the dominant influence in determining the pace of every aspect of internal and external economic activity, while Government institutions now provided the mechanisms by which much of the Indian economy was run. Industrial development, monetary conditions, resource allocation and even the supply of food had become important concerns of a bureaucracy that, before the First World War, had prided itself on its passive role in the economic life of its subjects. The growth of state intervention in the Indian economy was perhaps the most important feature of the economic history of the period, yet such intervention was not the result of a steady, cumulative process of administrative activity. For much of the inter-war period central Government tried hard to maintain the status quo of 1913. Its ultimate failure to do so was the result of the changed circumstances brought about by the need to fight two major wars, and by the structural changes in the internal economy that resulted from the disturbed conditions of the years between those wars.

During the First World War the need to supply an enlarged army, the problems of price inflation and the disruption of normal commercial activity brought about by shortages of railway equipment, shipping and finance for overseas trade compelled British officials to rethink their attitude to the colonial economy. Many of the administrative initiatives that resulted – advance purchase schemes to support prices and prevent speculation in raw cotton, tea and rice; the banning of the export of hides, jute, wool, cotton, foodgrains, oils and most metals except under official supervision; direct control of production and marketing of salt and coal – were only temporary expedients designed to deal with immediate crises. But others had a longer life and a larger impact. Steps were taken to ensure that the Indian economy made a full contribution to the Allied war effort. Most important of all, the production of war supplies in Government factories was stepped up and, under the aegis of a Munitions Board, direct requisitions of textiles and leather goods were made from Indian manufacturers.[1]

It was the problem of supplying a modern war from a base with only a rudimentary industrial infrastructure that brought home to the Government of India the weaknesses of its pre-war model for Indian economic development. By 1917 officials were becoming concerned about the inadequacy of Indian industrial production for war purposes, and about its reliance on imported inputs. Had Japan joined the Central Powers, it was believed, shipping difficulties would have meant that Indian factories ground to a halt.[2] As the Viceroy, Lord Chelmsford, reported to George V:

> We are of course handicapped by our inability to procure machinery and by the necessity we are under of establishing industries which should have been set up in pre-war days. For this we have to thank the ill-judged parsimony and the now discarded *laissez-faire* policy of those days.[3]

It was against this background of preparations for a siege economy that the Government of India sanctioned a major change in its industrial policy by setting up, in 1916, an Industrial Commission chaired by Sir Thomas Holland of the Munitions Board. The Commission was influenced by the need for better war production and also by a prediction that the post-war years would see a state of economic warfare which would favour those countries that had governments prepared to plan for autarchy. Its report of 1918, which is noteworthy for its clear exposition of a detailed and subtle plan for Indian industrial development, advocated that central Government play a major role in industrialisation by the investment of social overhead capital, the promotion of technical education and research, the provision of industrial banks and the supply of direct financial and entrepreneurial assistance to private industry where necessary.[4]

The Commission stressed that the central administration was the only level at which sufficiently bold and broad-ranging action could be taken. The Commissioners had been most impressed by the work of the Munitions Board and had seen in its work the first steps towards the implementation of their own proposals.[5] The Government of India took the same line and in 1920 the Munitions Board was converted into a Board of Industries and Munitions to frame detailed proposals for a Department of Industries which was, in turn, inaugurated as part of the central administration in 1921, under the direction of Sir Thomas Holland. Unfortunately, during the three years between the Commission's report and the establishment of the Department of Industries, events had conspired to rob the new industrial policy of its *raison d'être*.

Pushing through the plans of the Industrial Commission necessitated making industrial development a central Government department because, under the scheme of constitutional reform for India proposed by the British Government in 1918, central Government departments were to remain under the sole control of the bureaucracy. The Government of India was fully aware of this and was convinced that it was essential because no Indian minister in the provinces would have the time, the money, the authority or the will to implement the Industrial Commission's formidable list of proposals. The India Office supported this view, but others were less sure. To Indian politicians in the provinces the reservation of industrial policy to the centre called into question the reality of devolutionary, democratising reform, while a number of imperial policy-makers in London thought that industrial policy was the sort of subject that should be handed over to Indian ministers in the provinces because whatever they did with it would not matter much to the future of the Raj. Thus, in the final form of the 1919 Government of India Act, administrative efficiency was sacrificed to political expediency; industrial policy was made a provincial, responsible subject. Plans were kept in being for two central cadres of technical services to advise provincial governments, but local jealousies and financial stringencies had killed these off by 1922. After Holland's dismissal from the Executive Council in 1921 the Department of Industries was stripped of all its major responsibilities except the protection of labour.[6] Of the functions proposed for it by the Industrial Commission only the supplying of industrial intelligence and the creation of state factories remained. Provincial governments' jealousies of their autonomy meant that there was almost no demand for such intelligence, while the limited number of state enterprises for which funds were available achieved little.[7]

Once the need to further the imperial war effort in all possible ways ceased to be the basis of British policy towards India, the case for the new industrial policy was weakened considerably. The general change in the attitude of the central Government towards Indian economic development that had been caused by the war, of which the industrial policy was the major result, moderated in the post-war period. Government's role could never again be quite the same as it had been before 1914, but it could still descend some way from the peaks of interventionism reached in 1917 and 1918. The fate of the new industrial policy illustrates this, as do the twists and turns of official thinking over the related issue of tariff protection to stimulate industrial development.

Just as the strains brought about by war encouraged Government officials in Delhi and London to think in terms of autarchic post-war economies, so too the idea of creating an autarchic empire, by substituting imperial preference for free trade, gained adherents in the Government of India and in the British Government. The sometimes real, and often imagined, subservience of the Indian Government to London in matters of tariff policy before 1914 was recognised as a major cause of Indian discontent with British rule. Giving the Government of India independence in tariff policy would remove this grievance and, at the same time, prepare the way for a new system of Indian and imperial tariffs that could strengthen the links between the imperial and the colonial economy.[8] These plans attained formal expression in the 'Fiscal Autonomy Convention' of 1919:

> Where the Government of India are in agreement with a majority of the non-official members of the Legislative Assembly, either in regard to legislation or in regard to resolutions on the Budget or on matters of general administration, assent to their joint decisions should only be withheld in cases in which the Secretary of State feels that his responsibility to Parliament for the peace, order and good government of India, or paramount

considerations of Imperial policy, require him to secure reconsideration.⁹

During the war the Government of India was more in favour of fiscal autonomy, and of protective tariffs, than of imperial preference. After 1918 only desultory action was taken to respond to the recommendations of the British Government's Committee on Commercial and Industrial Policy After the War for a possible bilateral scheme of preferential duties. An Imperial Preference Committee was set up within the secretariat, but its sole important recommendation was for the establishment of a Fiscal Commission to consider a policy of protection for India. When this recommendation was accepted the protectionists in the Government of India and the India Office carefully packed the Commission to ensure that more weight would be given to protection than to preference.¹⁰

The Indian Fiscal Commission reported in 1922. The majority report ignored the question of imperial preference but mapped out a policy of 'discriminating protection' for import-substituting industries on a 'dynamic comparative advantage' yard-stick.¹¹ It recommended that tariff protection be extended to certain industries if it was likely that, given a period of freedom from outside competition, they would eventually be able to achieve economies of scale that would allow them to meet the competition of foreign rivals without protection. Such industries would have to show that they would enjoy adequate home demand and could obtain sufficient supplies of labour and materials, and that they could not match future foreign competition without a spell of protection. A Tariff Board was to be set up to hear specific cases and to make non-binding recommendations to Government.¹²

The Government of India accepted this majority report, although with some important modifications. Officials were concerned that too extensive protection might diminish the income available to Government from revenue tariffs, and were also anxious to retain control over policy. The majority of the Fiscal Commission had recommended that the Tariff Board be permanent and independent; the Government decided that it should be *ad hoc* and semi-official. As it was eventually set up, the Tariff Board was advisory and had no power to initiate enquiries; a recommendation from the Commerce Department was needed before it could hear evidence from any industry.¹³ Between 1923 and 1939 Tariff Boards conducted fifty-one enquiries and granted protection to eleven industries – iron and steel, cotton textiles, sugar, paper, matches, salt, heavy chemicals, plywood and tea-chests, sericulture, magnesium chloride and gold thread – and, under somewhat different criteria, to rice and wheat producers. While the way in which the Boards were set up and the briefs that they were given inhibited the formulation of a long-term, integrated protective policy, the measures that Government enacted on their recommendations did give real aid to all the industries listed above except, perhaps, heavy chemicals and plywood.[14]

The policy of discriminating protection provided some impetus towards import-substituting industrialisation and central Government's increasing reliance on customs revenue had a similar effect through raising the prices of imported goods. In 1914 Indian customs duties had been low, only 5 per cent *ad valorem* generally and 3·5 per cent for cotton textiles. In 1916 the general rate was raised to 7·5 per cent and in the next year the rate on cotton goods was raised to the same level. In 1921 the general rate, including the duty on cotton, was raised to 11 per cent, while the duties on sugar and on various luxury goods were increased to 15 and 20 per cent respectively. A further increase in the general rate to 15 per cent was imposed in 1922, although cotton was left at its old level. The duties on sugar and luxuries (motor cars and other vehicles, confectionery, certain items of cutlery, hardware and metal goods, clocks and watches and rich yarns and fabrics) were raised by a further 10 per cent. In 1931 the general rate was raised again, this time to 25 per cent. Certain classes of goods were now admitted at lower rates, most importantly machinery and railway plant and rolling stock (10 per cent), while luxuries went up again – for example motor cars to 37·5 per cent and wireless apparatus to 50 per cent. A special rate of 20 per cent (15 per cent for British goods) was fixed for low quality cotton textile imports in 1930, this rate being increased to 50 per cent for non-British goods in 1932 and 75 per cent in 1933. By the early 1930s some protective tariffs had also reached remarkable levels, imported sugar being charged at 190 per cent in 1931 – it is hardly surprising that imports of sugar mill machinery increased in real terms by 3000 per cent between 1928 and 1933.[15] Other industries which would appear to have become established in India as a direct result of changes in revenue and protective duties include paper, matches and rubber manufactures.

Government stores purchase policy also stimulated import-substitution in the late 1920s and the 1930s. In 1924 the Secretary of State had surrendered control over this policy to the Government of India; by the 1930s the bulk of stores were obtained by rupee tender in India rather than by sterling tender in London. This change was a blow to British exporters, and their position was not improved by a series of Government of India decisions in the early 1930s to give encouragement to Indian manufacturers – stores purchase officers were now instructed, in comparing goods of adequate quality, to prefer cheaper though inferior goods and, in comparing goods of equal price, to give preference to the products of Indian manufacturers made from Indian raw materials. Indian products made from imported raw materials were to be preferred to imported goods held in stock in India by branches of foreign manufacturing companies, and these in turn were to be preferred to simple imports. In addition, a discretionary allowance of 10 per cent of the total purchase price could be made in the case of products of Indian manufacturers in comparing the costs of their tenders with foreign ones of equal quality.[16] The total amount of stores purchased in India was not very great, rising from Rs. 1·64 crores in 1922–3 to Rs. 4.76 crores in 1934–5,[17] but such purchases were vitally important for certain sectors of industry – notably for suppliers of railway equipment, contracts for guaranteed purchases of steel rails and fishplates keeping the Tata Iron and Steel Company going in the late 1920s and throughout the depression. In 1931–2, 8 per cent of all railway stores and 12·5 per cent of such stores for state railways were brought in India; by 1938–9 these proportions had reached 28 and 46 per cent respectively.[18]

Changes in central Government policy in the 1920s and 1930s had created new opportunities for Indian manufacturers; yet the emasculated remains of the new industrial policy, revenue tariffs, changes in stores purchase rules and discriminating protection, did not represent, together or separately, a major new economic strategy. State factories and industrial intelligence had a minimal impact; stores purchase rules affected very limited areas of enterprise; revenue tariffs were imposed on fiscal, not developmental, criteria; protective tariffs were subject to stringent tests and stiff conditions. The policy of discriminating protection was potentially the most important new factor, but, in the 1920s at any rate, the Government of India was not prepared to follow it to its logical conclusion. Although Government decisions to accept or reject Tariff Board recommendations were sometimes affected by antiprotectionist pressure groups, in general the essence of the official position was neutrality. The advantage for Government of the Tariff Board system was that demands for protection were assessed on the basis of fairly objective criteria based on orthodox economic principles; administrative rather than political considerations could then determine the actions of Government. This was clearly demonstrated by the modifications that the Government had made to the structure of the Tariff Board system that had been proposed by the Fiscal Commission:

> The Secretariat wanted the Tariff Board to serve as a buffer between itself and interests demanding protection. The Government of India had learned . . . that it must avoid placing itself in a position where it would be vulnerable to direct pressure from Indian business interests. As the Government of India had recently obtained a degree of autonomy from his Majesty's Government, it was now even more vulnerable to pressure from internal interests. It was hoped that a semi-official Tariff Board would provide that buffer.[19]

The most important area in which the actions of central Government affected the colonial economy was in monetary policy. Here again we can see that for much of the inter-war period the great desire of the Government of India was for officials to play no active role in matters so important to the domestic economy. To achieve this objective meant finding an automatic, self-regulating system of currency management.

The First World War destroyed the gold exchange standard that had worked so well, at least from the point of view of Government, before 1914. The basis of the pre-war arrangements had been the free movement of funds between India and Britain that had made the payment of debts in London and credits in India possible. The smooth running of the mechanism for increasing the level of currency in India to match her credits with the rest of the world had lain at the heart of this system and during the war, with Indian exports in great demand and with the Government of India financing a substantial amount of 'imperial' war expenditure against payment in London,[20] it was this mechanism that broke down. Both the war expenditure and the favourable balance of commodity trade increased the Government's balances in London

Central Government Economic Policy, 1914–1947 65

while depleting them in India, but the normal methods of transferring these balances from Britain to India were a great deal more difficult in wartime. The shipping of gold was prevented by the hazards of war and by the embargo on such exports imposed by most belligerents, including Britain; buying silver and shipping it to India to mint new rupees was impeded by problems of supply, the growing number of other buyers and the reluctance of the United States, the major holder of silver bullion, to release their reserves. To meet this situation the Council Bills made available for the financing of Indian exports had to be rationed and stringent exchange controls brought into force to ensure that foreign demands for rupees were limited to payments for essential war supplies. In addition, the need to expand the currency to maintain war expenditure at a time of price inflation brought about by shortages without the possibility of acquiring bullion led to new techniques of currency management. The Indian authorities issued increasingly large amounts of currency notes against British Treasury Bills (bought by the Secretary of State out of his swollen London balances) and against Treasury Bills issued in India and exchanged with the Controller of Currency for paper money. In 1914 the gross note circulation in India had been Rs. 66·12 crores, 21 per cent of which was issued against securities rather than against bullion; in 1919 gross note circulation was Rs. 153·46 crores, 64 per cent issued against securities. In this period the number of British Treasury Bills in the reserves went up nine-fold and the number of Indian Treasury Bills doubled.[21]

The only long-term solutions to the problem of liquidity would be to allow the exchange rate of the rupee to rise or to declare rupee notes inconvertible into coin, but the Government was reluctant to do either. Inconvertibility, it was feared, would result in a complete collapse of confidence in paper currency and Government credit.[22] Raising the exchange rate was first discussed in the winter of 1916–17, but the idea was dismissed as profiteering at the expense of the British Government which was buying most of India's exports. Yet by August 1917 the world price of silver had risen so high that the bullion value of the rupee was greater than its face value, and the exchange rate was raised from 1s 4d to 1s 5d. The London price of silver continued to rise, partly due to the increase in the world price and partly to the fall in the sterling/dollar parity and, to prevent a loss on coinage, the rupee exchange was pushed up with it to 1s 6d in April 1918, 1s 8d in May 1919, 1s 10d in August 1919, 2s in

September 1919, 2s 2d in November 1919 and 2s 4d in December 1919.[23]

As early as December 1915 it had become clear to Finance Department officials that 'the practical suspension of the automatic action of our currency system' was in sight,[24] and in 1917 the Government found itself 'within measurable distance of a complete regulation of exchange by the state'.[25] By the end of the war there were few guidelines left for monetary policy. The exchange rate was floating ever upwards, the rupee was effectively on a silver bullion standard linked to a depreciating pound sterling and the bulk of the currency reserves was made up of investments which could not easily be sold off and which were declining in value as the exchange rate rose. The business of Government could only be carried on by expanding the currency against created securities and by maintaining a floating debt equivalent to 63 per cent of annual revenue.[26] The exchange rate, internal prices, credit rates and the level of currency now had to be determined by executive action rather than by an automatic currency system. Worse still, officials were becoming uncomfortably aware that some of the policies they had adopted in wartime were now having disruptive effects on the lives of their subjects. The expansion of currency against created securities to ease constrictions in the supply of short-term Government finance – to 'reach for the morphia syringe' as one official described the process[27] – was now recognised as one of the causes of price inflation.[28] Neither the Government of India nor the India Office felt capable of establishing a new policy on its own and so, in May 1919, a committee of experts was appointed under the chairmanship of Sir Henry Babington-Smith.

Put simply, the point which the 1919 Committee on Indian Exchange and Currency was asked to consider was what was the optimum level of the rupee exchange needed to ensure stability against rises in the price of silver while minimising disruption of trade. At first this point was discussed only in relation to a sterling-based gold exchange standard, since there was an almost universal ban on gold exports and no free market in gold bullion. While the Committee was sitting, however, the United States Government removed its embargo and a free market in gold was re-established in London. Thus a second fundamental question was introduced – should the Indian currency system be based on a full gold standard?

In its initial 'Statement of Case' to the Committee, the Government of India was only concerned with finding a sterling value for the rupee which would put it out of reach of rises in the London price of silver. Soon after this had been submitted, however, officials also became concerned about the rise of prices in India, which they saw as being at the root of the various civil disturbances of the previous two years – a high exchange rate, and a contraction of the currency to maintain it, was seen as a means of solving this problem too.[29] With only two exceptions, all sections of opinion consulted by the Committee agreed that a high exchange rate was the answer to Government's problems. The calculations on which the proponents of a high exchange based their case are interesting: the Governments' 'Statement' had not committed itself as to what might be a suitable rate; general opinion among the witnesses to the Commitee was that 2s gold would insulate the rupee from silver prices. It was accepted that too high an exchange rate might damage India's exports and expose her internal markets to a flood of imported goods, but everyone, Briton and Indian, official and non-official, expert and layman alike, assumed that world prices would continue to rise and that Indian exports of raw materials would find as insatiable a market during the period of reconstruction as they had in wartime. No one produced any hard evidence on which the Committee could decide at what point the rupee might become over-valued. A typical argument was that used by Sir David Barbour, an ex-Finance Member of the Government of India: 'It is not easy to say beforehand, but the rupee was at one time worth 2s and the business of the country went on at that rate; so I suppose it would again at the same rate.'[30] Three of the Indian witnesses called by the Committee (Manu Subedar, S. K. Bomanji and S. K. Sharma) represented the 'Bombay school' of economic opinion and gave evidence radically different from anyone else's. Their views – a 1s 4d rupee to raise prices, a gold standard and gold currency and a limitation of Council Bills to the amount needed for the Home Charges – were supported in the minority report of the Committee written by its only Indian member, Dadiba Dalal. The great weakness of the Bombay case so far as the majority of the Committee was concerned was that it ignored the socially disruptive effects of continued inflation and provided no practical solution to the problem of the high price of silver. While Subedar had argued for an immediate gold currency to replace the silver one,[31] Dalal had advocated a debased two-rupee piece.[32] The majority of the Committee regarded these ideas as unworkable,[33] while the Government of India assessed the evidence of Subedar, Bomanji and Sharma as 'frankly racial' and thought of Dalal's report as 'in the nature of a leg-pull'.[34]

The other dissident voice on the exchange question was that of Sir Lionel Abrahams, who had just retired after a long career at the India Office. Abrahams, the chief architect of the pre-war gold exchange standard, argued persuasively against fixing the rupee at any level while world conditions were so unstable and when no serious attempt had been made to assess the effect of any particular rate on Indian trade. Urging a flexible, pragmatic policy and a floating exchange rate, he asserted that 'it is better to guide your policy by a process of continuing enquiry . . . than to guide your policy by guesswork'.[35] These ideas were not well received, for both the Government of India and the Currency Committee wanted an automatic, self-regulatory system free from official interference. As the Committee's report commented: 'However complete the integrity and however great the intelligence on which official action is based, an automatic system, which does not depend upon such action for its operation, is greatly to be preferred.'[36] A gold standard independent of sterling was the best automatic system that the Committee could imagine and, once the United States had removed their embargo on gold exports, it seemed to be a practical possibility. An effective gold standard had been a long-standing demand of Indian critics of monetary policy and the Indian witnesses who had given evidence to the Committee all heartily approved the idea. The only serious opposition to it came from the City of London. Sir Brien Cockayne, the Governor of the Bank of England, had argued before the Committee that if the free import of gold into India were allowed once more then gold would simply vanish into hoards and 'the whole of the Empire's production of gold might be absorbed by India instead of being devoted to the use which we hoped it would be put in regulating the other exchanges'.[37] Cockayne wanted to conserve the Empire's stocks of gold to meet Britain's obligations in the United States and argued that because India enjoyed the privilege of being part of the Empire she ought to subordinate her hunger for gold to this higher purpose.[38] These views were supported by 'a leading London banker', who wrote to *The Times* that if the rupee were only linked to sterling,

> then we shall have all the benefits of India's large exports to help raise the general level of sterling. . . . The most effective way to

raise sterling to a gold level . . . is first of all to get the whole Empire on a sterling basis. Then we shall have the exports of the whole Empire concentrated on sterling, which in time would be pushed up to gold parity.[39]

This view of India as an imperial appendage was not popular with the Currency Committee or with officials. As F. H. Lucas, Financial Secretary of the India Office, pointed out in his evidence, 'speaking from the point of view of one who has to fight the battle for India', India had earned her export credits and ought to be allowed to take payment for them in whatever form she wished.[40] The Report of the Committee followed this line and specifically rejected the notion that 'in the interests of the Empire as a whole, it is desirable that the exchange system should be such as to facilitate and promote trade within the Empire rather than outside it and . . . to retain within the British Empire the financing of Indian trade.'[41] The Babington-Smith Committee recommended that a gold standard be set up in India with the rupee at 2s gold. Steps were suggested to encourage a gold coinage, free export and import of gold was to be allowed and a gold mint established. These proposals represented a simple and attractive solution to the complex financial and monetary problems of the Government of India. A gold standard rupee would be politically popular in India; it would ensure the automatic regulation of the currency system, do away with the need for Council Bills to finance more than the Home Charges, and make even more equal the partnership between the India Office and the Government of India. In February 1920 a joint communiqué was issued by the India Office and the Government of India announcing that this policy was in operation.

Unfortunately, events proved that 1920 was not a suitable year in which to attempt to reform the Indian currency system. The grotesque history of Indian currency in the next few months – the attempt to hold the value of the rupee in the face of a trade slump, a balance of payments deficit and massive speculation – is well known.[42] By September the new monetary policy lay in ruins. The rupee had been revalued at 2s gold, but its market value was now only 1s 10d sterling and this fell further during the next six months. Once more without a monetary policy the Government of India was at a loss in such matters as how to reduce prices, regulate the flow of currency and ease disruptions in the internal economy. All the balances built up in London during the war had now been spent in trying to support the exchange. Importers, who had ordered goods when the rupee was worth more than 2s 4d sterling and who now had to pay for them with rupees worth less than 1s 10d, were protesting vigorously and adding complaints to those of the nationalists who alleged that selling Reverse Council Bills to support the exchange had been a plot to hand out India's resources to British and expatriate businessmen.

Government monetary policy continued to be the subject of a long and bitter debate between officials and an important body of Indian opinion for most of our period. The chief question was the correct exchange rate for the rupee, but this subject was often used as a catch-phrase to summarise deeper issues. What was really at stake was the question of the purposes of Indian monetary policy as a whole and, in particular, the attitude that Government should adopt towards regulating the pace of internal economic activity.

Chastened by the experience of 1920, the monetary authorities in India consciously refrained from any action to influence the rupee exchange rate for four years, during which time the rate fell to 1s 3d sterling in early 1921 and then rose slowly to 1s 6d sterling by late 1924 as world demand for Indian exports increased. But eschewing influence on the exchange did not mean that the authorities could do nothing at all, and the imperatives of internal and external Government finance necessitated action which affected the level of currency circulating in India. Because of the world trade depression and the instability of the rupee exchange the Secretary of State was unable to sell any Council Bills until January 1923, yet his expenditure still had to be financed. This was managed in several ways: by raising loans in London, by using the money recovered from the War Office for imperial war expenditure in India and, most importantly of all for Indian conditions, by cancelling currency notes in India to release funds from the currency reserves in London for revenue purposes. In addition, measures had to be taken to reduce the Government of India's floating debt (over 60 per cent of revenue in 1921) and to cut down the number of currency notes issued against created securities. From 1921 onwards the Government whittled down the floating debt as and when it could by cancelling currency notes and the created securities that had been issued to support them, by paying off Treasury Bills and by converting short-term into long-term debt. This policy was made difficult to implement by the fact that the Government of India's budget was in deficit by a total of nearly Rs. 100 crores between 1918–19 and 1922–3, but the re-establishment of a budget surplus in 1923–4, thanks to severe tax increases and retrenchment of expenditure, enabled Government to redeem all Treasury Bills in public hands by July 1924.[43]

In pursuit of these aims, the Government of India managed to contract the currency by almost Rs. 52 crores between January 1920 and March 1923, although officials were very well aware of the dangers of squeezing Indian credit too hard, both for the sake of their own loan programme and the financing of trade. The Indian monetary authorities knew themselves to be ill-equipped to take decisions about the optimum level of circulating currency. The official in charge of expanding and contracting the currency was the Controller of Currency in Calcutta, aided by a Deputy in Bombay; to estimate whether money was likely to be too tight or too slack at any given moment, these officials had to make guesses about the character of the next monsoon, to assess the probable world demand for Indian exports and the Indian demand for imports and to make assumptions about price levels and banking and stock market trends. The Finance Department acknowledged the weaknesses of this arbitrary system – as Sir Basil Blackett, Finance Member from 1923 to 1927 pointed out, 'you cannot accurately gauge whether deflation is needed by the country by any method whatever'[44] – and they were alive to the dangers of contracting the currency too much. Even when Reverse Councils had been on sale in 1920 the Government had thought it inadvisable to contract the currency by the full amount of such bills sold (Rs. 47·14 crores were received for reverses, but only Rs. 36·68 crores' worth of notes were cancelled) because of fears of creating too great a stringency in the Indian money market.[45]

Between 1921 and 1924 an attempt was made to ease the high interest rates, brought about by the fluctuating seasonal demands of commodity traders, by setting up an automatic system of expansion and contraction against internal trade bills. In 1921 the Imperial Bank of India had been formed by a merger of the old Presidency Banks of Bengal, Bombay and Madras to act both as a Government and a private bank. The Imperial Bank held Government balances and provided 'ways and means' advances; it issued Treasury Bills and made advances from surplus Government balances to other banks against trade bills and other short-term credit instruments. In February 1922 the Government of India announced that it would issue specially printed currency notes to the Imperial Bank against internal trade bills deposited with it, these notes to be withdrawn and cancelled as the bills were paid off. Initially this arrangement was implemented for Rs. 5 crores' worth of notes when the bank rate reached 8 per cent; during 1923–4 the amount was increased to Rs. 12 crores to be issued in instalments as the bank rate rose above 6 per cent, with the full amount to be issued at 7·5 per cent. These provisions for 'emergency' currency had only a limited effect, for the amounts involved were small and the scheme of issuing it against *hundis* was inefficient since most of India's internal trade was not financed by such bills but by the far cruder instruments of cash credits and demand promissory notes.[46] The early 1920s also saw one other advance in the techniques of Indian currency management. In 1923 the Government of India began to purchase sterling exchange directly, by buying in small amounts from the Indian branches of the exchange banks that needed rupees to finance the shipment of exports. The Secretary of State objected to this development, being reluctant to see his control over the purchase of foreign exchange through the sale of Council Bills compromised but, by acting first and asking afterwards, the Government of India got its own way. The Indian authorities argued that buying exchange in India was cheaper and more flexible; within a short time this method of obtaining remittances had taken over from the more formal and rigid Council Bill system.[47]

From 1921 to 1927 the Government of India was without a clear-cut or theoretically sound monetary policy. Remittance needs required some currency contraction and the stringency that this, and Government's equally pressing need for loans, caused in the Indian credit market was offset by only partial palliatives. Officials were agreed that the solution to the problem was for Government to abdicate its control by re-establishing the rupee on an exchange standard and by linking it, preferably directly, to the international gold standard. Before this could happen the rupee ratio had to be stabilised – 'you cannot have an automatic currency until you have got your rate fixed,' argued the Finance Member[48] – but the traumatic experience of 1920 had taught that India could not go it alone. The rupee could not be stabilised until other major currencies, notably sterling, had returned to the gold standard.[49]

Improvement in trade and a slow rise of world prices following the depression of 1920–1 had pushed up the rupee exchange to 1s 4d sterling in 1923 and to 1s 6d sterling in October 1924. This development caused concern in New Delhi as officials began to be haunted by the memory of the 1919–20 crisis, when a sudden rise in the exchange had been followed by an even faster fall. Determined to remove any uncertainty, the Government of India began to expand the currency in the busy season of 1924–5 and to sell rupees to prevent the rate moving much above 1s 6d. This policy was again followed in 1925–6 as increased international trade caused the exchange rate to harden. Then, in 1926, the announcement that a Royal Commission was to be appointed to consider the future of the rupee exchange caused the rate to weaken as rumours of a future 1s 4d ratio encouraged remittance and speculation. The Indian authorities now decided that the existing 1s 6d ratio should be maintained by currency contraction until the Commission had reported – not in an attempt to influence its decision, but simply to prevent the disruption of trade that a fluctuating exchange rate would produce.[50]

The Government of India's monetary policy now came under renewed attack from within India. The most powerful section of Indian commercial and business opinion, that grouped around the Bombay cotton magnates, had always advocated a cheap money policy to stimulate industrial growth and welcomed currency inflation as a way of easing credit and raising internal prices and purchasing power. The official policy of maintaining the 1s 6d ratio in 1926 was seen as a device to stunt India's industrial growth and to open up the internal market to artificially cheapened imports. The Bombay cotton industry itself was in a bad way by the mid-1920s; the post-war stock market boom had caused many mills to become over-capitalised and the slump of 1920–1 had had drastic effects. A survey of 75 of the 85 mills in Bombay in 1923 estimated that 26 had made a profit in the previous year, 43 a loss and 6 broken even.[51] The unusually high price of raw cotton in 1923–4 pushed up production costs, while a slump in cotton prices in 1924–5 disturbed the up-country market for Bombay's goods. By 1925 unsold stocks of cotton goods were piling up in Bombay and there were increasingly loud protests about currency policy, which was seen as responsible.[52] As a Government official reported at the height of the storm:

> The absence of demand for [cotton] piece goods is generally attributed [in Bombay] to the effects of the currency policy of

Government . . . the better informed do not object so much to the high exchange as to the monetary policy which has crippled the buying power of the peasantry by restrictions imposed on the normal expansion of currency. The majority . . . contend that the present position has been brought about by Government's policy and that it is up to Government to come to the aid of the industry in meeting a situation brought about by its own action.[53]

When the Royal Commission on Indian Currency and Finance (Hilton-Young Commission) began to take evidence, the Bombay school's attack on Government policy concentrated into a lobby to fix the rupee exchange rate at 1s 4d. While the Government witnesses argued that prices in India had already adjusted to the higher exchange, and that any increase in the level of circulating currency following a devaluation would lead to socially disruptive price inflation, most Indian witnesses before the Commission tried to show that prices were already too low to sustain a healthy level of internal commercial activity, and that they would fall still further if the 1s 6d ratio were maintained. Both the Finance Department and its critics were agreed that once the internal economy had adjusted to a new level of prices it did not matter, within very broad limits, what that new level was because both outputs and inputs would conform to it. The argument over whether adjustment had yet taken place focused on two points – the level of wages in the Bombay cotton mills and the price of raw cotton and certain food-grains, notably pulses.

During the inflationary period of the war and the post-war boom, the wages of mill-hands in Bombay had soared. According to Sir Victor Sassoon, who represented the Bombay Millowners' Association before the Royal Commission, wages had risen from a base of 100 in 1914 to 231 in 1926.[54] The official figures showed a rise in nominal wages of only 87 per cent in the same period, equal to a real rise of 68 per cent taking increases in the cost of living into account.[55] Everyone was agreed that this problem was peculiar to western India, industrial wages in Bengal having increased by less than 50 per cent, but agreement was not universal about what relevance these facts had for the formulation of monetary policy. To Sassoon the 'stickiness' of wages in adjusting to now-declining price levels demonstrated the damage that deflating the economy could do to Indian industries and was therefore a major indicator of the need for reflation;[56] to Blackett, the Finance Member, this was an internal problem for the millowners and not one with which Government policy ought to be concerned.[57]

The controversy over the level of prices for agrarian produce was most wide-reaching. To the mill interest the fact that prices of major cash crops in western India were relatively lower than their pre-war level gave cause for concern, in that this was thought to be responsible for a depression in the market for Bombay cotton goods.[58] More generally, some of the Indian economists who appeared before the Commission argued that the lower level of prices of exportable cash crops impaired the progress of this, the most advanced, sector of agriculture, and pulled down the prices of crops produced for the internal market, intensifying the burden of debt on all classes of agriculturalists.[59] The official reply to this case was to point out what was seen as the full implication of the quantity theory of money: what was important was not the amount of money that a peasant received for his produce but rather the amount of commodities (or gold) that he could purchase with his surplus. With a lower price level, both the commodities bought and those sold would be cheaper by the same proportion, and although the gold cost of debts incurred before 1917 would be higher their rupee cost would remain the same.

This debate revealed two very different and equally overgeneralised conceptions of the rural economy. The Government and its supporters chose to assume that Indian agriculture ran on a fully cash-based marketing model; the Bombay school postulated a rural economy in which everything except cloth and bullion was produced on the spot and in which any surplus was turned into cash. Thus while officials thought that any agrarian adjustment to a new price level would produce no long-term changes, their critics maintained that the higher the internal price level the better since the peasantry sold more than it bought.[60] The discussion of this issue before the Commission revealed some remarkable ideas about the nature of agrarian life, epitomised by the surreal exchange between Professor C. N. Vakil, of Bombay University, and Sir Rajendra Mookerjee, a member of the Commission, over whether the peasant would rather have enough to eat but till his fields naked, or clothe his starving body so that he could beg his food.[61]

The Government and its critics were projecting that view of rural society which was necessary to support the rest of their respective cases. The official view was determined by the wish to see the 'natural forces' of the world economy free to transform Indian agriculture, while the arguments of the Bombay school only really applied to the rich cotton-growers of western India with whom they dealt so closely. The limitations of the Bombay model of the agrarian economy were brought out strikingly in the examination before the Royal Commission of D. P. Khaitan, a Calcutta-based 'nationalist' businessman, over the question of wheat prices. Khaitan failed to argue convincingly that a 1s 6d rupee damaged the wheat producer, as he was forced to admit that most Indian wheat was not exported and that much of it never entered the cash economy at all.[62] The case of the cotton cultivator was ideal for Bombay since cotton was an inedible cash crop hit by a fall in world prices, the trade in which was heavily influenced by credit rates abroad and in the Westernised internal banking sector; jute could have provided as good a basis for the anti-government argument, but jute prices were still high in 1926.

The report of the Royal Commission did not concern itself with the ideal interests of Indian agriculture, contenting itself with demonstrating that internal prices had largely adapted to the 1s 6d ratio and therefore recommending that rate. Similarly, the minority report of the Commission, written by Sir Purshottamdas Thakurdas in favour of a 1s 4d rupee, limited its argument to demonstrating that prices had not yet so adjusted. Both reports based their case on an examination of the index numbers of Indian prices, figures in which neither claimed any confidence as adequate statistical data. The majority report seems to have had the better of this somewhat sterile argument, especially as some of Thakurdas's calculations were suspect.[63] In any case, as Blackett pointed out to the Central Legislative Assembly, even if prices had not completely adjusted to the 1s 6d ratio they were certainly not adjusted to the 1s 4d one.[64] In 1927 the C.L.A. passed the Government's Currency Bill and the rupee was fixed at Rs. 13·33 to the (gold) pound sterling.

The most interesting of the many questions raised in the course of the ratio controversy is that of the role that Government saw for its monetary policy in the development of the Indian economy. There is no evidence to suggest that the Indian authorities advocated a high ratio to benefit British exporters or to make Government remittances to London cheaper. Officials did not expect any significant increase in imports as a result of fixing the exchange at 1s 6d, for they were convinced that prices had already adjusted to that level; if the rupee were devalued, it was argued, all internal prices would quickly rise by the same proportion as the increase in price of imported goods. The Finance Department's case had been influenced by a prediction that a lower ratio would increase Government expenditure during the new period of price adjustment, but officials saw this issue in terms of the interests of the Indian tax-payer, interests which they were already hard at work defending against the Secretary of State in the dispute about securing remittance by buying sterling in India rather than by selling Council Bills.

The most important difference of attitude between officials and their critics was over the role that Government could and should play in economic development. In keeping with the position they had held since the question had first been discussed in the 1890s, officials advocated a higher, rather than a lower, exchange rate in the interests of the consumer over the producer – although they had little idea of, and little interest in finding out about, what these neatly polarised categories really meant. More important, perhaps, was the fact that their experience since the collapse of the gold-exchange standard in 1917 had convinced officials that monetary policy ought to be passive rather than active; no amount of concern for the interests of Indian commerce, nor provision of emergency currency, could produce a monetary policy as efficient or as smoothly working as that which would result from linking the Indian currency system to the world economy through the gold standard. The idealised official picture of agrarian life based around a sophisticated cash-orientated market economy, reflected the Government's model for Indian development. The problems of industry and agriculture could best be solved, it was thought, by the fostering of Westernised banking institutions, a stable exchange rate and an integrated credit network. These prerequisites could only be achieved by fully integrating India into the world economic system and by keeping Government interference to a minimum. The prices of agrarian produce might be relatively lower in the 1920s than they had been before the war but that was seen as a world-wide phenomenon about which Government could and should do nothing.[65] The attitude of Government was encapsulated in a comment by an official in the Legislative Department on the millowners' case for a lower ratio:

> It has been suggested by Sir Victor Sassoon that the lowering of the ratio will increase the prices of agricultural products and consequently the purchasing power of the agriculturalist, and the

result will be increased profits to mills and to trade all round. This is a remarkable statement to make. If it were easy to create wealth by manipulating exchange, why do not other nations adopt it and where is the limit?[66]

A few years later many nations, including both Britain and India, were attempting to do just this.

The advocates of a 1s 4d rupee claimed to speak for the whole of India, but in fact represented a strong sectional interest. The Government of India, in supporting a 1s 6d rupee, also claimed to speak for the whole of India, but in fact represented nobody. The real case for 1s 6d was very simple – Government had to abdicate control of monetary policy in favour of an automatic system to ensure 'confidence',[67] and since prices were thought to have already adjusted to 1s 6d that ratio represented the *status quo*. Therefore a self-regulating exchange system could be established more quickly if the ratio were not altered again. Blackett was aware of Keynes's idea that exchange rates could be regulated by national monetary authorities to secure an optimum internal price level, but he thought the notion impractical because 'it leaves the Government in the same invidious position as they were in before the exchange was temporarily stabilised at 1s 6d and open to violent criticism from every quarter in every conceivable contingency'.[68] This desire for neutrality was the key to the Government of India's attitude.

To complete their abdication of control over Indian monetary management the Finance Department officials proposed to the Royal Commission that the rupee be placed on a gold standard, with a gold currency, and that a central bank be set up to run currency and remittance policy independently of Government.[69] The Commission's report rejected the first of these ideas, but took up the second. The Commissioners thought the plan for a gold standard rupee with a gold currency impractical, for they estimated that India would require over £100 million worth of gold bullion to start such a system with adequate reserves, and doubted whether this could be obtained without doing severe damage to the world financial system. As they pointed out,

> the evidence which we have received . . . has convinced us that it would be most imprudent not to take into account the possibility, indeed the probability, that unless great economy is exercised in

the use of gold, both in regard to its use as a commodity and its use as money, we have to look forward to a prolonged period of falling prices throughout the world.[70]

The British Treasury was also clearly opposed to a gold currency for India, fearing that the resultant redistribution of world gold stocks would impair its own attempt to re-establish sterling on gold at the pre-war parity.[71] Treasury influence on the Commission was only indirect, however, and it seems likely that the Commissioners reached their decision independently. In place of a gold coinage the Commission recommended a gold bullion standard for the rupee with a Government undertaking to buy or sell gold bars at the rate of 8·475 grains of gold to the rupee. The Commission claimed that this scheme had all the advantages of a full gold standard with a gold coinage, while being a great deal more economical in its use of gold:

> Since gold bars are to be given in exchange for notes or silver rupees, not for export only, but for any purpose, this is not an exchange standard; it is an absolute gold standard. Nevertheless the compensatory mechanism of the exchanges is preserved, because gold bars are not currency. When gold bars are given by the currency authorities for notes or rupees, the currency is contracted, while, on the other hand, when gold bars are given to the currency authorities for notes or rupees, the currency is expanded.[72]

The system was put into effect in 1927, but no one in India, official and non-official alike, had a clear idea of how it should work.[73] It was never seriously implemented, and in 1931, with foreign confidence in the rupee seriously damaged by the world financial crisis, the rupee was taken off the gold bullion standard and put on a sterling one.

The Royal Commission did support the Government of India's scheme for a central bank – the Reserve Bank of India – to improve techniques of monetary management and to secure Indian confidence in the running of the currency system. This proposal was given a key place in its report.[74] An official bill to establish such a bank was introduced into the Central Legislative Assembly in 1927, but there it foundered on the mutual distrust of Indian legislators and the Secretary of State.

In keeping with contemporary theory, the Commission proposed that the Reserve Bank be made independent of Government and of any interference by the executive. The plan was for a bank on the lines of the Bank of England with private capital and with a majority of the directors elected by the shareholders.[75] The India Office and the Government of India both accepted the plan and the Reserve Bank Bill was drawn up on these lines. Opinion in the C.L.A., on the other hand, was sharply opposed to a private bank; M.L.A.s wanted the capital of the bank to be subscribed by Government and insisted that a majority of the directorate be their own nominees. During the debate on the Bill the Government managed to patch up a compromise stockholders scheme – the capital of the bank to be made up of Government stock sold to the public in small lots; holders of such stock would then elect a minority of the directors with the rest nominated by commercial associations and by Government. M.L.A.s were to be *ex officio* members of the provincial boards of stockholders that would elect 10 of a directorate totalling 22 voting members. The India Office, however, refused to accept this plan and the Bill had to be withdrawn. A new Bill, on a shareholder basis, was put before the C.L.A. in 1928, but was defeated.[76]

The Royal Commission had proposed a Reserve Bank because 'only then will any danger of Government's remittance policy interfering with the proper management of the currency be eliminated'.[77] In popularising the idea in India, Blackett had prophesied that:

> At one stroke control of Indian currency and finance will be transferred . . . into the sole control of India . . . the atmosphere in which that control will be exercised will no longer be a Government atmosphere but an atmosphere permeated by the views of representatives of agricultural, commercial and industrial India.[78]

The problem was that some sections of opinion found this hard to believe, while others found it hard to accept. While Indian businessmen feared that the influence of the bureaucracy would still be paramount,[79] both European and Indian M.L.A.s were worried that, with a shareholder bank, 'control . . . will fall into the hands of a few self-seeking capitalists, European and Indian. Of the two, control by Indians, and especially the Bombay capitalists, is probably feared more even than control by European interests.'[80] India Office officials, in turn, were adamant that there should be no central bank at all if there was any danger that those who ran it might be prepared to jeopardise the meeting of India's external commitments for the sake of domestic economic expansion. With a shareholder bank this was deemed unlikely, for large sections of commercial opinion were involved in the external economy and because 'the Bank will be run by the Governor and the Deputy Governor', both of whom were to be appointed by the Viceroy, and 'the Board will be largely ornamental'.[81] The Secretary of State was prepared to make concessions to ensure that no one group of capitalists could gain control of the directorate,[82] but not to prepare the way for political influence. If that were allowed; it was feared,

> the effect . . . would be the setting up of a duplicate executive, representing the party in power [in the C.L.A.], and confronting the constitutional executive, with every disposition, and certainly full power, to hamper the latter at every step.[83]

The issue at stake in the debate over the constitution of an Indian central bank, of whether India's external commitments were to be protected at the expense of her internal economy, was one that was to dominate the minds of financial policy-makers for the next five years. It is probable, however, that even had some compromise been arrived at over the composition of the Reserve Bank board the Secretary of State would still have ended up by vetoing the legislation. During 1927 the C.L.A., encouraged somewhat by the Government of India, had proposed amendments to the Reserve Bank Bill to allow a gold coinage to be introduced in due course. To the Secretary of State this was an anathema, and a final confrontation over this point was only prevented by the defeat of the Bill in 1928 before these clauses were debated.[84]

With the failure of the Reserve Bank Bill, Government of India officials found themselves in an invidious position. They had a legal obligation to maintain the exchange, and were responsible for currency policy. Although in theory internal credit rates were regulated by the Imperial Bank, in practice Government action played a large part in determining them, while at the same time the Government had to rise long- and short-term finance to meet the requirements of its own exchequer. These responsibilities were closely interlinked and were intimately connected both with the supply of cash and foreign exchange to meet the Government's obligations and with the performance of the most politically sensitive sectors of the Indian economy.

Overshadowing all else in financial policy in the next few years was the Government of India's budgetary requirements in Britain, a summary of which is given in Table 3.1. Because of the need to supply the Secretary of State with funds to meet the Home Charges, the Government of India was the largest single dealer on the Indian foreign exchange market. To meet its obligations in London the Government of India needed to secure an adequate income in India and to purchase enough sterling remittance with the rupees thus raised. If sufficient revenue were not forthcoming the Indian authorities had to borrow to make ends meet; if they could not purchase enough remittance there were a number of options open: gold or silver could be shipped from official reserves and sold in

TABLE 3.1 Government of India Expenditure and Receipts in United Kingdom 1928–1934 (in £ '000s)

	1928–9	1929–30	1930–1	1931–2	1932–3	1933–4 (budget)
Expenditure						
Current	30518	32257	32428	32071	30354	30215
Capital	10402	12865	3919	2012	182	983
Other[a]	2201	1696	1651	17940	10928	6433
TOTAL	43121	46818	37998	52023	41464	37631
Receipts						
Net purchase of £	30810	15215	−339	26301	36946	21000
£ loans raised	9100	11940	25604	8966	9500	6000
Transfers through currency reserves	−5190	7904	6362	20906	−15527	−375
Reduction of balances	407	−1142	834	−10311	5946	8466
Other[b]	7994	12901	5537	6161	4599	2540
TOTAL	43121	46818	37998	52023	41464	37631

[a] capital portion of railway annuities, railway sinking funds, discharge of war loan, discharge of India stock and bonds, advances repaid and miscellaneous deposits.
[b] sale of silver, revenue in UK, Iraq drawings, supply of opium, receipts from War Office, etc.

Source: Sir George Schuster, 'The Sterling and gold resources of government and the problem of remittances' 30.10.39 [sic.] in T. 160 Box 519 F. 12471/05/4.

London, the Secretary of State could borrow on the London market, remittance could be made through the currency reserves. The success of internal Government finance was dependent on obtaining revenue and raising loans. The rates at which such loans were floated had a considerable impact on other credit rates in India, for Government stocks competed with industrial shares, while Treasury Bills were brought by banks as an alternative to making advances for trade and industry to private customers. One of the Government's problems was that its budget could easily be imbalanced by a slump in the internal economy which depressed revenue returns, and that it would then have to take fiscal action that would tend to deepen the slump. In a depression the Indian authorities had to increase their short-term borrowing to raise cash, but such action, by pushing up credit rates in general, also impaired the recovery of sensitive sectors of the internal economy. In addition, the bulk of the cash in hand of the Imperial Bank, the agency responsible for implementing credit policies to regulate the pace of internal economic activity, was made up of Government balances. When, therefore, the Government was in financial difficulty and its balances were low, the resources available to the Imperial Bank for reflation of the economy were reduced. Withdrawing currency to finance the Secretary of State by transfers through reserves also had the effect of tightening credit in India, as this was done either by drawing on Government balances at the Imperial Bank or by issuing Treasury Bills.

When economic conditions were favourable, as they had been for much of the 1920s, the Government could perform its complex role without too much strain; when, as at the end of the decade, a depression in all sectors of the internal economy coincided with a depression in the world economy, a number of major problems arose. Between 1930 and 1932 the Government of India was faced with a serious currency crisis which called into question all the assumptions on which its monetary policy had hitherto been based.[85]

The crisis of the early 1930s was dominated by the problem of the rupee exchange. By 1930 the rupee was chronically weak; refusing to buy below par the Indian authorities were able to purchase only £15 million worth of remittance between April 1929 and March 1930, and in the next financial year had to sell £300,000 more sterling than they were able to buy. The Secretary of State's commitments in London – £64 million over the two years – had to be met by remittance through the currency reserves, running down the home treasury balances and borrowing in London. The strain on the rupee was the result of economic depression and political upheaval. The collapse of world prices for agricultural products turned the terms of trade against India, sapped her balance of payments surplus and pushed down internal prices, thus promoting rural unrest and preparing the ground for agitations against rent and land revenue. The economic crisis thus produced, which affected indigenous industry as well as agriculture, complicated a political situation already confused and disturbed by the decision of the British Government to introduce sweeping reforms in central Government. The mere mention of such reforms weakened confidence in the rupee because it was widely believed that the transfer of control over monetary policy to an Indian minister responsible to an elected central assembly would lead to deliberate devaluation and an 'irresponsible' monetary policy.

From 1929 onwards the Government of India was faced with a flight of funds from India. In normal years an influx of long-term capital was an important item in balancing India's international account and in providing remittance for Government. In 1927 the Indian authorities, concerned about selling enough Treasury Bills without hampering the financing of trade and industry by banks, had begun a deliberate policy of increasing the attractiveness of its short-term interest rates to draw in capital from abroad and to induce the exchange banks to retain funds in India at the end of the trading season. This policy had had some success but its consequence was that when, in 1930, confidence in the rupee faltered and the head offices of the exchange banks began to put pressure on their branches in India to run down their balances, obtain rupees by borrowing locally rather than by importing sterling and secure immediate cover for every transfer of funds to India, the flight of short-term capital put both Government remittance and the funding of the floating debt in jeopardy.

Faced with difficulties in buying remittance to meet the Home Charges, and in borrowing funds to balance the budget, the Government of India was forced to contract the money supply by remitting through the currency reserves, to issue Treasury Bills at ever higher rates and, by running down its balances, to push up the Imperial Bank's rate for advances. As the depression in price levels deepened, and as internal economic activity ground to a halt, the Indian authorities began to have increasing misgivings about the appropriateness of this policy, but they could see no other way out. During 1930 and the early months of 1931, goaded by constant demands for funds from the India Office, they contracted the currency tighter and tighter, withdrawing Rs. 40 crores in 1929–30, Rs. 33 crores in 1930–1 and a further Rs. 25 crores between April and August 1931 (total circulating currency had been Rs. 494 crores in 1928–9). Even so, by May 1931 it was clear that a crisis point had been reached in external finance. The Secretary of State was in urgent need of funds, but there seemed to be no way of getting money to him. The rupee was at 1s $5\frac{13}{16}$d and no one would import sterling, thus providing remittance, unless the rate were forced up by another $\frac{1}{8}$d, a sterling loan had just failed and another could not be tried until conditions were more stable. The India Office suggested yet more contraction but, as the Government of India pointed out, there were no resources left to effect this with.

The Indian authorities were convinced that it was now time to attack the root causes of the currency crisis – the loss of confidence caused by political uncertainty and by the world depression in the price of primary produce. They now suggested that the British Government should provide a drawing credit for India of £50 million (the amount was increased to £100 million shortly afterwards) to show that 'they are prepared to back India financially while the constitutional changes are being considered'.[86] In early September 1931 the Finance Member, Sir George Schuster, suggested a still more radical solution. He proposed, with the use of a credit from the Bank of England, to ease the strain on the rupee, raise Indian prices, lower credit rates, give a boost to exports and placate nationalist opinion by devaluing to 1s 4d.[87]

The policy of contracting the currency and raising interest rates was an effect, rather than a cause, of the wider financial crisis. Government action was aimed at removing from the market currency made redundant by the collapse of export prices. When world prices for Indian produce had first begun to decline in 1928–9 the result had been to increase the amount of circulating currency and lower interest rates as the exchange banks and export/import firms found that they no longer needed all the rupees they had imported to buy up marketable export produce. By 1929–30, however, capital was being drained abroad because of speculation and as a hedge against an uncertain future. The authorities had then deliberately raised the bank rate, and drawn off surplus funds with Treasury Bills, to prevent purchasers of Indian goods from meeting their demand for rupees by borrowing in India, rather than by importing sterling, and to try to hold short-term funds in the country. At the same time the Government's budgetary problems reduced the balances at the Imperial Bank, thus limiting the extra cash available for financing trade and industry by internal credit agencies. The collapse in price of India's export staples affected liquidity and purchasing power in those sectors of the agrarian economy that supplied such goods. The landlords, rich peasants and traders, who normally bought up these products from the cultivators, now found it hard to sell them again and could neither supply nor obtain the usual rations of credit needed to keep alive the rural marketing networks in goods for export or internal consumption. In normal years the import of currency to buy up exports had helped to expand internal credit for financing the movement of crops. Now that external financial agencies were exporting currency this expansion was curtailed, while the actions of Government did little to help. The absolute fall in money supply was not all that large – by March 1932 circulating currency was 82 per cent of its March 1929 level, while taking the fall in prices into account the amount had actually increased by 24 per cent[88] – but the effect of contraction on the internal economy was exacerbated by the imperfections in the internal credit networks. Contraction of the currency directly affected industries now heavily dependent on bank credits, rather than on investments from the public; it also served to increase those problems of commodity marketing that the collapse of demand and prices, and the consequent financial difficulties of *shroffs* and indigenous traders, had caused within the agrarian economy. It was to prevent the flight of capital that Schuster had proposed a drawing credit in May 1931, and it was to aid the internal credit networks that he suggested devaluation in September.

Schuster's proposals represented a breakthrough in the history of Indian financial policy. For the first time the Indian authorities were now recognising that monetary management was necessary to protect the internal economy from the impact of world demand. The Government of India did not suggest devaluation of the rupee and reflation of internal money supply because Indian prices needed to be lowered to make her exports competitive abroad (as the theory of the gold bullion standard postulated), but because Indian internal marketing networks would not continue to function without such policies. The drawback to these new plans was that they needed London's consent, and this was not forthcoming.

In the summer of 1931 the India Office favoured a British Government drawing credit for India, but was opposed to any devaluation of the rupee. The Treasury, on the other hand, was initially prepared to accept devaluation, but was adamant that no credits, 'transferring the burden, even contingently, on to the shoulders of the British taxpayer',[89] could be extended. When the world financial crisis finally forced sterling off the gold standard in September 1931 the British Government decided that the rupee should be put onto a sterling standard at the old rate, which meant a substantial devaluation against gold.

This decision was not intended to solve the problem of Indian finance, or to mitigate the strain on the Indian economy caused by the Great Depression. And yet, by creating a premium in the sterling and rupee price of gold, the British Government did provide a way out of the impasse. The substantial gold exports from India, which began in the autumn of 1931 and continued for the rest of the decade, effectively solved the short-term problems of Indian currency and finance, providing the Government of India with enough remittance to meet all its commitments in London, and allowing the authorities to expand the currency and initiate a cheap money policy. Yet, ironically, there is no evidence to suggest that this development had been forseen in 1931. The gold exports, vitally important as they were, were unplanned and unexpected.

The devaluation of the rupee and sterling in 1931, added to the British Government's subsequent measures aimed at raising world commodity prices, undoubtedly helped India to recover from the depression. But the way in which India had been treated during the currency crisis did little to still official and non-official criticisms of London. The Government of India had argued that India's interests required the rupee to be devalued against other major currencies by more than British interests required sterling to be so devalued. Devaluing the rupee by 12 per cent (to 1s 4d) against sterling in the summer of 1931 might not have helped the Indian economy very much, but such action could well have helped to improve relations between Indian businessmen and the British bureaucracy and, by promoting political tranquillity, have brought lasting benefits to Britain herself. As it was, currency policy, which in 1931 Schuster had called 'the worst cause of discord in recent years',[90] remained a contentious issue in relations between Britain and India until 1947.

Out of the wreckage of his hopes for a new alignment of monetary policy in the early 1930s Sir George Schuster retrieved one crumb of comfort. In 1934 the Central Legislative Assembly passed a Bill to establish a Reserve Bank of India, which came into existence in 1935. The bank was given control of currency and credit policy and was responsible for managing internal and external public debt and for supplying remittance to the Secretary of State. Little of the sense of liberalism that had, in Government of India circles at least, been associated with the 1927 initiative now remained. The bank was set up on a shareholder basis. London only consented to it as a way of preventing any Indian finance member of a future federal government from having any influence on monetary policy. The Secretary of State was to retain ultimate control over the bank's activities, through the supervisory powers held by the Viceroy independently of his Council of Ministers. There was a statutory obligation for the bank to uphold the 1s 6d ratio.[91] Had there been a fresh financial crisis at a time of a responsible government in India, it is clear that the Viceroy would have been put under immense pressure to allow the bank to make concessions to Indian opinion, but such a government never materialised, not did any such crisis. The Reserve Bank performed its functions in the late 1930s at a time of limited economic prosperity, easy money and plentiful remittance.

The crisis of the Great Depression stimulated changes in official thinking on economic policy in other spheres too. Discriminating protection was deliberately extended outside the industrial sector in 1930 when it was decided, largely at the prompting of Punjabi agricultural interests forcefully represented on the Executive Council by Sir Fazl-i-Hussain, to impose a tariff on imports of Australian wheat to aid the indigenous producer. Ironically, this protective tariff actually damaged local industry by raising the input costs of the flour mills of Calcutta that had been processing the imported wheat.[92] In 1932 the same reasoning led to a tariff on imported sugar to protect cane-growers in India; this stimulated the cane-crushing industry as well, but cost the central Government Rs. 8 crores a year in customs revenue.[93]

Schuster was the Executive Councillor most anxious to adapt Government policy to changed circumstances. In addition to his proposals for currency, he initiated a series of debates within the bureaucracy about new ways in which the Government could help the internal economy. Few of his plans bore any fruit, however. In 1930 Schuster announced that the Government of India would be prepared to consider schemes of intervention to support prices, should any be suggested by provincial governments; none were.[94] He also urged sympathetic handling of the plans put forward by the Central Cotton Committee for action to provide special financial arrangements to buy up the 1931 cotton crop, and of those of the Indian Jute Mills Association in 1932 for intervention to control production. These schemes came to nothing, however, as they were opposed by Schuster's colleagues on the Executive Council and by the Imperial Bank.[95] Schuster's radicalism was part of a coherent scheme motivated by his conviction that 'the world is moving towards a stage where economic planning by Governments is becoming more and more necessary'.[96] His fullest statement of this view was made after he had left India, in a lecture to the Royal Society of Arts in 1935:

> [Economic planning] is an expression which has been much abused. . . . True, when the phrase implies ideas that a single Government, by its own action, either in the way of monetary policy or public works expenditure, or by any other 'panacea' can recreate prosperity and off-set all those world-wide conditions and maladjustments which have brought about the present depression, then it must be viewed with scepticism and cautious criticism. . . . But it is a very different thing to recognise that Governments in these days have got to accept a far greater responsibility for guiding the economic life of their countries than has ever been necessary before. However much any supporter of old-fashioned individualistic ideas may dislike Government interference of any kind, he is merely burying his head in the sand like an ostrich if he refuses to recognise the established fact that practically every Government in the world is now in actual practice interfering drastically with the flow of trade. And if these interferences are going on, surely it must be the duty of a Government . . . to keep itself informed and use its information to guide its peoples. . . . If interference has got to be undertaken at all . . . then it is only commonsense to urge that it must be done properly – that it must be guided by foresight and reasoned purpose.[97]

In June 1932 Schuster had confessed that he 'should like to see the G.o.I. attempting to devise something like a five year economic plan . . . even if it led to no practical result it would be good for the country that the attempt should be made'.⁹⁸ The first requirement was information. The degree of ignorance in official circles about the Indian economy was horrendous. In 1930, for example, Schuster had asked a conference of the Financial Secretaries of provincial governments, called to discuss the depression, what impact Government currency policy was having on the amount of credit available to the cultivator and indigenous trader – they were unable to give a reply.⁹⁹ To remedy such defects Schuster proposed the setting up of an Economic Advisory Committee, on British lines, and eventually an Economic Sub-Committee of the Executive Council was established to co-ordinate departmental action. In 1933 this sub-committee commissioned a plan for an economic census from two British economists – Prof. A. L. Bowley and Dr D. H. Robertson; their report strongly recommended extensive improvements in the Government's statistical organisation.¹⁰⁰ The Government of India did not move particularly fast on this matter, but a decision was eventually taken to establish a new permanent statistical and industrial intelligence unit under an Economic Adviser. This office started to function during the Second World War.

Financial stringency, as well as administrative opposition, prevented the implementation of any major public works programme that might have mitigated the impact of the depression. The Government of India's annual capital expenditure, which had run at an average of Rs. 27 crores between 1920 and 1930, declined to an average of under Rs. 6 crores between 1931 and 1939.¹⁰¹ Just before his term of office expired, however, Schuster did sanction two small non-remunerative capital schemes – the rebuilding of the Pusa Agricultural Research Centre and the establishment of a Civil Aviation Authority. The latter, at a cost of Rs. 40 lakhs, was allegedly based on 'Keynsian notions'¹⁰² – the stimulation of a depressed economy by the establishment of capital schemes to provide new employment and encourage investment. Yet the chief help that Government policy gave to Indian industry during the depression was by extending old-established practices – revenue duties were substantially increased in 1930 and 1931, while protection was granted to new industries on the principle, according to Sir James Grigg, Schuster's unsympathetic successor, of 'the most possible protection with the least possible justification'.¹⁰³

Schuster's basic position had been that, even if Government action could do little to help the internal economy, officials should at least be seen to be trying. With his departure in 1934 the motivating force of a new economic policy was gone. Grigg held firm to the orthodoxies of pre-depression British Treasury circles, declaring that he found Keynsian ideas 'either silly or vicious',[104] and had little sympathy for the concept of economic planning. As he told the C.L.A.:

> Whether economic planning is right or not, I for one am not going to stand for that form of it which consists in Government taking all the losses and leaving all the profits to others. And if there is any other form, I suspect that it is only that now in force in Soviet Russia and nowhere else in the world.[105]

Grigg's stance was based on the old model of Indian economic development that had provided the justification for the economic policy of central Government before 1914. He held to this in a strict, if somewhat pessimistic, form:

> The representative Indian is not to be found among the few tens of thousands of noisy politicians, journalists, stock exchange gamblers and clerks; he is an almost naked creature clad in a loin cloth and an umbrella who squats about among his crops by day and breeds like a rabbit by night. And in my view we have neglected the second class for the first. It's quite true that we have removed from the peasant the fear of famine and murder but what with his entire neglect of Malthusian teaching and the slump in agricultural prices his economic position is if anything worsened. As an antidote to the misfortunes of the cultivator we have played up the idea of a rapid industrialisation of India by means of stupendously high dutires but the effects haven't been too happy. The prices to the consumer have been grotesquely high . . ., import trade has been cut down enormously and . . . the ability of the agriculturalist to export still further reduced while, except in the case of steel, the enterprise and uprightness of the industrialist have been insufficient to enable the new industries to become established securely. Thus we have pleased nobody, not even the industrialist or the politician to whom we have been playing up.[106]

Even had Grigg been more willing to advocate interventionary policies there were other barriers to central Government action.

Provincial administrations were still highly jealous of their autonomy, as the Government of India discovered when it attempted to initiate a centralised system of industrial intelligence.[107] There was also the residual problem of money; the establishment of full provincial autonomy and the separation of Burma in 1937 affected central revenues and necessitated grants from the centre to the provinces. These developments cost the central budget Rs. 9 crores in 1937–8 and 1938–9 and Rs. 10 crores in 1939–40.[108] In keeping with Grigg's views, spare central revenue (about Rs. 3·5 crores) was diverted to a scheme of rural development. The central Government was thrown back once more onto the customs revenue, but the tariff increases of 1931 had brought this close to the point of diminishing returns. In view of these constraints, the central Government did little for the rest of the decade, contenting itself with encouraging the Reserve Bank to attempt the integration of indigenous bankers into its credit network, commissioning a report on the shortcomings of co-operative societies, reorganising the income tax structure and passing amendments to the Companies Act to regulate the running of joint-stock banks.

The outbreak of war in September 1939 created a series of severe problems for central Government economic policy. World war again disrupted the equilibrium between external and internal economic pressures, and broke up the established patterns of monetary management, industrial production and agricultural marketing to such an extent that the Government of India was compelled to abandon *laissez-faire* completely, although not always successfully.[109] At the heart of the changes that occurred in the Indian economy between 1939 and 1945 were the demands of the imperial war effort. The Indian army increased nearly ten-fold; much of the equipment needed to supply these new troops was produced in India and, in addition, nearly £300 million worth of materials (mostly textiles, clothing and ordnance) was made in India for distribution in the Allied war theatres in the Middle and Far East. The war effort had a dramatic effect on many aspects of life in India and presented the central Government with a series of unprecedented economic problems. The most important of these was the price inflation, far greater than that of the First World War, that resulted directly from the impact of the war.

In 1939 the Government of India had agreed with the British Government that India's defence expenditure should be divided between them. The Indian exchequer was to pay a fixed amount equal to the effective costs of the army in peacetime (Rs. 36·77 crores), with an addition to allow for any rise in prices, a lump sum (Rs. 1 crore a year) towards the cost of maintaining Indian troops overseas, and the cost of all war measures regarded as being taken in India's exclusive interest. The British Government was to pay for the extra expenses caused by the use of Indian troops outside India plus, up to 1943, the whole cost of capital outlay needed for industrial expansion for the war effort. These arrangements meant, in brief, that the Indian Government met the cost of all forces in India (Indian and Allied) plus the cost of all supplies and equipment for them up to the level fixed as necessary for India's local defence, while the British Government paid for any troops and supplies needed in India above this level and for Indian troops and military equipment used outside India. Since Burma had been separated from India by the 1935 Government of India Act, most of the cost of the fighting there fell on the British Government. Indian and British defence expenditure in India during the war is given in Table 3.2.

TABLE 3.2 Defence Expenditure in India 1939–1945 (in Rs. crores)

	1939–40	1940–1	1941–2	1942–3	1943–4	1944–5	1945–6
Chargeable to India	49·54	73·61	103·93	267·14	395·86	458·32	395·32
Chargeable to H.M.G.	—	53·00	194·00	325·48	377·87	410·84	374·54
Total	49·54	126·61	297·93	592·62	773·73	869·16	769·86

Source: N. C. Sinha and P. N. Khera, *Indian War Economy* (Calcutta, 1962), *Appendix XXXII*.

The 1939 agreement did not solve all the Government of India's financial problems regarding defence, for costs had to be paid for in India as they occurred; Britain was under an obligation to pay her share, but cash could not be shipped out to India in wartime. The British Government's debts to the Government of India were met in the first years of the war by cancelling out India's sterling debt and railway annuities held in London. By 1942 these bonds had been almost completely paid off and the British Government paid for new Indian recoverable expenditure by issuing sterling Treasury Bills to the London office of the Reserve Bank. Debt repayment and sterling balances did not increase the revenue of the Government of India and, although increasing taxation, floating long-term rupee loans and stepping up small-savings schemes allowed the Finance

Member to meet all the defence expenditure chargeable to India in full, it was not possible to finance the expenditure incurred on behalf of the British Government in this way. Most of the cost of this had to be met by expanding the money supply against Government securities, first against Treasury Bills issued to the Reserve Bank in India and later against the sterling balances held by the Bank in London. Although this new money was technically covered by adequate reserves its effect tended to be inflationary, for it increased purchasing power without increasing the supply of goods available for purchase. The inflationary potential was large – the amount needed to be covered in this way totalling Rs. 1457 crores between 1939 and 1945. Overall, total money supply (notes in circulation, bank deposits and cash holdings and deposits with the Reserve Bank) rose from Rs. 317 crores in August 1939 to Rs. 2190 crores in September 1945.[110]

India's war effort did not simply increase purchasing power without increasing consumer goods; the country's role as a major supplier of war materials actually diminished the goods available to the civilian population. The volume of imports fell sharply during the period of hostilities, while industrial production expanded significantly only in those industries that supplied the war effort. The result was a savage increase in the price of consumer goods on the internal market, as indicated by Table 3.3. The demands of the

TABLE 3.3 Indices of Relative Price Movements 1939–44
(August 1939 = 100)

	Rice	Wheat	Cotton manufactures	Kerosene
December 1941	172	212	196	140
December 1942	218	232	414	194
December 1943	951	330	501	201
December 1944	333	381	285	175

Note: Rationing was introduced during 1944.

Source: A. R. Prest, *War Economies of Primary Producing Countries* (Cambridge, 1948), p. 46.

war effort also gave considerable impetus to the development of India's industrial potential, but its contribution to actual expansion was not equally great. As Table 3.4 shows, the output of important industries in India during the war varied considerably. Those

TABLE 3.4 Indices of Indian Industrial Production 1939–1945
(1937 = 100)

	Cotton textiles	Jute	Steel	Chemicals	Paper	Cement	Matches	Paint	Sugar
1939	104·3	92·4	125·0	103·9	135·1	152·9	87·0	147·1	62·5
1940	103·6	96·1	125·5	133·3	169·7	152·1	90·0	165·6	106·0
1941	114·8	92·4	131·1	153·2	185·4	185·8	76·4	241·9	108·2
1942	102·0	99·5	136·7	138·7	180·9	194·5	60·0	233·5	78·4
1943	117·0	84·4	141·5	138·6	179·2	188·4	68·8	251·3	95·3
1944	122·9	86·7	139·6	126·3	192·7	182·1	68·1	259·3	97·1
1945	120·0	84·4	142·9	134·1	196·5	196·5	90·2	232·4	85·5

Source: *Report of the Fiscal Commission 1949–50, Vol. I*, p. 21.

industries which were already in existence worked to full capacity, but the shortages of capital goods and skilled manpower prevented a major breakthrough. Even so, some new plant was built and a few basic industries were established, notably in ferro-alloys, metal fabricating, chemicals and machine tools, although many of these new articles were produced in very small quantities. A rapid expansion of small-scale industries also created new sources of supply for heavy industry, especially of such consumer and intermediary goods as hardware, piping and new types of textile products. Although industrial expansion in strategic materials expanded, the bulk of such goods never entered the civilian economy. The system of Government requisitions was much more efficient and extensive in this war than it had been in 1914–18. As the Government of India Mission to the United Kingdom of 1945 (Hydari Mission) pointed out, 'since September 1939 India had progressively taken more and more from her civilian economy to meet Defence requirements'.[111] It was estimated that all mill production of wool textiles, all factory production of leather and footwear, all organised production of timber, nearly three-quarters of steel and cement production, over two-fifths of paper production, about one-sixth of cotton textile production and the whole of the 'normal' quota of 600 million yards of cotton yarn had been directed away from the civilian economy to serve military requirements. In addition, every engineering workshop that could produce ordnance or structural materials was at work on Government contracts. The industries that produced the consumer goods most in demand on the civilian market did not expand as fast as did strategically important ones. This was partly the result of deliberate Government policy in the licensing of new factories and the cutting down of non-food crop production. The decline in imports increased demand for indigenous manufactures, but local producers were unable to keep pace. Table 3.5 gives an indication of the decline in civilian consumption of consumer staples. An alternative method of calculation shows that the supply of cotton goods available for civilian consumption fell by more than 23 per cent, while both imports and home production of kerosene had fallen by over half their peacetime levels by 1943–4.[112]

The most important item on the internal market was food. In 1942 a major crisis arose in this commodity as prices soared, producers hoarded and transport was disrupted; local shortages became major famines and millions died in Bengal. The scarcities of

TABLE 3.5. Indices of Goods Available for Civil Consumption in India 1939–40 to 1945–6

(1938–9 = 100)

	1939–40	1940–1	1941–2	1942–3	1943–4	1944–5	1945–6
Rice	109	92	103	97	121	111	104
Wheat	95	101	91	92	103	97	108
Other cereals	105	116	106	121	118	107	na
Sugar[a]	162	121	86	106	123	95	97
Tea[b]	122	115	93	226	173	31	na
Cotton piece-goods[b]	96	88	84	60	82	81	84
Iron and steel[b]	100	na	81	40	63	63	80
Cement	62	49	47	16	57	55	141
Paper and pasteboard	95	80	59	33	30	39	58
Kerosene	103	97	86	54	42	47	61
Wool manufactures[a]	100	26	31	13	4	18	37

[a] annual pre-war average = 100.
[b] in calendar years (viz. 1939–40 = 1939); 1938 = 100.

Source: Calculated from figures in N. V. Sovani (ed.), *Reports of the Commodity Prices Board* (Poona, 1948), p. 38.

the second half of the war continued at the end of hostilities. The problem was one of supply, rather than of production; total output of food-grains had remained more or less constant, while the increased demand of foreign soldiers and the decreased supply of imports did not affect the general picture very much. It was the distributive system that broke down. Caught in an inflationary spiral, producers and merchants invested in commodities (by hoarding) rather than in the purchase of non-existent consumer goods. For the rest of the war the problem of feeding the towns and deficit food-producing rural areas became as important for central Government as fighting the Japanese.

The Government of India was slow to react to the disruptions of the internal economy caused by wartime events. In the first years of the war the Finance Member refused to admit, in public at any rate, that the existing arrangements for war finance created an inflationary potential, stressing instead that the shortages of supply were a complete explanation of price rises. By 1943, however, both the Finance Department and the Reserve Bank had realised that something would have to be done to reduce purchasing power and to persuade Indians to invest in Government loans rather than in commodities. The options were limited. Taxation, especially the Excess Profits Tax, was increased in an attempt to mop up surplus purchasing power and new savings schemes were introduced, including ten-year Defence Savings Certificates and National Savings Certificates. To aid investment in Government loans a control was imposed on the issue of industrial shares in May 1943 and sanction was withheld from any company not producing goods essential for the war or the civilian economies. The net increase in public debt raised in India between 1939 and 1945 was Rs. 1136·17 crores: Rs. 521·36 worth of long-term debt, Rs. 40·14 crores worth of Treasury Bills and Rs. 574·67 crores worth of small savings.[113] In addition it was agreed in 1943 that the British and United States Governments should finance some of their war expenditure in India by the sale of gold through the Reserve Bank. These sales were kept up until the middle of 1945, and totalled over Rs. 140 crores' worth. American war expenditure was almost exclusively financed in this way. These actions had a limited, although beneficial, effect; the rate of increase of the money-supply, which was 325 per cent between September 1940 and September 1943, was nearly halved for the last two years of the war.

Measures to control the prices and supply of consumer goods had to be more drastic. They involved the central Government in increasing intervention in the most convoluted and sensitive areas of the internal economy. Between October 1939 and September 1942 six Price Control Conferences had considered the problem of regulating the prices of consumer goods, but with little practical result. The provincial governments were unwilling at this stage to intervene in internal marketing and were more anxious to prevent any impositions by central Government which would compromise their autonomy. When the food crisis struck in the summer of 1942 the first set of ameliorative measures were based on the false assumption that a shortage of production was the problem, and were organised on the well-worn, but somewhat irrelevant, principles of famine relief. Ineffectual efforts were made, on a provincial basis, to fix maximum prices, to restrict movement and forward operations in wheat, and to establish regional committees to co-ordinate the supply and regulate the price of other food-grains. Early in 1943 the Government of India formulated a 'Basic Plan' for the movement of stocks from surplus to deficit provinces, while the provincial governments did the same for surplus and deficit districts.

These schemes could not work without control over procurement as well as over distribution. The provincial and central administrators began in this field by trying to work by remote control; grain dealers were licensed and contracts placed with them for the movement of grain – the merchants proved unco-operative and the next step was for Government officials to purchase grain from the cultivators and then to sell it to the merchants for distribution. This system, too, broke down and by 1944 direct requisitioning had been established in most provinces with local administrators doing all the work of procurement, storage, transport and supply through rationing and 'fair-price' shops. By the end of the war legitimate food-grain marketing was a Government monopoly. The increase of official intervention in the marketing of other consumer goods followed the same pattern. Simple price control of sugar, cotton and kerosene merely encouraged the growth of a black market and, by the last years of the war, had been supplemented by partial rationing and some direct control of production, marketing and distribution. In addition, faced with shortages of capital equipment for industry, central Government attempted to regulate industrial expansion by vetting issues of new capital, controlling the establishment of new plant by a licensing system and regulating imports and the spending of foreign exchange.

Central Government intervention in the wartime economy was by no means completely effective. Provincial jealousies, over food stocks in particular, inhibited the establishment of a nation-wide distributive system. Official food procurements came to rely on food imports, since these could be controlled more easily than local production. Yet, by 1945, the cumulative effect of the war measures had been to force the Government of India into a new role in regulating the internal economy. Before 1943 the central Government had been reluctant to abandon the appearance of *laissez-faire*. In December 1942 the Viceroy had pointed out that 'drastic steps such as wide-spread requisitioning [of food] are . . . not likely to yield results comparable to the panic they would create'.[114] Reviewing the prospects of increasing India's industrial production of war materials by direct intervention, the Government of India had argued in the same year that 'we do not regard high powered control as constitutionally feasible'.[115] The next three years demonstrated that the strains of war made intervention on an unprecedented scale both necessary and possible. By 1945, as one contemporary observed noted:

> The role of the general administrator has altered with a vengeance. In addition to his other duties, he has now become a

monopolist, the only wholesale dealer in grain throughout the province with full control over all retail dealings, except for small quantities within village boundaries and was responsible for the conduct of the majority of grain retail shops in the province.[116]

Industrial licensing, controls of investment and price controls of consumer goods all helped to change fundamentally the relationship between central Government policy and the internal economy of India.

The ending of the war did not mean that intervention could be abandoned. The money supply was still inflated and, as the attempt to de-control food in 1947-8 showed, the dislocation of internal economic networks caused by the war continued into peacetime. In addition, the central Government had emerged from the war with a commitment to an active policy of economic development, especially of industrial development. From 1942 onwards a wide-ranging debate had been going on about the economic future of India after the war, and specifically about the uses to which the sterling balances should be put. By 1945 the Government of India secretariat had hammered out something that approached a coherent plan of post-war economic reconstruction using the sterling balances to purchase capital goods and Government loans and deficit finance to provide aid to new industries, including the nationalisation of the heavy industrial sector if adequate private finance were not forthcoming.[117] This plan necessitated continued intervention. Central Government licensing of industrial undertakings and foreign exchange quotas was to be the means of official influence over industrial development, while creating money to provide capital investment meant continued controls over profits and prices to prevent inflationary disruption.

The war years had witnessed a further breakdown of the system by which the Indian economy had worked before 1913. An increased demand based on considerations other than those of free competition had stimulated intense, if unbalanced growth. Production of cotton and jute had decreased under Government pressure and food crops for internal consumption had become the leading sector of the agrarian economy; Indian industries supplied a totally protected home market in which price made no difference to demand, either for military stores or consumer goods. At the same time rural investment was switched into commodities, industrial profits soared, cheap money was available and those sectors of the established internal marketing networks that survived the Depression had to adapt to direct requisitioning. As one analyst of these changes has put it:

> The Indian economy mainly consists of two imperfectly welded sections, an international economy superimposed on a primitive subsistence economy. What enabled the delicate mechanism of internal production and trade to carry on from year to year in prewar days was the assurance of imports of machinery and consumer goods in sufficient quantity. When these imports were no longer available the whole economy was threatened with collapse.... What ensured supplies of foodgrains in peacetime was the existence of fairly steady prices and a sufficient supply of acceptable exchange-media. When these normal relationships were disturbed, or even when it was thought that they might be disturbed, the whole economy was threatened with breakdown, for any reduction of supply due to these causes is, *ipso facto*, concentrated on the urban areas.[118]

This breakdown threatened most acutely between 1939 and 1945, but it was not simply a product of the war. It had been precipitated by changes in the internal financing and marketing networks in India throughout the inter-war period, and in particular by the collapse of traditional linkages between the local and supra-local economy during the Depression. The increased importance of joint-stock banks, with interests in industry and in the Treasury Bill market as well as in trade, in providing credit for the marketing of agrarian produce, and the decline of the indigenous banking system were important developments. At the same time, this process of substitution of banking networks was not perfect, so that gaps appeared in the internal marketing process that, eventually, only the Government could provide the institutional apparatus to fill. The apotheosis of this process was reached in 1943 when the Government, unwillingly and in a piecemeal fashion, was forced to take action that brought it into a self-consciously dominant position of influence over all aspects of economic life.

Government activity had always had a significant impact on some sectors of the Indian economy – a more important one, indeed, than most officials realised. Even before 1914 the Government had been the largest dealer on the foreign exchange market, the largest borrower of internal capital and the largest single depositor in domestic banks. During the 1920s direct purchasing of foreign exchange for Government remittance in India, the development of a short-term capital market and the establishment of the Imperial Bank of India, which used Government balances to make advances to other financial institutions, took this further. The creation of the Reserve Bank in 1935 did not reduce the impact of Government's actions because the Reserve Bank, like the Imperial Bank before it, was heavily dependent on Government balances for cash, while its exchange purchases were based on Government's needs. Since, at the same time, other Westernised banking institutions were extending their operations downwards into the indigenous banking sector, the impact of Government intervention in the Westernised sector to secure its own requirements had a potentially larger impact on the economy as a whole. The development of financial institutions that occurred in the inter-war period, notably the 'modernisation' of banking networks to integrate agricultural marketing into the rest of the economy and the growth of large institutions with interests in both trade and industry, had been part of the Government of India's long-term development plan for the economy since before 1914. It had been thought that once these goals had been achieved, hostile criticism of *laissez-faire* economic policy would collapse; ironically, because this growth was accelerated in the 1930s and 1940s thanks to a crisis in India's external and internal economies and in the relationship between them, its result was that *laissez-faire* had to be abandoned for ever.

The Government of India's economic policy between 1914 and 1947 was subject to two important constraints. Firstly, there was the bureaucracy's isolation from the people it ruled. Intervention in the domestic economy meant sacrificing the interests of some sectors to the needs of others. Such was the case, naturally, with not intervening (in certain circumstances), but this was never seen as so pressing a problem. The central Government's difficulty was that, as non-representative, largely alien, administration it had only limited opportunities for testing the political climate, and no way of binding support to itself by means of a party structure. The advantage of the 'free market' model of economic development, which the Government of India clung to except when put under the extreme pressure of a world-wide war, was that it allowed Government to keep a low profile. *Laissez-faire* was attractive for practical, as well as for theoretical, reasons. Secondly, the Government of India never had much room in which to manoeuvre. The theoretical debate about the pace of Indian economic activity in the inter-war period, symbolised by the ratio controversy and the discussion of devaluation during the Depression, was subsidiary to meeting its immediate revenue and remittance requirements. Government policy was always interventionary in pursuit of these short-term needs, but the economic changes of the inter-war period meant that they now set central Government apart from important sectors of the internal economy. Only after 1939 did the pressures on Government to control prices, secure war supplies and mop up surplus purchasing power, coupled with the repatriation of all India's sterling public debt, result in an involvement with the internal, rather than the external, economy. After the Second World War, as after the First, the Government of India found that the impact of its economic policy on the lives of its subjects was immensely heightened. The sterling balances accumulated between 1914 and 1918 had been spent in an attempt to abdicate this dominant position; by using them to establish a new exchange rate and an 'automatic' exchange standard the Government had attempted to deflate the economy and mitigate the effect that its need for short-term finance and created money had had on internal economic activity. After 1945 the Government could not abdicate – normal economic activity could not go on without the institutions it provided – while the existence of sterling balances much larger than those of the earlier war meant that detailed decisions about the future of the Indian economy would have to be made within the secretariat. By 1945 the central Government needed an economic plan, if for no other reason than to co-ordinate its own inescapable responsibilities – and thus the performance and development of the entire Indian economy.

4. The Imperial Government and the Indian Economy: The Official Mind of Decolonization, 1914-47

The last chapter has attempted to describe and analyse the role of the Government of India in the development of the Indian economy during the last thirty years of British rule. It is now time to turn our attention to the activities of the imperial Government in London in the same period, and to assess the ways in which changes in the political economy of the Raj altered the objectives of metropolitan policy-makers and influenced the actions they took to secure them. To do this we have to concentrate on imperial policy, on the official mind of decolonization in India. Whitehall was the summit of the pyramidal structure by which the Indian empire was governed; although those at the top were not always the masters of events they did hold overall authority and accept overall responsibility for decisions.

Ideally, an analysis of the official mind which shaped British India policy ought to be based on a series of detailed studies of each major decision taken, following through every aspect of the complicated bureaucratic, executive and legislative process. Unfortunately, there is a notable dearth of useful research at this level.[1] Faced with this the only practical approach is to work backwards from the declared intent of major acts of policy, paring off the obviously particular and ephemeral influences to reach the residual core. Thus the working definition of the official mind used in this chapter is that of the lowest common denominator of the objectives of British policy-makers, modified by an appreciation of the limitations which changes in Britain's position in India and the world imposed on the purposes of policy. We have already defined the objectives of British policy as the maintenance of India's imperial commitment to provide a market for British goods, supply men and materials for imperial defence and obtain the sterling remittance needed to meet Home Charges and interest payments.

The ability of the Government of India to fulfil these obligations depended on its being able to balance external and internal demands for its revenue resources. To a large extent, then, the history of the last three decades of the Raj is the history of Indian public finance. Figures for the revenue, expenditure and public debt of the Government of India tell us much about the difficulties faced by British officials and politicians in shaping constitutional, as well as economic, policy for India in this period. Conclusions drawn from a study of these figures are implicit in much of the analysis that follows. For the sake of convenience, however, tabular statements of these statistics have been grouped together in an appendix at the end of the chapter.

The true nature of India's imperial role was demonstrated by the quality and quantity of commercial, monetary or strategic resources that the British Government could draw on at times of imperial crisis. However, in bargaining for these resources, British demands were not simply based on a crude assessment of British needs. London was only prepared to bully New Delhi over tariff policy when imperial policy-makers were convinced that the political and economic consequences of disappointing British commercial interests were greater than those of alienating Indian business opinion. When the Government of India could prove that, for financial or political reasons, it could not maintain the Indian army as an 'imperial fire-brigade', then British strategic planners were prepared to limit the imperial role of Indian troops or even, in the last resort, to pay for their services. Only over Indian monetary policy did British Governments refuse to compromise for most of our period, and that was because the Treasury was convinced that the British tax-payer would be left to foot the bill should the Government of India ever default on its sterling debt.

The role which India played in supporting the imperial system only became apparent at times of imperial crisis. Between 1914 and 1947 there were four such crises – those of the two World Wars, that of the early 1920s, when a trade depression coincided with the British realisation that the cost of holding their new empire in the Middle East was prohibitive, and that of the early 1930s, when the Great Depression and the disruption of established patterns of international investment and capital flows pushed sterling off the gold standard.

In 1914 no one doubted that India had a major role to play in any scheme of imperial defence. The Indian army of around 160 000 fighting troops, one-third of them British, represented half the British world-wide military strength. Since the 1860s imperial defence plans had concentrated military might on two centres only – Britain herself and India. The Indian army had proved its worth in the second half of the nineteenth century in fighting minor wars, and supporting imperial troops in major ones, in East Africa, Egypt, The Sudan, Persia, Afghanistan, Burma and China. There were, however, clear limitations on the type of opponent that the Indian army could tackle. By the early years of the twentieth century it had been accepted in London that the Indian army was not strong enough to take on that of a major power – specifically that of Russia. Reforms and modernisation schemes designed to fit the local army for large-scale warfare were proposed by the Commander-in-Chief, India, in 1904, but had to be abandoned for want of cash.[2] In 1913, following the report of the Army in India Committee, the Government of India declared that the primary functions of its army were two-fold:

> While India should provide for her own defence against local aggression and, if necessary, for an attack on the Indian Empire by a great Power until reinforcements come from home, she is not called upon to maintain troops for the specific purpose of placing them at the disposal of the Home Government for wars outside the Indian sphere, although – as has happened in the past – she may lend such troops if they are otherwise available.[3]

A few days before the outbreak of war in 1914 the Indian Army Council decided that India could spare two infantry divisions and one cavalry brigade for service overseas in the imperial cause and, in the autumn of that year, these troops were sent to France as an expeditionary force. The next four years saw a remarkable expansion of the Indian army. In 1914 Indian revenues supported 80 000 British officers and men and 230 000 Indian troops (including non-combatants); during the war the Indian authorities recruited more than 800 000 fighting troops and over 400 000 non-combatants. The pre-war Indian army establishment of Indian troops was mainly made up of 155·5 cavalry squadrons and 138 infantry battalions; by October 1918 a further 121·5 cavalry squadrons and 203·5 infantry battalions had been raised. Nearly one million men were despatched overseas during the period of hostilities – more than half of them to Mesopotamia (Iraq), and substantial numbers to France and Egypt.[4] In addition to supplying men India provided materials for the imperial war effort. The Indian Munitions Board purchased more than Rs. 37 crores' worth of ordnance, clothing and other military supplies between April 1917 and October 1918.[5] The exigencies of war, and especially the disastrous Mesopotamia campaign of 1916, revealed to the Government of India how ill-equipped and under-supplied its army was in comparison to those of its major opponents and allies. During the second half of the war the Indian army acquired, for the first time in the case of some native troops, regular rations and adequate medical services.

These new arrangements, in addition to new levels of pay introduced during the war to stimulate recruitment, substantially increased the cost of the army to the Indian tax-payer. Yet the Indian exchequer did not have to meet all the costs of this increased military activity in the imperial cause. In the late nineteenth century there had been considerable debate between the Government of India, the India Office and the British Treasury over who should pay for Indian troops serving overseas. Although at this time India was still widely regarded in London as 'an English barrack in the Oriental seas from which we may draw any number of troops without paying for them', the Government of India disapproved of this role, as did a strong section of parliamentary opinion at home.[6] Ever since the Abyssinia expedition of 1867 the principle had been laid down that the Indian Government should pay the normal costs of troops serving overseas, while the imperial Government met their 'extraordinary' costs, plus the full cost of raising new troops in India to replace those abroad should this prove necessary. As the Treasury had pointed out in 1885: 'The Indian Exchequer will bear whatever expenses would in ordinary course have fallen upon it if the troops had remained in India, but it must be relieved from all expenses which, but for the expedition, would not have been incurred.'[7] During the 1870s, 1880s and 1890s the Government of India had waged a paper war of attrition against this division of responsibilities, arguing that the imperial Government ought to meet the full costs incurred when Indian troops were used in campaigns that had no bearing on India's security. London finally accepted this principle in 1896, the Treasury agreeing to pay the full cost of that year's operations in Mombassa, and the India Office prepared a formula laying down that the proportion of the expenses borne by the Government of India should depend on the extent to which Indian interests were at stake in the result of the campaign.[8] This left only the question of who was to decide whether or not Indian interests were involved; in 1900 the Commission on the Administration of the Expenditure of India surveyed the question and came to the conclusion that India ought to pay the ordinary costs of troops sent to Egypt, Persia and the Gulf, Afghanistan, Central Asia and Siam, and some of the cost of troops sent to East Africa.[9]

At the start of the First World War India was asked to provide troops for Europe and Egypt (these latter being quickly transferred to the Western Front). Under the 1900 arrangements, the Government of India need not have paid any of the expenses of these troops. However, following a non-official resolution in the Imperial Legislative Council, the Indian authorities offered to treat the expeditionary force to France as if it were going to an area in which India had a substantial interest – in other words, they offered to pay the ordinary costs of these troops, leaving extraordinary expenses and the cost of raising replacements to the imperial Government. This offer was accepted by London and the agreement formalised by parliamentary resolutions in the House of Commons in October and November 1914. For the next three and a half years financial arrangements for the Indian army continued on this basis in all theatres with the Government of India being responsible, in brief, only for the normal expenses of the troops that made up its peacetime army. All other expenses were met by London until April 1918, when the Indian Government agreed to expand its commitment to cover the local costs of seven divisions (100 000 men) of the troops already recruited in India during the war, of another seven divisions to be raised by July 1918 and of a further seven divisions to be raised in 1919. The signing of the armistice in November 1918 meant that London was not able to take full advantage of this offer.[10]

Before April 1918 the imperial war effort had involved the Government of India in a small amount of extra expenditure/on defence because of the need to meet new standards of pay and equipment; in the last summer of the war costs rocketed as India fulfilled her new commitments. Defence expenditure in 1913–14 was Rs. 31·9 crores; the imperial war effort cost an extra Rs. 2·96 crores in 1914–15, Rs. 8·36 crores in 1915–16, Rs. 9·46 crores in 1916–17, Rs. 10·22 crores in 1917–18, Rs. 29·68 crores in 1918–19 and Rs. 4·85 crores in 1919–20.[11] Total military expenditure in India from 1913 to 1920, and a breakdown of the Indian and imperial share in it, are given in Table 4.1. Military expenditure

TABLE 4.1 Government of India and British Government Net Defence Expenditure in India 1913–1920 (in Rs. crores)

	1913–14	1914–15	1915–16	1916–17	1917–18	1918–19	1919–20	1920–21
Defence expenditure of Government of India	29·84	30·65	33·39	37·48	43·56	66·72	86·97	87·38
Defence expenditure in India of H.M.G.		13·84	24·02	57·77	103·17	138·38	94·11	82·00
Government of India defence expenditure as percentage of total	100·00	68·89	58·16	39·35	29·69	32·53	48·03	51·59

Note: Sterling converted in rupees at rate of £1 = Rs. 15.

Source: *Statistical Abstract for British India 1911–12 to 1920–1*, pp. 188 and 195 note.

cost the Government of India Rs. 224 crores between April 1914 and March 1919, while the imperial Government contributed a further Rs. 337·3 crores. Yet, even though London was responsible for a good deal of the cost of India's war effort, the increased demands that were made on the exchequer necessitated the raising of new taxation, as did her other major contribution to the imperial cause – the taking over, in March 1917, of £100 million worth of British Government War Debt. The Government of India provided £78 million of this immediately, by meeting that amount of imperial expenditure in India without taking payment in London, and agreed to assume responsibility for interest payments on the balance. To raise the money to meet both the defence expenditure and the repayments the Indian authorities issued a large rupee loan in 1917, the interest on which had to be met from future revenue, and increased taxation. During the war all tax levels were raised, the most important increases being in excise, customs and income tax; in addition, a super-tax was imposed for the first time in 1917. The burden of taxation (excluding land revenue) per head of population rose from just over Rs. 1·5 in 1914–15 to just under Rs. 2·5 in 1918–19. The Government of India incurred over Rs. 105 crores' worth of new net permanent debt during the war years, and over Rs. 108 crores' worth of net floating debt. Its annual expenditure on interest payments, which ran at around Rs. 1·8 crores from 1914–17, increased to Rs. 10·9 crores in 1917–18 and to Rs. 12·2 crores in 1918–19.[12]

These new commitments had to be paid for: the cost presented itself in two forms – the need simply to find adequate finance to sustain India's effort during the war, and the need to assuage the Indian political demands and agitations that had grown out of the sufferings and disturbances caused by her role as an imperial appendage. The resources to meet both were found by reducing India's future role in the imperial system, although this was not fully apparent until the early 1920s. Britain had been able to command extensive support from India in her time of need, but the strains that this had caused meant that in more normal times British imperial interests in certain vital fields would be subordinated to Indian domestic requirements.

The first sign of this had come in 1916, for in March of that year the Government of India proposed to London a 7·5 per cent general tariff on imports and also suggested that the tariff, but not the excise, on cotton goods be raised to the same level. The British Government refused to allow any increase in the cotton tariff but did accept the need to increase the general rate. British cotton manufacturers were not to escape for long. The Government of India's £100 million gift of March 1917 had to be paid for both morally and materially and the British Cabinet now accepted that Lancashire would have to play its part in this – the Indian authorities had only agreed to take over so much of the British War Debt on the understanding that the cotton tariff would then be raised to 7·5 per cent. With some reluctance the Cabinet in London accepted this bargain, while insisting that the excise on locally produced cotton goods be raised to the same level as the tariff on imports.[13]

The most important effect of the war on Indian affairs was the acceleration of various schemes of constitutional reform, culminating in the Government of India Act of 1919. This legislation was largely based on the joint report written by the Viceroy (Lord Chelmsford) and the Secretary of State (Edwin Montagu) in 1917 which had argued that the only way to win Indian co-operation for British rule was to give representative Indians a greater measure of responsible executive power. The 1919 Act set up autonomous dyarchic provincial administrations in which Indian ministers responsible to elected legislatures had control over some Government departments. The bureaucracy's hold over the centre continued intact, although the elected element in the central legislature was increased and its rights of discussion widened. Perhaps the greatest advance of the 1919 Act was its acceptance of the notion that the Indians who were to co-operate in Government should be elected by a general, if restricted, franchise. British policy-makers now saw that the best chance of survival for the Raj lay in the development of a 'free-market polity', rather than in the continuation of the old policy of the bureaucracy ruling in conjunction with the selected representatives of particular interest groups.[14]

It is interesting that, in the discussions surrounding the 1919 Act, no one considered how the reforms might affect India's imperial role. The British Cabinet, the heart of the imperial policy-making process, never faced the Indian problem head-on;[15] to many of its members the purpose of constitutional advance in India was defensive – not to reward India's efforts during the war, not because any milestone had been passed in the evolution of Indian political opinion, but because 'if the Government does not take charge of the operation, someone else will . . . and there may easily grow up a disaffection that would soon become dangerous'.[16] It was clear to the Government of India, to the British Government, and even to the self-consciously liberal Montagu that 'the Government of India . . . was concerned with the supreme interests of the country and was not the right sphere in which to initiate constitutional changes'.[17] Montagu's famous declaration of 1917 that the policy of the British Government was 'the progressive realisation of responsible government in India as an integral part of the British Empire'[18] did not imply any formal weakening of India's imperial commitment. As Montagu himself pointed out to the House of Commons in February 1922, such advance was conditional on Indian 'good conduct' and, in the imperial context, this included loyalty to the empire and preparedness to put the interests of the imperial power above those of India alone. If Indians refused to use their increased power to play a part in the imperial system, Britain could and would return to coercion.[19]

In practice, the 1919 reforms did affect the Government of India's ability to respond to imperial demands. The Act created a Central Legislative Assembly in which Indian politicians could debate government policy more fully than ever before. Although M.L.A.s had no power to pass or reject legislation without the

Viceroy's consent, the Government of India now had to take into account the force of Indian opinion consistently, articulately and constitutionally expressed. Indian control of provincial government, it was thought, would not affect India's imperial role as the areas of government to be handed over – education, local government, public health, labour and industry – were of purely domestic concern. But this was a miscalculation. For the reforms to work in the provinces the Indian politicians there had to be given increased financial resources. This meant overhauling the centralised system of public finance, and any increase in the resources available to the provinces meant a diminution of those available to the centre. Once Indian participation in provincial government was permitted financial decentralisation became essential; the only way to do this was to separate provincial and central revenue. In 1920 arrangements were made whereby the provinces were to receive all receipts from land revenue, irrigation, excise and general stamp duties while the central Government was to rely on opium and salt duties, income tax and the revenue tariff. These arrangements cost the centre Rs. 10 lakhs – to compensate for this the provinces were to make annual contributions to the central exchequer totalling Rs. 9·83 lakhs, leaving them with an increased revenue of Rs. 8·67 lakhs.[20] This settlement, known as the Meston Award, caused great annoyance to the provincial governments, who resented paying 'tribute' to the Government of India, and the system of provincial contributions lapsed in 1927–8. To raise substantial amounts of new revenue the Government of India now had to depend on income tax and customs tariffs: raising income tax would be unpopular in India, raising customs tariffs would be unpopular in Britain. In the political circumstances of the 1920s it was to be Lancashire, not Bombay, that would suffer the more.

Of itself the 1919 Government of India Act produced no new formal limitations on India's imperial role, but that role was not itself formal. It was simply a reflection of the Government of India's ability at any given point to respond to the demands of British policy-makers for commercial, financial or military assistance, balanced by the domestic demands of Indian opinion and the limitations of its own exchequer. Thus when, in the early 1920s, the Government of India took up an attitude which severely damaged British military and commercial expectations, this stance was based on the traditional considerations of financial stringency and

The Official Mind of Decolonization 1914–47

domestic political pressure, not on any new formal constitutional arrangements.

From 1920 to 1923 the Government of India faced a major financial and exchange crisis brought about by the collapse of the rupee exchange and the depression in world trade of 1920–1, coupled with a need for heavy military expenditure to fight an Afghan war and meet troubles on the frontier. The central Government's budget was in deficit by a total of Rs. 84 crores between 1918 and 1922; this, and the collapse in the exchange, forced it to borrow in London to meet commitments there, but by mid-1922 Indian loan stock was becoming unpopular in the City.[21] The only acceptable long-term solution was to increase revenue and to decrease expenditure, but increasing revenue meant raising tariffs while decreasing expenditure meant cutting the army budget: thus the domestic financial crisis compromised the Government of India's imperial commitment. As we have already seen, the general customs tariff was raised from 7·5 to 11 per cent in 1921 and to 15 per cent in 1922; cotton duties were included in the 1921 increase, but not in the later one; special duties on luxury goods of up to 30 per cent were also imposed. These increases were, by and large, popular in India, while the Secretary of State in London gave them his full support. The Lancashire cotton manufacturers, and other British manufacturing interests, protested in vain. Raising the Government of India's revenue was not enough, however; some cuts in expenditure were also necessary. It was unfortunate that, just as the Government of India decided that the army was the best place to make these, the British defence planners discovered a new, extensive and expensive imperial role for the Indian army to perform.

In 1918 the British had found themselves heirs to the old Turkish provinces and Russian spheres of influence in the Near and Middle East.[22] Britain and her Arab allies had conquered Palestine and Syria, and had helped to liberate the *Hejaz*; the Indian army had occupied Mesopotamia, had overawed the Persians and had supported Ibn Saud in Arabia. At the same time, the collapse of Russia and the fear of a Turkish and German eastward thrust had stimulated the Government of India to send troops to hold a line between Batum on the Black Sea and Baku on the Caspian, which in turn had fostered hopes of protection among the newly created independent republics of Georgia, Armenia, Azerbaijan and Dagestan. British policy-makers now began to think of the advantages of retaining these new outposts of empire, advantages which were clear to Lord Curzon: 'You ask why should England do this? Why should Great Britain push herself out in these directions? Of course, the answer is obvious – India.'[23] Ironically, Montagu was the recipient of this homily. It was the Foreign Secretary, rather than the Secretary of State for India, who thought that the future of the Empire depended on the creation of a buffer zone stretching from Cairo to Peshawar for the defence of India.

Such grandiose schemes seemed to be important in the frantic atmosphere of the closing months of the war. But in the cold light of peacetime, with a financial crisis and growing demands for social reform in Britain, with rebellions to be faced in Ireland and Egypt, and with the Turks and the Russians moving against the new outposts of empire, a line had to be drawn between necessities and luxuries. By the end of 1919 informal control had been deemed sufficient for Persia and South Russia; in Iraq, too, the fear of Russian or Turkish invasion, and of the commercial infiltration by French and American oil companies, was not strong enough to outweigh the £30 million a year needed to maintain a British garrison.[24] In June 1920 the Secretary of State for War and the Chief of the Imperial General Staff reported to the Cabinet that British forces were overstrained in this theatre and that withdrawal was the only way to prevent an eventual disaster. Six months later the Cabinet authorised the withdrawal of British troops from Persia to the line of defence of the Basra oil-fields, and the cutting of the Iraq garrison to a minimum.[25]

There was only one alternative to a curtailment of direct British control in the Middle East – the employment of the Indian army in its traditional role as a cut-price imperial garrison. In the summer of 1920 India was supplying ten infantry battalions for Iraq, nine for Egypt, seven for Palestine, six round the Black Sea and smaller formations in Malaya, North China, Hong Kong, Aden, Cyprus and the Persian Gulf. To compensate for the withdrawal of British troops from Iraq the Government of India was now invited to provide an additional 39·5 battalions of infantry and pioneers, four regiments and a troop of cavalry, ten companies of sappers and miners and four companies and a troop of signallers. The Viceroy was warned that this contribution was only a beginning, and he was required to meet it immediately – before any arrangements for sharing the cost had been made.[26]

The Indian reaction to these proposals was sharp and decisive. In

1919 military expenditure had kept the Indian budget in deficit; New Delhi now calculated that the new demands would increase the cost of its army to £60 million a year – 40 per cent of India's net revenue. The Viceroy argued that such a commitment would cause a complete breakdown in the political situation in India, the C.L.A. would refuse to vote any new taxes and the Indian members of the Viceroy's Executive Council would resign. Therefore, the Government of India explicitly rejected any 'obligation to supply permanent overseas garrisons to mandated territories';[27] the Secretary of State for India supported this stand, and further pointed out:

... we must definitely get out of our heads the vague idea, too often entertained, that India is an inexhaustible reservoir from which men and money can be drawn towards the support of Imperial resources or in pursuance of Imperial strategy.[28]

Indian garrisons in Iraq were not all that was at stake here. In the dark days of 1919 the British Government had decided to revise fundamentally India's formal role in the system of imperial defence. A new Army in India Committee (Esher Committee) was set up to investigate the future of the Indian army and to examine the tortuous chain of command over it, especially the relations between the Chief of the Imperial General Staff, the War Office, the India Office, the Government of India and the Commander-in-Chief, India. The Esher Committee was specifically asked to consider what problems would arise in Indian and imperial defence policy if India achieved Dominion status. The Committee's report of 1920 recommended that the solution to all difficulties was to make the Indian army responsible to the imperial, not the colonial, Government: the Secretary of State for India and the Viceroy were no longer to be allowed a decisive voice in military planning, the Military Department of the India Office was to be abolished and greater powers were to be given to the C.I.G.S. and to the Commander-in-Chief, India, to impose policy on the India Office and the Government of India. When the Indian army was used in an imperial role, civilian officials were to be bypassed and orders to go directly from the C.I.G.S. to the Commander-in-Chief, India.[29] The Esher Committee Report began, ominously: 'Novel political machinery created by the Peace Treaty has enhanced the importance of the Army in India relatively to the military forces of other parts of the Empire, and more particularly to those of the British Isles.'[30] It went on to hint that, as mobilisation in Britain came to a halt, the Government of India should prepare itself to intervene in the Near and Middle East, and even in Eastern Europe, should the occasion arise.

Both the India Office and the Government of India protested loudly about the implications of this new policy. They emphasised the political and financial limitations on using Indian resources for imperial ends, and stressed the importance of retaining the full powers of the Secretary of State and the Viceroy in the chain of command. Both made it clear that the Indian army should not, normally, be used outside India's borders and that its costs must be scaled down, not boosted to meet British requirements. It was pointed out that Indian moderates, and even British expatriates, were very sensitive to the 'exploitation' of the Indian army and that, even though the direct costs of Indian troops abroad might be met by the imperial Government (although the Esher Committee report was unclear on this point), the problems of demobilisation, compensation pay for overseas service and the uncertainties of future commitments would all increase the defence expenditure of the Government of India.[31] In a despatch to the Secretary of State the Viceroy quoted with approval a recent resolution of the C.L.A. that

> the purpose of the Army in India must be held to be the defence of India against external aggression and the maintenance of internal peace and tranquillity ... it should not as a rule be employed for service outside the external frontiers of India except for purely defensive purposes or with the previous consent of the Governor-General in Council in very grave emergencies.[32]

After a flurry of memoranda and much bitter argument between the India Office and the War Office the whole matter was taken up by a sub-committee of the Committee for Imperial Defence; this eventually reported in June 1922 and its recommendations were approved by the Cabinet in January 1923. The new proposals cancelled out the Esher Committee plans almost completely. The Viceroy and the Secretary of State for India were restored to a central position in the Indian army command structure, and were to be consulted on the political and financial situation in India before any Indian contribution to imperial defence was considered. The C.L.A. resolution on the Esher Committee report was singled

The Official Mind of Decolonization 1914–47

out as 'stating accurately and concisely the objects for which the Army in India exists'. On the employment of the Indian army overseas:

> The principle should be generally accepted that, except in the gravest emergency, the Indian Army should be employed outside the Indian Empire only after consultation with the Governor-General in Council. . . . The view of the Government of India that the Indian army should not be required permanently to provide large overseas garrisons is supported. Units required for such purposes should be maintained in addition to the establishment laid down for the Indian Army, and the whole cost, direct or indirect, of recruiting and maintaining such units should be borne by His Majesty's Government, or by the dependency or colony requiring their services.[33]

This position held for the rest of the decade; the Indian army could still play a limited imperial role, but at London's expense. In June 1921 the Government of India had, in fact, laid down clearly its own version of the Indian imperial military commitment, a commitment more extensive than that later proposed by the Cabinet:

> We are ready to accept as a permanent liability the obligation, which we undertook before the war, to provide from the Indian Army the battalions required for garrison duties in China, the Malay States, Colombo, and Aden. As regards the Mandated Territories [Palestine and Iraq], we are prepared . . . [to supply troops for them] on the clear understanding that all charges connected with the active battalions . . . will be borne by His Majesty's Government. . . . [It is necessary that] we should receive early and definite orders as to the extent that we shall be asked to provide such garrisons as a quasi-permanent arrangement.[34]

By 1923 the financial and political crisis in India had forced British policy-makers to revise their ideas about how India could be made to fit into the imperial system. For their military obligations, the Government of India had won acceptance of a return to the arrangements that had governed the use of the Indian army in 1913. Yet although this had been done by a series of what looked like formal agreements, it represented only a truce in the clash between

Indian and imperial opinion. In times of peace the level of the Indian military budget continued to be the subject of protest by Indian politicians; in times of war the extent of India's military commitment to the imperial cause would continue to be decided by short-term calculations based on the immediate crisis. The issue at stake in the post-war years was the attempt by the War Office and the Esher Committee to increase India's responsibility for imperial defence by linking her army to an integrated imperial defence force. The Government of India's victory on this occasion did not mean that the attempt would not be made again when a new global threat emerged to the security of the British Empire.

Much the same state of affairs existed for tariff policy in the 1920s. The Fiscal Autonomy Convention, which held that the Secretary of State should avoid interference in budgetary policy when the Government of India and the C.L.A. were in agreement, remained only a convention. While some Secretaries of State, Montagu and Benn for example, were prepared to give the Government of India the benefit of the doubt every time, others were less generous. As Lord Peel pointed out in 1923, the India Office expected to be consulted on tariff matters before these were raised in the C.L.A. and, therefore, before the Government of India and the central legislature could be in agreement over them.[35] Under the terms of the 1919 Government of India Act the India Office could still interfere in tariff policy, even after this had been agreed by the Government of India and the C.L.A., to safeguard imperial interests and to maintain any fiscal arrangements involving Britain as well as other parts of the Empire.[36] Between 1923 and 1929 many of London's old taboos about Indian tariff policy were broken, 'discriminating protection' was introduced and the cotton excise abolished. Yet this did not mean that, in other circumstances, the British Government would willingly continue to deny itself influence over Indian fiscal policy. When a major commercial crisis arose in Britain in the early 1930s, the Fiscal Autonomy Convention was to come under considerable pressure from London.

The purpose of the Convention had not been to loosen the commercial ties between Britain and India but to set them on a new, and politically more secure, basis. In the words of the parliamentary Joint Select Committee on the 1919 Government of India Bill:

> Nothing is more likely to endanger the good relations between India and Great Britain than a belief that India's fiscal policy is

The Official Mind of Decolonization 1914–47 119

dictated from Whitehall in the interests of the trade of Great Britain. That such a belief exists at the moment there can be no doubt. That there ought to be no room for it in the future is equally clear. India's position in the Imperial Conference opened the door to negotiations between India and the rest of the Empire, but negotiation without power to legislate is likely to remain ineffective. *A satisfactory solution of the question can only be guaranteed by the grant of liberty to the Government of India to devise those tariff arrangements which seem best fitted to India's needs as an integral part of the British Empire.*[37]

In 1919 it had seemed that India's commercial commitment was also to be considered in an imperial context, but there was no real equivalent for tariff policy of the Esher Committee. On the eve of the Imperial War Conference of 1917 the British Government's Committee on Commercial and Industrial Policy After the War had issued an interim report urging the British Government to make a statement of faith in the idea of imperial preference and recommending that any future British customs duties include some measure of this. However, the final report of this same committee in 1918 marked the death of any notions of increased imperial solidarity that had been canvassed during the war; rather than looking to an autarchic imperial future the committee produced what has been called 'a document of Great Britain's national economic policy'.[38] British Governments of the 1920s were prepared to give an imperial preference on any customs duties that they imposed, but they were not ready to contemplate imposing duties for the sake of giving preferences, nor to sacrifice the interests of British agriculture and industry for the sake of Dominion or imperial producers. Thus, while the 1923 Imperial Economic Conference resolved that 'all possible means should be taken to develop the resources of the Empire and trade between Empire countries',[39] following the Conservative débâcle of the 1923 Tariff Reform election no major political party in Britain was prepared to offer a systematic scheme of preferential agreements.

The Government of India was as unconvinced as most British politicians of the usefulness of a closed imperial economic system. At the 1923 Imperial Economic Conference, for example, the Government of India representative argued that India's extensive trading links outside the Empire made imperial preference of dubious economic value to her. At this conference the Indian delegate did vote in favour of the resolution urging closer imperial economic cooperation, an action which the rest of the Viceroy's Executive Council found disturbing and from which they implicitly disassociated themselves.[40] By 1930 the Indian administration had given small preferences to certain British steel and cotton imports, but always denied that this had been done out of any regard for the principle of imperial preference. As the Commerce Member, Sir Geoffrey Corbett, pointed out to the 1930 Imperial Economic Conference:

> I have already explained that it is foreign goods that are replacing British goods in the Indian market. It follows that it is frequently against foreign goods that Indian industries require protection. In some lines there is really no competition at all between British goods and Indian goods. In other lines the measure of protection required is far less. . . . In our schemes for protecting the steel industry and the cotton textile industry . . . we have recognised this difference and we have fixed differential duties for British and foreign goods. It should be clearly understood that we have done this solely in the interests of the Indian consumer, and in pursuance of our principle of granting the minimum protection required by Indian industry. . . . India is prepared to consider favourably all schemes designed to encourage the development of trade with all other countries of the British Commonwealth. But she is not prepared to depart from her present policy of discriminating protection. . . . We are, therefore, unable to commit ourselves to any general scheme of tariff preferences within the Empire, but we must reserve complete freedom to deal with each case as it arises.[41]

In contrast to commercial and military policy, which were to some extent considered in an imperial context immediately after the First World War, the gold standard rupee of January 1920 gave the Government of India's monetary policy formal independence of sterling and of any possible future imperial monetary standard. This independence was maintained even after the abandonment of the gold rupee, and was strengthened by the abandonment of the Council Bill sale system of settling India's international accounts. In 1920 some opinion both in the City of London and among the 'imperial visionaries' in the British Government had wanted to tie the rupee to sterling and to prepare the way for a currency and

The Official Mind of Decolonization 1914–47

monetary system exclusive to the Empire.[42] The Treasury was always opposed to such schemes in general, however, and the Babington-Smith Committee had rejected them for India in particular. The gold bullion standard rupee of 1927 maintained India's formal monetary independence – although the fact that the bulk of her foreign exchange reserves were held in sterling means that she can be seen to have been part of the *de facto* sterling area. However, sterling's return to the gold standard in 1925 limited the importance of this link and the Hilton-Young Commission of 1926 re-affirmed the Babington-Smith Committee's stand by clearly rejecting a sterling standard for the rupee because of the damage that any crisis in the British economy might then cause to the Indian one.[43]

The autonomy that the Government of India enjoyed in fiscal and monetary affairs in the early 1920s had been based on judgements and opinions formed during the British and imperial economic crisis of 1917–21; the fact that these economies faced no new major upheavals during the rest of the 1920s helped to ensure that this position was maintained. As the world slid into depression after 1929, however, India's role in the imperial economy had to be reviewed anew. In the crisis of 1917–21 policy-makers had been struck by the strengths, or potential strengths, of the Indian export economy and of the rupee, and by the corresponding weaknesses of the British export economy and of sterling. In the crisis of 1930–1 these relative strengths and weaknesses were seen as reversed and policy, especially currency policy, had to be adapted accordingly.

The Great Depression of the early 1930s represents the third major imperial crisis in which India was involved in the twentieth century. Events in this period conspired to strike at the heart of the established relationship that still existed between the British, imperial and world economies. The decline in the price of primary produce on the world market lowered demand for imported goods in many of the countries with agricultural economies that were the traditional markets for Britain's export staples, thus exacerbating the problems of industrial stagnation and unemployment that had bedevilled important sectors of the British economy since 1918. Faced with reduced or non-existent balance of payments surpluses in commodities, the governments of countries with agriculturally-based economies had difficulty in meeting their debt obligations in London; this helped to tighten the spiral of weakening confidence that forced sterling off the gold standard in September 1931 and seriously damaged London's role, and the invisible earnings gained from it, as the major financial centre of the world. In these circumstances British policy-makers began once more to take an active interest in the ways in which Empire countries managed their economic affairs. Thus the subject of India bulked large in the official mind once more, specifically the problems of Indian tariff and monetary policy.

The slump in commodity prices in the early 1930s hit India hard. The value of her exports of merchandise (excluding precious metals and government stores) fell from Rs. 361·34 crores in 1929–30 to Rs. 257·85 crores in 1930–1, to Rs. 181·90 crores in 1931–2, to Rs. 152·86 crores in 1932–3.[44] India never suffered a visible balance of payments deficit during this period but, as in 1920–3, the depression in exports combined with poor harvests and political agitation led to agrarian unrest, a flight of capital, a lack of confidence in the rupee and a financial crisis for the Government of India.

The effect of the onset of the Depression was to cause a potential decline in the Government of India's revenue, rather than a substantial increase in its expenditure. The customs revenue on imports, which had provided 44 per cent of the central Government's total revenue receipts in 1928–9, was the most vulnerable item. As the value of India's imports of merchandise steadily declined (falling by over half between 1928–9 and 1931–2) the fall in customs receipts that would have resulted had the rates not been raised was potentially disastrous. Even with considerable increases in revenue tariffs in February 1930, January 1931 and September 1931, the income derived from customs duties on imports still fell from Rs. 40·92 crores in 1928–9 to Rs. 36·08 crores in 1931–2.[45] The most contentious issue that arose from proposals to increase tariff rates was that of the fate of cotton manufactures. In the early 1930s successive British Governments were very concerned about the contraction in Lancashire's sales to India as a result of the depression, uncompetitive prices and a boycott of British goods, for sales of British cloth in India slumped from 1248 million yards in 1929 to 376 million yards in 1931.[46] Yet the Government of India was not prepared to treat cotton as a special case, for the tariff on cotton textile imports had been second only to that on sugar as a revenue earner in the late 1920s, providing 15 per cent of customs revenue on imports (and over 6 per cent of the central Government's total revenue) in 1928–9. As it was, despite, and in part because of, increases of between 220 and 270 per cent in the cotton tariff between January 1930 and October 1931, the Government of India's receipts under this head fell by almost half between 1928 and 1932.[47]

The Labour Government of 1929–31 was probably more under the influence of the Viceroy over matters concerning India than was any other British Government of our period and, although the Cabinet was concerned about the effects in Lancashire of any increase in cotton tariff, it decided that it could not overrule Lord Irwin when, in February 1930, the Government of India announced that it was going to increase the import duty on cotton textiles to 15 per cent.[48] In January 1931 the Viceroy announced another increase in the general tariff rate, including the cotton tariff, from 15 to 20 per cent. The Cabinet now argued Lancashire's case strongly, warning that increased tension between Britain and India on this issue might jeopardise the work of evolving constitutional reforms. The British Government wanted a clear preferential rate for British goods, but the Viceroy opposed any such move. Knowing the strength of Indian opinion on this issue, Irwin pointed out that Indian tariff policy had to be justified in terms of India's interests alone and warned that imposing imperial preference would only increase the effectiveness of the boycott of British goods. Faced with an official and non-official revolt in India the Cabinet backed down, although they did secure a small preference of 5 per cent for British low quality cotton imports.[49]

The real crisis over the cotton tariff came in September 1931. The Government of India, in financial difficulties again and under pressure from London to balance its budget to boost confidence in the rupee, proposed a further 5 per cent increase in all tariff levels. By now the National Government, dependent in practice on Conservative support, was in office. The influence of the Lancashire manufacturing interest was substantial – the 60 Conservative MPs from that county were the largest and best organised pressure group in the House of Commons, while the opinion of Lord Derby, the county's largest magnate, carried weight in the House of Lords and in the Conservative Party. Whereas the Labour Secretary of State, Wedgewood Benn, had taken shelter behind the Fiscal Autonomy Convention, claiming that it was his duty to look 'from the standpoint of India with a view to advancing the interests of India' in tariff matters,[50] his Conservative successor, Sir Samuel Hoare, thought that as 'an extreme measure in a time of national emergency' the Convention could be set aside.[51] Hoare frequently warned the Viceroy that both he and Baldwin thought that the Convention should be modified and, in times of great stress, threatened that it might be altered significantly under the new constitutional proposals.[52] But although Hoare thought that the Government of India's new tariff proposals were 'disastrous upon [sic] Lancashire',[53] there was little that he was able to do about them. The Cabinet complained to the Viceroy and then threatened him, proposing first a 5 per cent excise on Indian manufactures to nullify the protective effects of the new tariff, and then an increase in the rate on non-British goods to 40 per cent.[54] But the new Viceroy, Lord Willingdon, refused to be bullied. He argued that any dictation by London of Indian tariff policy would cause a storm in India, and revealed that three of the Indian and two of the British members of his Executive Council were prepared to resign if the Cabinet's proposals went through.[55] In the face of this opposition there was little that the British Government could do but give in with the best grace it could muster.

By the end of 1931 the National Government had accepted that it could not interfere directly in the general tariff policy of the Government of India and that this method of maintaining a British commercial advantage was closed to it. The stick of imperial command now had to be replaced by the carrot of bilateral consultation. Writing, as Chancellor of the Exchequer, to disabuse a prominent Lancashire Conservative leader of the hope of forcing New Delhi to improve the position of British cotton textiles in the Indian market, Neville Chamberlain pointed out in January 1932 that 'an agreement by assent... is the most hopeful line of approach'.[56] Considering the uncompromising attitude towards Indian monetary policy taken up by the Treasury at this time these views have a special irony, and demonstrate the prominence that the issue of the rupee had assumed in the official mind.

Deliberations about the financial side of India's imperial commitment were inextricably linked with the whole question of further constitutional reform. The problems of Indian finance in this period were both short- and long-term. The short-term crisis, as we have seen, concerned the problem of providing the Secretary of State with sterling funds to meet his commitments in London at a time (1930–1) when the reduction of India's commodity trade surplus, the flight of capital from India, the lack of confidence in the rupee and the reluctance of foreign investors to buy Indian loan-stock made capital hard to raise in London and remittances hard to obtain in India. This crisis was only resolved in the winter of 1931–2 by the revival of India's export trade thanks to sales of large amounts of gold from private stocks.[57] The long-term problem was that of ensuring that Indian finances continued to be run in such a way that the British Government's interests could not be put into jeopardy by any future Government of India in which central departments were to be made responsible to an elected legislature. The transfer of control over financial and monetary policy was recognised, both in London and New Delhi, as the most important part of any scheme for the reform of Indian central Government. Discussion of the reform of financial management was dominated by the intractable problem that the British Government and powerful sections of Indian opinion had clearly defined interests in this aspect of Indian policy that were mutually exclusive. The depression in the world economy that lasted throughout the period of the consitutional discussions, and the short-term crisis in Indian finance of 1930–1, strengthened these interests and deepened the divide between them.

In the early 1930s all sections of Indian commercial, financial and political opinion were convinced that the disruptions caused by world depression were being exacerbated by policies (high interest rates, currency contraction and holding the rupee exchange) aimed at maintaining India's external obligations at the expense of her internal economy. A number of solutions were proposed, the most important being external debt repudiation (part of the Congress platform for Civil Disobedience) or readjustment of the external debt between the British and Indian Governments, the latter becoming liable only for loans contracted in the interests of the internal economy (an idea being widely canvassed in Indian business circles in 1930),[58] coupled to a devaluation of the rupee. It was not only Indian business interests that favoured devaluation. By 1933, when the issue was being freely discussed in connection with the forthcoming Reserve Bank of India legislation, a large body of British expatriate and home opinion also supported such a move. The entire board of the Imperial Bank, both Britons and Indians, were now in favour of devaluation to 1s 4d at most, as was a substantial section of expatriate opinion in Bombay and Calcutta, some interests in the City of London and even, at least according to E. J. Bunbury (an enthusiastic expatriate campaigner on this issue), the Governor of the Bank of England himself.[59]

All those, of whatever race, who had an interest in the expansion of the Indian domestic economy as a market for imported or indigenously produced goods, or for the employment of loan capital, could see the advantages of devaluation and of policies aimed at raising incomes and internal purchasing power. The Government of India had a somewhat different perspective. While prepared, although not always willingly, to follow London's line on currency and monetary policy, officials in New Delhi were aware of the connection between financial stringency and political intransigence in India. In 1933 Lord Willingdon asserted, with typical exaggeration, that the refusal to devalue supplied 'probably the strongest hotile motive in India'.[60] More soberly, but more suggestively, Schuster had stressed in 1930 that:

> We feel very strongly that the demand made by the Indian public that policy as regards Finance and Commerce should be carried out in accordance with preponderant opinion in the country is one of the most important factors in the political situation, and the practical satisfaction of this demand might create an entirely new political orientation in India.[61]

Lord Irwin had pointed to the same conclusion in January 1931 when he told the Secretary of State that the future management of financial policy was the most important issue to be faced in any new scheme of constitutional reform. If it were announced that finance were to come under the control of an Indian minister, he argued, this would be taken to mean devaluation; if power to alter the ratio were withheld from a reformed Government there would be no hope of reconciling the most important sections of Indian opinion to such reforms.[62]

Policy-makers in London could see the force of this analysis, but they were not prepared to draw the same conclusions from it. The immediate financial and political crisis in India in 1930 and 1931 forced the British Government to consider precisely the question of India's imperial financial commitment and its own stake in the political economy of the Raj. The answer was found to revolve around the provision of defence, the sterling debt and salaries and pensions. As an India Office memorandum pointed out in June 1931:

> If a Federal Government were established in India, the aggregate

charges under these three heads (Defence, Service of the Debt, and Salaries and Pensions) would, at a very conservative estimate, absorb three-quarters of the total revenues of the Federation, and a very large proportion of these payments would have to be made in sterling. This fact illustrates vividly the direct interest which the British Government must continue to retain in the financial administration of India, and explains why it is necessary to impose such measures of Parliamentary control as may be sufficient to ensure that these obligations are met . . . There is no escape from the conclusion that so long as the British Government retains obligations which absorb so large a proportion of the total revenues of India, it must retain a direct interest in the financial administration of the country. This by no means implies that financial administration must remain under close or detailed control, but merely that provision must be made to ensure that the financial stability and credit of the country will be maintained, as unless this can be ensured the obligations falling on the British Government could not be met. This, from the purely British point of view, is the primary object of the [financial] safeguards.[63]

By the summer of 1931 the India Office and the Treasury were agreed that, in the words of an India Office official, 'the financial stake of His Majesty's Government and the British people in India remains, for all practical purposes, as a permanent obstacle to anything that could reasonably be termed financial self-government'.[64] This financial stake was particularly dear to the official mind: during the currency crisis of 1930–1 British policy-makers insisted on the Government of India contracting the money supply to make remittances, maintaining a 1s 6d rupee and keeping control of Indian finance in their own hands, but they did not do this to secure British commercial interests, or even to protect British bondholders or retired I.C.S. men as such; their concern was that, should India ever default on her debt and pension obligations, it would in practice be impossible for the British Government to avoid taking over these commitments and meeting them out of its own exchequer. It was the British tax-payer, rather than the British bondholder, that London's policy was designed to protect. As Ramsay MacDonald noted in September 1931, 'if we agree to a responsible Finance Minister, His Majesty's Government will eventually have to take over India's sterling obligations *per-*

manently'.[65] Both Chancellors of the Exchequer during this period, Philip Snowden and Neville Chamberlain, were of the same opinion.[66]

The crisis of 1930–1 had shown that the main threat to the Government of India's ability to meet its obligations in London was a failure of foreign and expatriate confidence in the rupee: London feared that any future attempt to devalue the rupee, or to transfer the power to effect devaluation to an Indian minister responsible to an elected legislature, would lead to a renewed collapse of confidence. To prevent this the India Office and the Treasury ensured in December 1930 that the Federal Structure Sub-Committee of the First Round Table Conference laid down that the essential financial safeguard for a reformed constitution must be the grant of special powers for the Governor-General to maintain the credit of India, ensure the supply of funds for defence, foreign affairs and debt servicing, supervise foreign borrowing and prevent discussion in the legislature of any unsuitable proposals affecting currency and exchange. The Viceroy was to act in these fields as the agent of the Secretary of State, not as a constitutional monarch dependent on the support of his a ministers.

The 1930 proposals for financial safeguards included the establishment of a Reserve Bank, free from political influence, to manage currency and credit policy and remittances. In 1927 it had been thought that setting up such a bank would boost Indian confidence in the impartiality of monetary policy; London policy-makers were still aware that this was an important aim but they were now more anxious to secure the confidence of foreign and expatriate interests than Indian ones. However, a Reserve Bank could be made to serve this purpose too, provided that its constitution was carefully supervised. During the criss of 1930–1 even a closely circumscribed Reserve Bank looked too risky however – removing the management of currency policy from the Secretary of State to any sort of central bank would weaken confidence to some extent, and India's finances were so shaky that the risk could not yet be taken. By the autumn of 1932 the situation was more stable and in October the India Office surveyed the possibilities again, coming to the conclusion that financial policy could eventually be transferred, but not until a Reserve Bank with adequate reserves had been established, the Government of India's short-term debt position had improved considerably and the depression in the Indian economy was over. The Treasury was now consulted and officials from that department drew up a detailed list of desiderata, laying down the essential conditions for a central bank as being currency reserves of £100 million, a permanently balanced budget, the ear-marking of resources to meet the £133 million worth of sterling and rupee debt maturing in the next six years, internal tranquillity and prosperity and an assured export surplus in commodities other than bullion. Once these conditions were met, the Treasury argued, a Reserve Bank could be set up and control over financial policy, with safeguards, could be transferred to India no less than three years later.[67] One Treasury official reviewed the problem literally in black and white terms and concluded that, with a 'white man's' Reserve Bank and proper safeguards, even a 'black Finance Minister' could do no harm.[68]

For the last two months of 1932 a Cabinet Committee considered the whole problem of future constitutional advance in India. Here, as the Secretary of State told the Viceroy, the only outstanding issue was 'how far we can reconcile the demands of political expediency with the needs of stable finance'.[69] When the full Cabinet met to take a decision on its committee's deliberations it was finally agreed that a pledge should be given to transfer control over finance to India, although with no definite date given, subject to the safeguards set out in 1930 and provided that a Reserve Bank had already been established and was working properly. The Treasury's fears that even this decision would lead to a collapse of confidence in the rupee went unheeded and the Chancellor eventually admitted that, while he thought no one in India capable of running monetary affairs satisfactorily, political necessity made the transfer of control on such terms essential.[70] The Cabinet's pledge was made public in the British Government's White Paper on Indian constitutional reform, published in March 1933.[71] The preconditions that had to be met before a Reserve Bank could be established were those that the India Office had decided on in October 1932; yet these qualifications did not, in practice, represent an obstacle to the setting up of such a Bank. It was decided early in 1933 that the administrative process needed to draft a Bill should be set in motion, and two committees of experts – one official and one joint official and non-official – set in London that summer. A Reserve Bank Bill was introduced into the Central Legislative Assembly in the autumn and was passed early in 1934. The bank itself came into existence in April 1935, to coincide with the implementation of the new Government of India Act.[72]

The constitution of the Reserve Bank of India followed the lines that London had laid down in 1927–8. The bank was non-political, with directors appointed by local boards elected by the shareholders. There was no state capital invested in the bank, although the Viceroy had power to appoint the Governor, the Deputy Governor and four of the twelve voting directors. The bank managed a rupee fixed to sterling at the established ratio and the Viceroy remained the only authority able to alter these arrangements. In the discussions that had been held with Indian opinion, both in London and in the C.L.A., the shareholder principle and the ratio question had come in for a great deal of criticism. Demands for a state bank were revived, and for power to be given to its directors to alter the exchange rate and currency standard of the rupee as they saw fit. Indians were not united on the state bank issue, however, and a number of businessmen-cum-politicians were prepared to sacrifice the ratio question to get some sort of central bank straight away. The Government of India was thus able to pilot London's Bill through the C.L.A. virtually unscathed, the only concession necessary being that of providing by statute for a London office of the Bank to manage the British end of the Government of India's foreign financial dealings, taking them out of the hands of the Bank of England. In addition, at the instigation of the Government of India, the Reserve Bank Act of 1934 contained a sop to Indian opinion on the ratio question in the form of a promise in its preamble that this issue, and that of the currency standard, could be reopened when world economic conditions were more stable.[73]

As the Secretary of the Indian Finance Department pointed out in 1933, 'primarily the Bank is to operate as a constitutional safeguard'.[74] Officials in India noted, with some amusement, that London's insistence on a shareholder bank meant that, although central banks were supposed to protect currencies against depreciations caused by spendthrift governments, the elected directors of the Reserve Bank would be drawn from the ranks of businessmen and industrialists who were the chief advocates of currency depreciation and easy money.[75] In any case, the Government of India had known for some time that the creation of a non-political central bank would not exclude the influence of the legislature from currency management.[76] However, the India Office had no doubts about the soundness of its plan: the Reserve Bank Act of 1934 and the Government of India Act of 1935 were not thought to take any real control of Indian financial management out of the hands of the

Secretary of State because the financial safeguards, including the safeguarding of the ratio and all that that implied, and the Viceroy's power to nominate the Governor of the Reserve Bank were reserved to 'the Governor-General in his discretion', in which capacity he remained under the orders of His Majesty's Government, and so in this way it was hoped 'to secure official control at all vital points'.[77] There is also some evidence to suggest that the first Governor of the Reserve Bank, Sir Osbourne Smith, was made to promise that he would work to uphold the established ratio.[78]

Great strain was put on India's domestic economy because she was forced to maintain her imperial financial commitment at a time of depression. This led to considerable political agitation concerning the demand that Indians should be given a greater say in their own affairs. The 1935 Government of India Act was designed to meet this demand, but the belief in London that any real transfer of control would inevitably lead to default, either through repudiation of debt or loss of confidence in the rupee, meant that, in practice, no such transfer was allowed. The financial safeguards of the 1935 Act and the establishment of the Reserve Bank of India represented instead a refinement of formal control, rather than a switch from control to influence. The Act succeeded in transferring the Finance Department without transferring finance: as one Indian businessman had pointed out in 1931, the functions of an Indian Finance Minister under the new constitution 'would be mainly to collect revenues and hand them over to the Viceroy for disbursement towards military, home charges, civil expenditure etc., etc.'[79] – control of central Government on those terms was not particularly attractive to Indian political leaders. The terms of the Act were dictated by the interesting conclusion reached when the British Government considered its stake in India's financial affairs – for it became clear that this stake was neither positive nor dynamic, but rather the short-term, defensive aim of ensuring that the British tax-payer did not have to foot the bill for India's debt repayments and pension obligations. When the Treasury and the India Office realised in 1931 that the British Exchequer would be unable to avoid covering the debts of a defaulting India, one door to wide-reaching constitutional advance slammed shut. It was not to be reopened until 1945, when India had replaced her sterling debt of £350 million with sterling balances of almost four times as much.

Within the Empire as a whole the economic crisis of the early 1930s led to a revival of interest in an exclusive trading and monetary system. This idea never achieved as tight a grip on actual policy-making as way as on the rhetoric of the policy-makers but, at least from the departure of sterling from the gold standard in September 1931 until the Imperial Economic Conference at Ottawa ten months later, it was a major force in determining British and imperial attitudes to economic policy. India played a full part in the discussion of a new imperial commercial and currency bloc and, for commercial policy at any rate, the idea of imperial solidarity produced a fresh line of approach to the problem of maintaining her imperial commitment.

As the world economic crisis deepened Government of India officials, concerned about falling prices, shrinking export markets and the danger of tariff wars and competitive devaluations, began to look more favourably at schemes of imperial preference. Although the principle expounded by the Commerce Member at the 1930 Imperial Economic Conference, that 'any scheme of economic co-operation . . . must be based on mutual self-interest and not merely on sentiment',[80] still held the field, by the summer of 1931 New Delhi was becoming aware that imperial preference could bring advantages to India. As the Commerce Member noted in May of that year:

> The basis of modern commercial and industrial economies is *an assured market*, which guarantees large scale, and consequently cheap, production. India requires such a market now-a-days, even for her raw materials, for the tendency of her foreign customers is to develop sources of supply in their own colonies and dependencies. More and more, therefore, India will have to look to the other parts of the Empire for her market, and in return she will be able to offer a large market for Empire goods.[81]

Britain's continuing formal control over Indian tariff policy was seen as the chief obstacle to this development – only if Whitehall was prepared to treat India in the same way as it treated Dominions would any satisfactory scheme of imperial preference, including British goods, stand a chance of being accepted by Indian opinion.[82]

This necessary change in London's attitude came about early in 1932. By then, as we have seen, the British Government had realised that it could not use the bare fact of India's subordinate status to force through substantial concessions for British exporters in the

Indian market. In January 1932 the Cabinet committee which was considering Britain's major economic problem – the likely continuing deficit on her balance of trade – reported that the best solution was a 10 per cent levy on imported goods. Dominion products would only be granted preference 'if an adequate return could be obtained' in the form of Dominion preferences for British exports, these to be negotiated at the Imperial Economic Conference to be held at Ottawa in July 1932. The committee did not consider the problem of India as a special case, but concluded that 'it could be arranged . . . for preferences to be given to Indian products on lines similar to those proposed for Dominion products'.[83] The British Government's announcement of its Import Duties Act of February 1932, which implemented the 10 per cent levy and laid down that Dominion and Indian goods would remain exempt only until 15 November unless mutual preferential agreements were concluded at Ottawa, gave discussions of imperial preference at the Imperial Economic Conference a new urgency. For the Government of India, as for the Dominion Governments, the Ottawa Conference became the forum for negotiating continued access to the British market on favourable terms. As the Secretary of the Indian Commerce Department put it, 'the sole ground on which the Government of India have accepted the invitation of his Majesty's Government . . . [to attend the Ottawa Conference is] the existence of the United Kingdom Import Duties Act and the date November 15th'. The only question for the Indian delegation at Ottawa was 'whether or not it will be in India's economic interests to give and receive tariff preferences'.[84]

At the Conference the Indian delegation concluded an agreement with the British representatives which gave preferences of between 7·5 and 10 per cent to a wide range of British goods exported to India. In return, the British guaranteed free entry for some Indian goods and margins of preference for the most important Indian exports, including tea, cotton, jute and tobacco. It has been calculated that, at current volumes and 1928–9 prices, Indian preferences on British goods were worth about £55 million while British preferences on Indian goods were worth about £47 million, although it is debatable whether such calculations are of much relevance.[85] It is important to realise, however, that what the Ottawa Conference did not do was to usher in a comprehensive system of imperial preference leading to a closed inter-imperial trading system. All the agreements made at Ottawa were bilateral only; after 1932 the British Government's actions revealed that it was prepared neither to sacrifice British agriculture nor British interests in non-Empire countries for the sake of Dominion producers. It is, indeed, probable that the increase in the proportion of Indian and Dominion exports that went to Britain in the early 1930s was the result of the relative stability of the British market during the Great Depression, rather than of the preferential trade agreements concluded at Ottawa.

For India in particular the Ottawa discussions represented a new approach to old problems rather than a fresh initiative on the making of commercial policy in an imperial context. Furthermore, the stress of the negotiations was as much on securing entry for Indian goods to the British market as vice versa. The bilateral agreements that the Indian delegation negotiated in July 1932 were limited: only that with Britain was of importance and even this ignored the subject of preferences on goods that enjoyed protection in India, thus excluding the two most contentious issues of Anglo-Indian trade – cotton manufactures and iron and steel. The iron and steel problem was settled by negotiations between British industrialists and the Tata Iron and Steel Company, which produced a cartel scheme in 1934; the cotton question was resolved, temporarily, by the Lees-Mody Pact of 1933, arranged between the Lancashire and Bombay millowners after the Government of India and the India Office had combined to suppress a Tariff Board report that opposed imperial preference.[86]

At Ottawa, and in the subsequent agreements of 1933 and 1934, the Government of India accepted the principle of imperial preference; but this was not, in practice, a very great concession. Like the Dominion Governments the Indian administration was committed only to giving a margin of preference to British goods, and showed itself ready to achieve this by raising the tariff on foreign manufactures rather than by lowering it on British ones. This policy, an implicit recognition of the fact that many British exports were uncompetitive on the Indian market, did nothing to improve the prospects of British manufacturers hoping to challenge the position of indigenous industries. Further, it soon became clear that an exclusivist imperial trading system would not suit India very well, for no imperial country could provide a market to rival that of Japan for India's important exports of raw cotton.

The Ottawa Agreement was ratified by the C.L.A. in November 1932. In 1935 the British and Indian Governments signed a

Supplementary Agreement on iron and steel and cotton tariffs to run during the life of the Ottawa pact. The C.L.A., however, refused to sanction this and, in 1936, ordered the Government of India to renounce the 1932 Agreement as well. Negotiations to find a replacement now began and, in 1939, a new Anglo-Indian Trade Agreement was signed. The Bill to implement this was thrown out of the C.L.A., but the Viceroy passed it by certification. The details of these various negotiations need not concern us here.[87] What is important for our argument is to note that the British Government was able to secure favourable treatment for British exports to India, but that this had to be done by negotiation. In such negotiations the British Government was still bound by the old constraints of the need to conciliate Indian opinion while securing concessions for British manufacturers, and thus found it hard to approach the problem in the most economically rational manner. As the President of the Board of Trade reported to the Cabinet on the 1939 Agreement: 'looked at purely from the trade point of view, the Treaty was unfavourable to us; as his colleagues were aware, however, the negotiations had been carried out on lines decided by the Cabinet from the wider point of view'.[88] Secondly, and perhaps more importantly, in negotiating new trade agreements with India the British Government found itself constrained by the need to secure a market in Britain for Indian goods. The preferential treatment, or guaranteed purchase, of Indian exports in Britain had to be kept on, for without this source of foreign currency earnings, it was feared, the Indian export economy would be unable to provide the remittances needed by the Government of India, leading to a new threat of default and another major rupee crisis.

The fixing of the rupee to a sterling standard in 1931 had made India, for the first time in her history, a full member of the sterling area at a time when that area had the capability of becoming a more distinct currency bloc that it had ever been before. After 1931 the British authorities were able, by using an Exchange Equalisation Account of foreign currency reserves accumulated in London, to exert some influence on the exchange rate of the pound against other major world currencies and against gold. The sterling area of the 1930s was not as closed a system as it was to become after the Second World War – sterling was still freely convertible into other currencies although investment outside the sterling bloc, and even inside it, was strictly controlled – nor was the Exchange Equalisation Account the equivalent of the dollar pool of the 1940s and early 1950s, being designed only to prevent undue fluctuations in the exchange value of sterling, although in practice it was used also to keep the sterling rate down against other major currencies (which meant selling sterling rather than buying it). The reserves of foreign currency and gold on which it was based were obtained by the Bank of England, subject to a Treasury guarantee against any losses, by open dealings on the London market and from its own reserves.[89]

When the rupee had been linked to sterling in September 1931 officials in the Indian Finance Department had looked forward to the creation of a new type of sterling currency bloc, one in which a committee of the representatives of all member states would be set up to review overall policy and in which such policy should be directed towards raising prices by deliberate devaluation.[90] Some India Office officials supported this idea, but the balance of opinion in the Treasury was set against it.[91] By the summer of 1932 the British authorities had decided what their external currency policy was to be – to hold the pound at around \$3·40 (gold), to make their 'ultimate objective' a return to the gold standard as soon as circumstances permitted (although without stating a possible exchange rate or a definite date) and, in the meantime, to create as strong a sterling bloc as possible, led by Britain. Other countries were to be induced to join the sterling area, which was to be run by informal discussions between central banks, 'not by the method of conference, but by good management of sterling . . . and by consideration of the needs of others'.[92] The level of the sterling exchange was to be determined by consideration of optimum price levels, the most important of which was the level of prices in Britain where a large national debt and the rigidity of wage costs made falling prices 'peculiarly dangerous'.[93] The only Commonwealth or Empire country that was specifically considered in this debate was India, but only because Treasury officials thought that 'the most powerful single force' working towards raising world prices was the flow of gold from there. A depreciated rupee, and hence a depreciated sterling, was seen as the best means of encouraging and continuing that flow.[94]

The Dominions, and India, hoped that currency policy would be fully discussed at the Ottawa Conference and that the British authorities would commit themselves to a definite policy to raise the prices of primary commodities. This expectation that the British Government would be prepared to risk its perceived interests for the sake of those of the other members of the sterling area, or that there would be any formal system of joint control in the new currency bloc, proved over-optimistic. The only concession that the British Chancellor was prepared to make was the general expression of a wish to see world prices rise, and a promise that British short-term credit policy would be directed towards this end. Inflationary finance of public expenditure was specifically ruled out, however, and stress was placed on the control of production as the best way to raise prices. The Chancellor alleged that world conditions were still too disturbed for the British Government to be able to stabilise the sterling exchange, or to return to gold, nor was it possible to predict what exchange rates either outside or inside the sterling area might prove to be the best.[95]

The British Government held to this position for the rest of the 1930s. Until 1935–6 British authorities employed a defensive exchange policy, focusing on the short term and being concerned mainly to prevent upward fluctuations of sterling against gold. In 1936 policy switched to a more active management of the exchange, but this was designed to aid the re-creation of a stable world currency system, which involved negotiations with the Americans and the French, rather than to serve the needs of the rest of the sterling bloc as such.[96] So far as British relations with India were concerned, the integration of the rupee into the sterling area in 1931 was a way of enabling India to maintain her traditional financial commitment – by creating that confidence among foreign holders of rupees which would allow her to meet her sterling obligations – rather than a move towards constructing a new role for India in a different type of world sterling system.

The fact that the central provisions of the 1935 Government of India Act never came into effect undoubtedly helped the British Government to maintain a hold over Indian currency and commercial policy in the late 1930s. Without the Viceroy's powers of certification in tariff matters, which were to be removed when a federal central Government was established, the 1939 Anglo-Indian Trade Agreement would probably never have come into effect. Similarly, a federal legislature would have been able to put considerable pressure on the Reserve Bank, and on the Viceroy, to devalue the rupee against sterling in the last years of the decade. In one important way, however, the 1935 Act did impair the Government of India's ability to satisfy London's demands, for the implementation of full provincial autonomy in 1937 necessitated a further reshuffling of the revenue allocations of the central and provincial Governments to the advantage of the latter. Between 1935 and 1940 the adjustments required by the new constitution cost the central exchequer more than Rs. 24 crores.[97] The Government of India was able to meet these demands only so long as no new external commitments were imposed on its revenues. Yet at the same time one part of its triple imperial role was being revived as London policy-makers grappled with the problem of imperial defence at a time when a major war against Germany, Italy and Japan seemed likely.[98]

The imperial crisis of the Great Depression had stimulated London to turn to an imperial solution to solve the problem of Britain's declining balance of payments. Yet the next few years had shown the limitations of an autarchic imperial economy and British commercial and financial policy had taken on a wider focus once more. By the end of the decade, however, a new crisis dictated a tightening up of the imperial connection again, as the British prepared to fight an imperial war which they knew they could not tackle alone. In 1937 a new Defence of India Plan resurrected India's role in imperial defence. The Government of India was now ordered to be ready to equip, send and maintain two infantry battalions in Egypt and Hong Kong and one each in Burma, Singapore and Iraq in case of war. The 1937 Plan did not pass without comment in New Delhi; the Viceroy refused to make its terms public for fear of the political reaction in India and for the next two years he argued with London about its details, finally being told by the British Cabinet in July 1939 that India had to bear some of the burden of defending Egypt and Singapore because these represented the western and eastern gateways to India.[99]

At the heart of the process by which India was re-integrated into a comprehensive system of imperial defence lay the old problem of public finance. The political difficulties and financial constraints of the late 1920s and early 1930s had prevented the Government of India from implementing any important reform or re-equipment schemes for its army. By 1937–8 the Indian army was judged inferior to that of Egypt, Iran or Afghanistan; there were no ordnance factories in the country and severe shortages of armoured cars, wireless and mobilisation equipment and ammunition.[100] Indian officials knew that they could not repair these deficiencies from tax revenue.[101] From 1933 onwards they had begun to put pressure on the British Government to pay more for the Indian army; however, it was impossible to succeed in this without modifying the position reached by the Government of India and the C.L.A. in 1921, and accepted by the British Cabinet in 1923, that the Indian army should not be thought of as part of the imperial defence force. Only by accepting an imperial role could New Delhi hope to get London to pay for the modernisation of its army, and in the late 1930s the British Government was happy to invest some money in India for the sake of achieving the smooth integration of Indian troops into its global defence plans.[102]

This two-sided process began in 1933 with the report of the Garran Tribunal, set up to consider whether the British Government should contribute towards the training costs in the United Kingdom of British troops stationed in India. The tribunal declared that the Government of India should be paid £1·5 million a year on this score, but only on the basis of an admission that the defence of India and the defence of the Empire as a whole could not be dissociated. In 1938 this reasoning was extended when the British Government increased its annual contribution by £500 000 and provided an additional grant of £5 million for equipment in return for an undertaking by the Government of India to maintain one division of infantry and four air squadrons, equipped to modern standards, to be used as reinforcements anywhere east of the Mediterranean under the command of the Imperial General Staff. In the winter of 1938–9 the Chatfield Committee, appointed by the Committee for Imperial Defence, reviewed the whole problem afresh and reached a conclusion reminiscent of that of the Esher Committee twenty years before. The plan for an Imperial Reserve Force separate from the rest of the Indian army was now scrapped; instead, the whole of the Indian army was to bear, together with the rest of the imperial military force, a 'joint responsibility' for the defence of India and of the strategic points from Suez to Singapore vital to that defence. The 'conditional obligation' that was thought still to govern the position of the Government of India in supplying troops for imperial purposes was to be replaced by a complete subordination of India's defence policy to the needs of the United Kingdom by bringing the Indian army under the control of the Imperial General Staff. As the Committee put it:

> The more completely the defence planning of the two Governments [of India and Britain] can be co-ordinated and merged in the general War Plan, the less will be the need for defining in any

general formula the degree of obligation resting on the Government of India.[103]

To fit the Indian army for this role the British Government was to make a grant of £25 million and a loan of a further £9 million (a total of Rs. 45 crores, slightly more than the Government of India's effective defence expenditure for 1939–40) for modernisation and for the setting-up of a programme to make India self-sufficient in explosives, ammunition and light armaments.

By 1939 the Government of India had accepted the obligation to make one infantry division available for service in Egypt, the Anglo-Iranian oil-fields, Singapore, Malaya and Burma as an integral part of its defence planning. On the outbreak of war there were two Indian infantry brigades in Egypt and one each in Singapore and Aden. Immediately thereafter one further brigade was sent to Malaya and two more, plus a Divisional Headquarters, to Egypt.[104] The only question that the Chatfield Committee had left unresolved was that of who should pay for Indian troops such as these fighting in an imperial role. This was decided by the Defence Expenditure Agreement of November 1939, which laid down that the Government of India was to contribute a sum equivalent to its normal peacetime defence expenditure plus the cost of all war measures undertaken to defend purely Indian interests, while the British Government was to pay the rest.[105] It can be argued that during the Second World War the British Government obtained the services of the Indian army cheaply, for even the £1335 million that it paid out from 1939 to 1946 was less than the market cost of the two million soldiers and large amounts of supplies and stores that it received in return. Yet the 1939 Agreement did prepare the way for a radical change in the financial relationship between Britain and her most important imperial possession: by 1947 India's sterling public debt had been paid off and she had amassed sterling balances of over £1300 million, more than seventeen times the annual revenue of the Government of India and almost one fifth of Britain's gross national product.

In the late 1930s the need to revive India's imperial military role supplied another constraint on any further constitutional advance in central Government. The Chatfield Committee were fully aware of the dangers of allowing nationalist politicians any measure of control over defence policy. The essential assumption on which its recommendations rested was that a settled defence policy can and will be laid down, in accordance with the principle that responsibility for the defence of India rests through the Governor-General and the Secretary of State for India with the British Government and with no one else; and that this responsibility will in no respect be weakened whatever political pressure is brought to bear on the Government of India either before or after the coming of Federation.

There was to be no 'whittling away of the responsibility of the British Government for the defence of India', for on this obligation rested the logic of the case for integrating the Indian army into the imperial defence force.[106] By 1939 the nineteenth-century role of India as an 'English barrack in the Oriental seas' had been restored, although the basis on which its troops were paid for had changed considerably. During the Second World War the British Government was able to maintain India in this newly re-established subordinate position in order to achieve the short-term objective of victory against the Axis powers. That victory was duly obtained, but the cost of achieving it was that, after 1945, India was lost to Britain and to her Empire.

In the first half of the twentieth century the benefits which Britain could obtain from her rule in India were diminishing, and the size of the sacrifices that Britain had to make to maintain these benefits was increasing. By 1945 each part of India's triple imperial commitment had been badly eroded, so that very little remained. However, it would be wrong to interpret this period as one in which India had become a steadily and consistently declining asset which, by the late 1940s, the British were happy to abandon. To do so would be to distort the way in which British officials thought about India and to ignore the full range of options that they could consider.

In the first place, India's imperial commitment did not decline in a continuous and gradual manner, it rose and fell in the process of crisis and response. Secondly, if we look at this commitment from the Indian end we can see that it was subservient to two even more important pillars of the Raj – money and politics. The fundamental problem of the Government of India was that it could only maintain its position by balancing imperial and Indian demands on its scarce revenue resources. This feat had to be managed without a safety-net, for Indian revenues were not large enough to satisfy both claimants. There were only two possible ways to resolve the problem – either to stimulate the Indian economy and so increase India's capacity for taxation, or to secure the support of Indian politicians and persuade them to moderate their demands for the sake of the imperial connection.

As we have seen, grave difficulties stood in the way of the former solution. Political and administrative necessity, and ideological predilection, dictated a 'free market' model of economic development; the remittance needs of the Government of India required that the external economy be supported at the expense, if need be, of the internal economy. The disastrous consequences of interventionism in the period 1916–21, in particular the experience of attempting to establish a new ratio for the rupee in 1920, remained as a nightmare in the official mind throughout the inter-war years. In addition, it was recognised that active attempts to change the framework of Indian society could make the British too many enemies and not enough friends. Significantly enough, the only two far-reaching schemes for Indian economic development which were considered before 1945 both originated in London and had political as well as economic objectives. In 1933 some private opinion in London suggested that any award made to India by the Garran Tribunal should be devoted to subsidising a scheme of village-level rural uplift which would act as a counter to Gandhi's All India Village Industries Association.[107] Late in 1942, Stafford Cripps, perhaps smarting at his failure to secure nationalist support for the war effort, proposed that massive amounts of British capital should be pumped into India to develop her economy. This plan was not just concerned with economics, however. As Cripps pointed out, a revival of paternalist imperial Government might change the basis of Indian political alignments to Britain's advantage:

> If the British Government could enlist the sympathy of the workers and peasants by immediate action on their behalf, the struggle in India would no longer be between Indian and British on a nationalist basis, but between the classes in India on an economic basis. There would thus be a good opportunity to rally the mass of Indian opinion to our side.[108]

However, his plans came to nothing.

If the Government of India could not easily increase its resources it could try to minimise conflict over their allocation. The British had long since discovered that they could not afford to rule India by naked force, the Raj had always depended on a measure of Indian co-operation or acquiescence. From the 1860s successive concessions of constitutional reform had given representative Indian leaders administrative power (to attract support, and to encourage those who knew native society to devise new forms of taxation) and had attempted to construct a framework in which Indian politics could develop in a manner that would strengthen, rather than weaken, the Raj. Thus by 1919 Indian ministers responsible to elected legislatures had been established in the provinces, while in 1935 the British completely withdrew from the provincial scene and even adopted a new plan for central Government that included some Indian responsibility. The legislative and executive powers given to Indians by the 1919 Government of India Act had not directly affected the imperial commitment. By the late 1920s, however, the growing extremism of Indian politics and the shortcomings of dyarchy had forced imperial policy-makers to make plans for further advance, including some transfer of power at the centre. Thus London was compelled to assess, for the first time, the nature of its interest in India and the extent to which this could be secured by informal influence rather then formal control.

The creation of the 1935 Government of India Act was a long and complex process which stretched over eight years and the life-time of three British Governments. It involved a parliamentary commission, three Round Table Conferences, a Consultative Committee, a White Paper and a joint parliamentary select committee. No British Government of this period had a clearly thought-out or consistent policy for Indian constitutional reform; London's plans were determined by a large number of short-term stimuli thrown up by events in Britain and in India. The Conservative Government of 1925-9 successfully shelved the Indian problem by appointing the Indian Statutory Commission; the minority Labour Government of 1929-31 produced liberal rhetoric but no real solution; the National Government of 1931-5 was more interested in conciliating the rebels within the Conservative Party than those in India.[109]

Not until 1933 was the National Government convinced that it would have to hand over some of the powers of central Government to representative Indians. To ensure an Indian administration that would be stable and not too anti-British it devised a scheme for Federation in which the Indian Princes could be used to balance the nationalist influence in British India. Central Government was to be run by Indian ministers responsible to a bi-cameral legislature (roughly two-thirds elected by British India and one-third nominated by the Princes), but they were to have only limited powers. The Viceroy was to be a constitutional monarch bound to follow the advice of his ministers in some respects, but he was also to have independent powers to protect the irreducible minimum of British interests. These included the army budget, debt repayment, the Home Charges, prohibition of any commercial legislation that might discriminate against British products or businessmen on racial grounds, and the right to prevent the introduction of any Bill that would upset established currency and credit policy. As Lord Linlithgow, who had been closely concerned with this plan, put it in 1939: 'After all we framed the constitution as it stands in the Act of 1935 because we thought that the best way – given the political position of both countries – of maintaining British influence in India.'[110] Such attempts to solve the Indian problem failed. It had been hoped that regular hand-outs of political power would buy support but, in practice, this tactic merely increased the demand for further advance. The analysis of Indian politics on which the British based their constitutional plans was false; it was supposed that Indian political development would follow the Westminster model of national parties internally unified and distinguished from each other by broad issues of principle,[111] but this did not happen. The Indian response to British constitutional initiatives was often negative – Indian political leaders either demanded specific reforms for the sake of sectional, incompatible interest groups, or else turned their backs on the whole apparatus of British rule in the name of nationalism. Some politicians, including many of those who called themselves nationalists, did participate in the political institutions provided by their rulers, but the British attempt to encourage a 'free market' polity by administrative reform was never successful. While British plans depended on the emergence of broadly based parties which would weld together a disparate and fragmented colonial society, the institutional structure of local and provincial self-government which they provided was not strong enough to facilitate this. By the 1930s the official framework for political integration had been supplanted by the institutions of the Indian National Congress, the chief opponent of British rule.[112]

One important theme of British India policy for the last thirty years of the Raj was the attempt to create a context for relations between Britain and an increasingly autonomous Indian Government. Two scenarios were possible – either the Commonwealth model based on the example of Canada, or the 'empire by treaty' tactic that had proved successful in Egypt and Iraq between the wars.[113] For most of the inter-war period it was implied that Dominion status was to be the basis of the relationship between Britain and a self-governing India. The British Government's declaration of 1917 (made by Edwin Montagu) established that London's goal was 'the progressive realisation of responsible government in India as an integral part of the British Empire', while Lord Irwin's announcement of 1929 laid down 'the natural issue of India's constitutional progress' to be 'the attainment of Dominion status'. Yet the Dominion status that Montagu and Irwin had in mind for India was never quite the same as that of Canada or Australia. In 1917–19 the British were only prepared to concede fiscal autonomy to India because this was the only way of enabling the Government of India to participate in an autarchic post-war imperial economy and, as we have seen, the Army in India Committee of 1919, when specifically asked to consider the problems that would arise in Indian and imperial defence policy if India achieved Dominion status in the future, recommended that the Indian army be brought under the direct control of the Imperial General Staff. In 1930–2 the British Government was only prepared to allow India increased freedom, as they saw it, over tariff and monetary policy because the Ottawa Conference and the creation of a sterling area separate from the gold standard produced the expectation that Britain's interests could be secured by other means. In the late 1930s the British Government, still in theory wedded to the ideal of Dominion status for India, achieved the subordination of India's defence policy to the needs of the United Kingdom by bringing the Indian army once more under the control of the C.I.G.S.

In the 1920s and 1930s, then, the actions of British Governments at times of imperial crisis show that they did not intend Dominion status for India to result in her becoming one of the 'autonomous Communities within the British Empire, equal in status, in no way subordinate to one another in any aspect of their domestic or external affairs' that the Balfour Declaration of 1926 had described. Dominion status for India was a fine phrase, but London policymakers were, in practice, only prepared to hold to it so long as India's commerical, currency and military policy options were predetermined by other influences over which British interests had the whip hand. The idea of Dominion status was used, as Irwin suggested that it could be to Baldwin in 1929,[114] to mollify Indian political opinion and to induce Indian politicians to co-operate in the self-governing institutions by showing that Englishmen considered Indians to be their equals. Even in the 1930s it was apparent that the British government's special interests in India would have to be secured by formal agreement, rather than by depending on sentimental ties alone, and by the early 1940s it was becoming clear to London that the limited Commonwealth model for decolonization was now played out. Massive election victories by the Indian National Congress in 1936–7 had shown that it would never again be practicable to devise a solution to the problem of Indian constitutional advance that was not acceptable to the nationalists, and the Congress had, in 1929, specifically rejected Dominion status in favour of complete independence. In 1942 the British Government realised that the right to leave the Commonwealth would have to be granted to India in any new scheme of self-government.[115]

The early 1940s saw another major change in British thinking. In the inter-war years Whitehall had tried to devise schemes of constitutional reform that would both attract the support of Indians willing to accept continued British influence and at the same time would supply a network of executive institutions that would enable these allies to dominate the domestic political scene. Both the 1919 and the 1935 Government of India Acts contained detailed plans to shape the structure of Indian governance in the medium or long term; final decisions on both were made in London with Indian political opinion being given only an advisory role. The contrast between these two Acts and the two constitutional initiatives of the Second World War years – the Viceroy's 'August offer' of 1940 and the Cripps Mission of 1942 – is clear. These latter two schemes were both, in essence, short-term exercises, attempts to attract Indian support for the war effort by adjusting the existing constitutional machinery while leaving the issue of further advance to be decided after hostilities had ceased. Both also introduced a new plan for determining the shape of a future constitution – this was to be decided by a Constituent Assembly of representative Indians and only checked over afterwards by the British Government. By the time of the Cripps Mission it had been further decided that the British Government's obligations (to minorities, the Native States, etc.) and interests were to be safeguarded by a treaty to be concluded between London and the Constituent Assembly as part

The Official Mind of Decolonization 1914–47

of the constitutional package. Since India was now to be free to leave the Commonwealth once her new constitution came into force, it was to be the treaty, rather than Dominion status, that would determine her future relations with Britain.

The terms of the Cripps Mission did not succeed in attracting the support of the Congress or the Muslim League for the war effort, yet they remained as the basis of British policy when the Labour Government began to discuss possible lines of advance in 1945–6. Officials and politicians in London had now to give some thought to the contents of any treaty that would be a condition of granting India her independence. It was recognised that two-thirds of India's traditional imperial commitment could be dealt with in other ways. The future commercial relationship between India and Great Britain would have to be settled by agreement, but neither this, nor the question of the future status of British expatriates in India, could be made a condition for granting independence. By the end of the war India's sterling debt had been repaid, so the earlier fears of the Treasury that a self-governing India might default were no longer relevant. India was now Britain's largest single sterling creditor, but the Prime Minister and the Chancellor of the Exchequer were clearly of the opinion that the question of sterling balances should be kept distinct from that of India's independence. As Attlee told the Cabinet in February 1946, 'there could be no question of offering, at this stage, concessions on the financial side in order to secure a political settlement'.[116]

The purpose of the treaty proposed in 1942 had been 'to cover all necessary matters arising out of the complete transfer of authority from British to Indian hands' and to make provision for the continued protection of those in India for whom the British Government thought itself to have a special responsibility, especially the minorities.[117] By 1945–6 the British Government had realised that it could do little for the minorities, or for the Princes, by statutory means, while the only important interest that could be covered by treaty was that of defence. India was still thought to have a vital role to play in post-war schemes of imperial defence, whether or not she remained in the Commonwealth. When asked their opinion in March 1946, the British Chiefs of Staff had stressed that 'it is clear that in the future we shall have to rely to an even greater extent upon reservoirs of manpower such as India can provide'. India was also thought important as a source of supplies and as part of a network of bases to defend the Persian Gulf, the

Indian Ocean, Southeast Asia and the Middle East. The Chiefs of Staff proposed that, under the terms of a defence treaty, India undertake to defend her frontiers and coastline, maintain internal security and provide troops, in peace as well as in war, 'for use in those British territories outside India the security of which is of direct importance to the defence of India' – in other words, permanent garrisons in Malaya and Burma and temporary ones in the Middle East. She was also to make bases available to British troops, ships and aircraft and, in return, would receive aid in training and equipping her army.[118]

These proposals, which were remarkably similar to those of the 1937 Defence of India Plan, were accepted by the British Government just before its Cabinet Mission departed for New Delhi.[119] They contained, however, a logical flaw that was eventually to destroy them, for their success depended on the maintenance of internal security in India. The Chiefs of Staff had pointed out that 'a contented and politically stable India is of the greatest importance to us in order to ensure the security of India as a military base and as a source of manpower and industrial war potential';[120] yet in 1946–7 law and order was collapsing in the subcontinent as communal unrest and distrust seemed to be preparing the way for civil war. To counter this, and to maintain communications, the Chiefs of Staff proposed that the treaty include provisions for British troops to be garrisoned in India permanently. This was the only way of securing British objectives, yet the Cabinet decided that to insist on it would prejudice the forthcoming discussions with Indian leaders and instructed the Cabinet Mission to agree to such a plan only if it were suggested by the Indian negotiators.[121]

The problem that the British faced in trying to secure the place of India in imperial defence was that they also had an important negative military interest in India. In the absence of a political settlement, law and order in the subcontinent could only be maintained by a substantial military presence and the British Government, anxious to bring its troops home, cut down on defence spending and with major strategic concerns elsewhere, could not accept this alternative. The military planners, both in India and in the United Kingdom, knew this as well as did the politicians. As the Viceroy, Lord Wavell, pointed out to the Secretary of State in March 1946, the treaty provisions set out in the directive to the Cabinet Mission 'should only be those for which we are prepared to risk a breakdown. . . . This will mean such an unlimited and dangerous military commitment that I am sure we must not risk a breakdown on the matter of military demands.'¹²² The Chiefs of Staff agreed:

> [We] assume that our primary political object is to grant India independence. . . . If this is accepted it follows that we cannot afford to allow the negotiations to break down and therefore cannot classify any of our needs as essential, if by this is meant that we would rather abandon the negotiations than modify our requirements.¹²³

Despite these glimpses of realism, the terms of reference of the Cabinet Mission included securing agreement on a treaty, to be a condition of the transfer of power, that included satisfactory provision for the defence of Southeast Asia.¹²⁴ Although the Cabinet Mission failed, the treaty idea lived on for the first few months of 1947 until, in circumstances that are still somewhat obscure, it was dropped in May in favour of Dominion status for the two successor states with the right to leave the Commonwealth if they wished. The events of April–May 1947 have been much discussed. Too much attention, however, has been focused on the side issue of what this episode reveals about Nehru's psychology;¹²⁵ this has obscured the main point – that the transfer of power limited by a treaty was now replaced by Dominion status, largely because it could not be agreed with whom a treaty should be made. Given the changes in the Congress attitude, Dominion status was now the best way of securing the British Government's chief aim, that of getting out of India before the explosive internal situation blew up in its face. By 1947 this dominated British thinking about India, as summed up by Linlithgow's remark to Wavell in December 1946 that 'we ought to run no risk of India becoming a second Palestine for us on a larger scale'¹²⁶ and Dalton's confession to his diary in February 1947 that:

> If you are in a place where you are not wanted, and where you have not got the force, or perhaps the will, to squash those who don't want you, the only thing to do is to come out. . . . The Tories are making a good deal of hoot about India, but I don't believe that one person in a hundred thousand in this country cares tuppence about it, so long as British people are not being mauled about out there.¹²⁷

In the spring of 1947 it may have seemed that keeping India in the Commonwealth, especially in a Commonwealth that was still based on common loyalty to the British Crown, would make it possible to retain her as part of an imperial defence network. Even after May 1947 the British Government continued negotiations with Indian and Pakistani leaders for some sort of formal co-ordination of defence policies in a Commonwealth context.[128] Yet these came to nothing and, by the time of the London Conference of 1949 at which India and Pakistan were admitted to the Commonwealth on a long-term basis as sovereign republics owing no allegiance to the British Crown, the idea of the Commonwealth acting as a third super-power in strategic terms had been dropped. There were a number of reasons for this. The increasing economic problems of the British Government, and its failure to create a sphere of influence in the Middle East by renegotiating treaties with Egypt and Iraq in the winter of 1946–7, cut down the options and opportunities of British policy-makers. Within India the logic of events that has hastened the end of British rule pursued the imperial power beyond the grave. The threat of communal civil war was converted, in 1947–8, into bitter if undeclared hostilities between India and Pakistan. It was no longer possible for the British Government to conclude defence agreements with either embattled government for fear of becoming involved. By 1949 India and Pakistan had created an important precedent in Commonwealth affairs–for the first time two Dominions had fought a war against each other. Ironically, it was this rivalry, and the desire of the successor states to ensure that the other did not secure any diplomatic advantage, that provided an important motive for their decisions to remain in the Commonwealth.[129]

In 1942 British policy-makers had rejected the Commonwealth model for decolonization in India in favour of the Egyptian model of empire by treaty, and in 1947 they reversed their position. The reasons for these contradictory decisions were the same. Both years were times of intense external and internal crisis for the Raj and on both occasions the dominant aim of British policy was to shore up the immediate position while leaving the future vague. In 1942 talking about an eventual treaty seemed to be the best way of preventing discussions about what might happen when the Raj came to an end, discussions that might make it more difficult to secure the support of Indian leaders for the war against Japan. In 1947 the problems associated with treaty-making seemed to be blocking the speedy exist of British personnel, and so Dominion status was substituted for the treaty, although the question of whether the Congress would have agreed to accept Dominion status in May 1947 if its leaders had not become convinced that the only alternative – a treaty – would be less to their advantage is an interesting one.

This episode is but the final illustration of the fact that the British had no long-term strategy for decolonization in India. The process which resulted in the transfer of power was the outcome of a series of short-term decisions, for officials thought of their interests in India in a limited and precise way. Yet, although their concerns were limited and precise, they were spread over a wide range of topics and the standard accounts of the last thirty years of the Raj, which concentrate on constitutional and political developments pure and simple, are inadequate to explain either the events or the workings of the official mind of decolonization.

The progress of constitutional advance in India was determined by the need to attract Indian support for British rule, to swell Government revenues and maintain political tranquillity, leaving the Government of India free to fulfil its imperial role. Thus the changes in the imperial role assigned to India by policy-makers in London were the most important single regulator of the development of constitutional reform. The limiting of India's imperial commitment, and thus the acceptance of further measures of non-official control in Indian government, was not a simple evolutionary process. India's true place in the Empire was only revealed in times of imperial crisis and the strains imposed by each successive crisis left India's imperial role altered. Even before the First World War it has been clear that, to survive, the Government of India has to balance imperial and domestic claims upon its scarce resources. The strains caused by India's participation in the World Wars of 1914–18 and 1939–45 and the financial crisis of 1930–2 boosted domestic pressure on Government to the point where a measure of constitutional reform and some limitations on the imperial commitment had to be imposed after each.

Since the British could not increase the Government of India's resources, they had to buy off Indian opposition to the imperial commitment by political reform. In switching from formal control to informal influence they were not simply seeking Indian co-operation for its own sake: granting Indians greater autonomy to control some aspects of policy was the only way that any advantage at all could be extracted from India, given the changes in Britain's position in the world, the strictures of Indian governmental finance and the course of Indian political development between 1914 and 1947. By 1947 the Raj had become an anachronism; it is perhaps significant that, of the many nineteenth-century prophecies of the ending of British rule in India, Attlee, in the parliamentary debate on the transfer of power, should have selected that of Elphinstone:

> We must not dream of perpetual possession, but must apply ourselves to bring the natives into a state that will admit of their governing themselves in a manner that may be beneficial to our interests as well as their own, and that of the rest of the world. . . .[130]

This was the dual mandate of British rule in India. Given the limited nature of the interests of the official mind, it can be said to have been successfully achieved by 1947, although perhaps more by default than by application.

STATISTICAL APPENDIX TO CHAPTER 4

TABLE 4.2. Central Government Revenue and Expenditure 1914–1945 (in Rs. crores)

	Current account		Capital account				Misc.	Overall surplus/deficit[a]
	Revenue	Expenditure	Outlay	Permanent debt	Other debt	Other[a]		
1914	+101·59	−98·12	−21·75	+·18	+4·02	+6·99	−·89	−7·98
1915	+94·33	−97·00	−20·03	+4·09	+11·12	+6·13	−·25	−1·61
1916	+99·18	−100·96	−10·12	+3·57	6·69	+6·98	−2·15	+3·19
1917	+118·80	−107·58	−5·23	+6·65	−3·47	+1·97	−8·32	+2·82
1918	+139·72	−127·59	−156·89	+103·86	+59·27	+·54	−11·02	+7·89
1919	+153·80	−159·53	−9·56	−21·89	+58·09	−1·81	−19·03	+·07
1920	+163·67	−187·32	−15·74	+7·17	+23·58	−·93	+6·01	−3·56
1921	+170·67	−196·68	−29·00	+37·69	−18·38	−5·64	+23·92	−17·42
1922	+81·19	−108·84	−25·22	+42·27	+23·24	−5·76	+6·73	+13·61
1923	+89·30	−104·31	−21·59	+66·23	−26·21	−9·11	+7·52	+1·13
1924	+101·47	−99·07	−24·13	+37·14	−4·96	−10·15	+5·45	+5·75
1925	+102·75	−97·06	−16·70	+11·73	+11·73	−9·95	+1·22	+3·72
1926	+100·89	−97·57	−27·53	−4·03	+20·58	−8·15	+10·77	−5·04
1927	+97·89	−97·89	−31·66	+3·32	+23·99	−5·89	+1·15	−9·09
1928	+92·50	−92·50	−35·06	+4·39	+22·79	−7·77	+·17	−15·48
1929	+92·50	−92·82	−30·89	+28·02	+18·31	−12·72	−2·91	−·51
1930	+96·83	−96·56	−32·02	+20·40	+39·98	−7·18	−3·37	+18·08
1931	+86·25	−97·84	−16·63	+46·98	−11·39	−10·97	−6·00	−9·60
1932	+83·65	−95·40	−8·55	−·48	+44·03	−12·63	−1·46	+9·16
1933	+87·57	−86·02	−1·86	+22·72	−27·32	−5·89	+4·73	−6·07

The Official Mind of Decolonization 1914–47   153

TABLE 4.2 (contd)

	Current account		Capital account				Misc.	Overall surplus/deficit
	Revenue	Expenditure	Outlay	Permanent debt	Other debt	Other[a]		
1934	+80·12	−80·12	+·41	−4·91	+14·68	−2·24	−2·97	+4·97
1935	+83·59	−83·23	−2·44	+3·81	+19·82	−2·10	−15·01	+4·44
1936	+83·09	−83·09	−9·26	−22·07	+·78	−·03	+17·65	−21·93
1937	+79·11	−80·89	−2·64	+13·53	+30·91	+·24	−7·11	+6·09
1938	+86·57	−86·57	−3·28	−5·90	+9·05	+4·02	−1·21	+2·68
1939	+84·47	−85·11	−9·07	−3·24	+13·55	+2·53	−1·30	+1·83
1940	+94·57	−94·57	−4·62	+13·56	+24·49	+2·15	−4·97	+3·49
1941	+107·65	−114·18	−6·93	+28·56	+26·81	+1·81	−45·66	−1·94
1942	+134·56	−147·26	−·99	−97·99	+94·16	+3·16	+15·62	+1·26
1943	+177·09	−288·87	−78·55	+16·04	+212·53	+7·49	−43·44	+2·29
1944	+249·96	−439·86	−64·51	+240·01	+18·79	+14·92	+46·11	+65·42
1945	+335·70	−496·25	−81·73	+203·11	+185·33	+22·38	+14·07	+182·61

Note: Dates represent financial years from April to March; 1914 is year ending March 1914 etc. Overall surplus/deficit figures given here have been calculated from the rounded sub-totals, and thus differ slightly on occasion from those given in the source, which are calculated from the full sub-totals.

[a] net loans and advances and capital contributed by railways.

Source: *Banking and Monetary Statistics of India*, pp. 872–5.

The Official Mind of Decolonization 1914–47   155

TABLE 4.3. Central Government Debt 1913–1945 (in Rs. crores)
(as on 31 March)

	Rupee debt			Sterling debt	Total
	Funded	Unfunded	Floating		
1913	142.84	30.80		268.76	442.40
1919	199.06	51.04	108.68	303.79	662.57
1924	358.81	72.21	51.77	263.94	746.73
1929	391.74	127.31	43.15	471.74	1033.94
1934	435.43	198.43	59.24	512.15	1205.25
1939	438.53	225.13	46.30	469.12	1179.08
1945	1219.09	265.62	86.71	67.58	1639.00

Source: *Banking and Monetary Statistics of India*, p. 881.

TABLE 4.4. Percentage of Revenue and Expenditure by Major Heads: Central Government 1919–1940

Revenue	1919–20	1924–5	1929–30	1934–5	1939–40
Land	12.5	0.3	0.3	0.2	0.1
Opium	3.5	2.8	2.3	0.6	0.4
Salt	4.4	5.4	5.1	6.6	8.6
Stamps	4.3	0.2	0.2	0.3	0.3
Excise	4.2	0.3	0.4	0.3	0.2
Customs	17.1	33.3	38.6	43.1	41.7
Income tax	13.6	11.6	12.6	14.4	13.2
Posts	7.0	0.8	0.01	1.0	1.3
Railways	24.0	27.1	28.0	26.5	27.1
Irrigation	3.1	0.1	0.1	0.01	0.01
Other	6.3	18.1	12.39	6.99	7.09
Expenditure					
Direct demands	5.0	4.2	3.1	3.3	3.1
Interest	5.9	14.2	12.5	10.9	9.5
Posts	5.1	0.2	0.6	0.7	0.6
Civil depts.	5.7	7.7	9.6	9.1	8.8
Railways	7.0	23.1	23.4	26.6	23.6
Irrigation	2.3	0.2	0.2	0.05	0.1
Civil works	1.2	1.3	1.9	2.0	2.1
Military	65.1	45.2	44.6	40.8	40.0
Other	2.7	3.9	4.1	6.65	12.2

Source: *Governments of India Revenue and Expenditure Accounts, 1919–20 to 1934–5, Statistical Abstract for British India 1930–31 to 1930–40*.

TABLE 4.5. Percentage of Revenue and Expenditure by Major Heads: all Provincial Governments (excluding Burma) 1924-40

Revenue[a]	1924-5	1929-30	1934-5	1939-40
Land revenue	37·5	33·2	36·6	30·7
Excise	22·7	22·2	18·6	13·6
Stamps	15·7	15·7	15·1	11·1
Forests	4·5	4·5	3·5	3·2
Registration	1·5	1·5	1·5	1·3
Irrigation	8·4	9·2	10·1	11·9
Other	9·7	13·7	14·6	28·2
Expenditure				
General administration	13·5	12·3	11·8	11·7
Justice	6·8	6·0	5·9	5·3
Jails	2·6	2·5	2·4	2·2
Police	14·2	12·7	13·6	12·6
Education	13·1	14·1	14·2	14·0
Medical	3·8	4·1	4·1	4·1
Public health	1·9	2·2	1·8	1·9
Agriculture	2·2	2·8	2·6	2·9
Industries	0·8	1·0	0·9	1·3
Co-operation				1·0
Civil works	8·6	10·9	8·6	8·7
Debt services	3·8	3·7	3·8	2·2
Direct demands	10·7	10·7	9·3	10·5
Other	18·0	17·0	21·0	21·6

[a] Excluding contributions from Central Government.

Source: As Table 4.4.

I am grateful for help from Mr C. Emery of Trinity College, Cambridge, with Tables 4.4 and 4.5.

5. Postscript: The Economics of Decolonization

To understand the economic factors that led to the decision to decolonize India we must concentrate on the problems and purposes of the colonial Government. The Government of India was the mediator between imperial and domestic demands for the use of colonial resources. Attacking the administration in New Delhi was the prime purpose of nationalist agitations against British rule, while maintaining that administration was the chief aim of imperial policy, an aim to which securing India's imperial commitment had to be subordinated and for the sake of which that commitment had to be modified.

In his book *An Economic History of West Africa*, Prof. A. G. Hopkins has constructed an economic model for colonial expansion and contraction based on the rise and fall of the open economy.[1] A colonial open economy is described as one which is based on substantial exports of a limited range of primary produce in exchange for imports of consumer goods. Expatriate or metropolitan interests usually dominate one or more sectors of such an economy and control the economic policy of its Government. Open economies have free trade, or low tariffs, so that the only restriction on the volume of imports is the purchasing power of local consumers; they also have satellite monetary systems, without a central bank, in which the expansion of money supply is closely linked to the performance of the foreign trade sector and the operations of overseas banking institutions. One of the most important features of an open economy is its ready response to outside influences:

> An increase or decrease in export earnings will be accompanied by roughly parallel movement in expenditure on consumer

imports. Quantitative changes occur easily enough but qualitative, structural transformation is far more difficult. The circularity of the system is reinforced by restrictions on the volume of investment, which is limited by the level of export earnings, by the tendency for capital to be leaked abroad, by the cautious nature of bank-lending policy, by the colonial tradition of maintaining a balanced budget, and by the conservative attitude of the large expatriate firms. Such investment as there is in an open economy tends to be directed into the existing export sector rather than towards new projects outide it.[2]

By contrast, closed economies in the non-industrialised world are characterised by the adoption of measures to limit their sensitivity to outside influences and to assist diversification. Economic policy is orientated towards satisfying domestic interests and an independent monetary system, headed by a central bank, is capable of creating money for internal circulation without acquiring foreign exchange, can implement contra-cyclical policies to soften the effects of extreme booms and slumps and use the techniques of deficit financing to increase Government expenditure. Hopkins argues convincingly that colonial Governments in West Africa tried to create open economies in the first decades of their rule, up to 1930; from 1930 to 1945, however, the strains imposed by the impact of depression, war and instability in the world economy resulted in increased difficulties for colonial rule, a partial change-over to policies designed to produce closed economies, and pressures on the colonial Governments that led to decolonization in the late 1950s and early 1960s. Political independence, in its turn, has led to a more complete transition to closed economies in many West African states:

> The motivation and timing of the movement for political independence were related to the inability of the colonial system to cope with the demands made upon it. It is important to stress that this failure did not occur simply because the colonial economy was immobile and unresponsive, ⋯ . [the] problem was rather that African expectations were expanding too fast to be contained within a colonial system, whatever its attributes.[3]

There are obvious parallels between this analysis and events in India. In 1913 the Indian economy had many of the features of an

The Economics of Decolonization

open economy and the position of the Government of India was secure; in 1947 the Indian economy was somewhat closed, and was becoming more so, while the British Raj was being speedily dismantled. Some differences of emphasis must be stressed, however. The Indian economy was never quite so open as were those of West Africa, for it was never so dependent on foreign trade for the disposal of agricultural surplus or for the acquisition of consumer goods. The switching of investment between the main sectors of the internal economy – agriculture, trade and industry – was inhibited by the success of the traditional marketing and credit-supplying institutions, which limited the impact of the world economy on producers, and by the Government's essentially conservative social policies which hampered the growth of capitalist agriculture. Further, the Indian economy had had, since the 1860s, an important industrial sector; expatriate interests controlled only a small segment of the economy; there were limitations on the control that London could exert over economic policy and the Indian monetary system had a measure of independence from that of the sterling area.

Despite these qualifications, we can say that the smooth functioning of the apparatus of British rule in India, if not of the Indian economy as a whole, depended on the existence and expansion of an open economy – for the Government of India could only operate successfully given a colonial economy with a large commercialised sector capable of maintaining itself without the need for constant supervision or intervention. The expansion of the foreign trade sector was, perhaps, the ideal form of economic development for the colonial Government, for this provided the Indian administration with easy access to its two major financial requirements – indirect tax revenue (from excises and customs dues) and foreign currency to meet its commitments in London. In the inter-war period the colonial Government needed an economy that imported substantial amounts of foreign goods (to provide customs revenue) and that earned large sums of foreign exchange on commodity or capital account. It also needed to maintain confidence in the stability of the Indian currency of foreign holders of rupees, for a flight of capital from India could eat up all the foreign exchange earnings of Indian exporters and more besides. This, in turn, meant that the Government of India had to continue the colonial economy's links, via the Secretary of State, with the London capital market. As Sir George Schuster pointed out in 1933:

> Hitherto, a main support of the whole structure [of Indian public finance] . . . has been the responsibility of the British Government for Indian loans. So far as the currency position has been concerned the ultimate defence, on which subconciously public faith has depended, has been India's credit in London – India's general power to raise funds in London – rather than the physical assets of the currency reserves, and it is doubtful whether any margin of static currency reserves . . . can fully replace this factor as a support for public confidence.[4]

The collapse of India's foreign currency earnings from her export of primary produce in the late 1920s and early 1930s put great pressure on the economic foundations of British rule. The depression in prices affected the domestic economy as well as the external one, and the tensions that resulted convinced some members of the Government of India, and most Indian and expatriate businessmen and politicians, that action would have to be taken to protect the internal economy from the decline in world demand by depreciating currency, obtaining a drawing credit in London, initiating price support schemes and so on. Such suggestions, however, strained relations between New Delhi and London and, since the Indian authorities could not implement these plans without the British Government's support, the new initiative was quashed. This, in turn, led to increased tension between the colonial Government and its subjects, intensified Indian demands for the closure of the domestic economy and fuelled the political agitation against British rule.

So far as the Government of India was concerned, the open economy was saved by the gold exports of the early 1930s. Yet things could never be quite the same again. The revenue tariffs imposed to balance the budgets of 1930 and 1931 had had a considerable protective effect and the past profits of the open economy – gold holdings bought with the proceeds of foreign trade – were now, for the first time on a large scale, being channelled into those activities, such as sugar refining and cement manufacture, that would benefit from the spread of a closed economy. Even more important was the way in which the economic upheavals of the Great Depression and the Second World War broke down the established systems of marketing and credit-supply, and the mechanisms by which food and raw materials were extracted from the rural areas and exchanged for consumer goods and bullion from the towns and from the international economy. These upheavals succeeded in eroding institutional barriers to the diversification of credit in the internal economy and helped to create, for the first time, a fairly well integrated national money market in India. This was a development which might have done much to remove the impediments to Indian economic progress, but because it was achieved by a series of explosive crises – of the rural economy in the 1930s and of the urban economy in the 1940s – it did not create a smoothly-working, well-integrated financial system. By 1943 not only was the Indian domestic economy largely closed to the world, but also the rural and urban sectors of the internal economy were largely closed to each other. With the import of bullion impossible, and with the war effort consuming most of India's production of commodity goods, food producers invested by hoarding and, with non-food producers facing starvation, the Government had to intervene on an unprecedented scale.

By 1945 the Government of India was unable to restore an open economy in India, nor could it easily withdraw from its involvement in the institutional linkages of the internal economy. By now, of course, New Delhi had less need of an open economy than it had had in the inter-war period, for it had no foreign currency requirements for remittances and it had become experienced in tapping other sources of revenue than customs duties. To what extent, then, can the changes in the structure of the Indian economy, and in its relationships to the imperial and international economies, be seen as a cause of decolonization?

There are a number of points that must be considered here. As we have seen, the destructive impact of world economic forces on the Indian domestic economy between the wars was exacerbated by the Government of India's continuing need, for its own purposes, to maintain an open economy in India. The strains that resulted from this, especially during the early 1930s, helped to increase opposition to British rule both among the masses and among opinion-formers. In addition, the impact of changes in the world economy in the 1930s and 1940s on both Britain and India had, by 1945, severely limited the advantages that Britain could look to from continuing the Raj, and had encouraged them to seek their aims by informal influence rather than by formal control. The immediate problem of maintaining law and order in India in 1945–7, which we have suggested became the dominant factor in determining British decolonization policy in those years, was made worse because of the tensions that had arisen in both town and countryside owing to the collapse of the established economic structure in the last two decades of the Raj. Although there seems, in theory, no reason why a colonial Government could not maintain a closed domestic economy, requiring constant intervention, as well as it could work with an open economy that could be run by *laissez-faire* (provided that it had no large foreign exchange requirements), we may take it as axiomatic that this was the case. Certainly the history of both West and East Africa in the 1950s suggests it.[5] In India there was the additional problem that by 1945 the Government of India was badly placed to ensure the smooth running of the domestic economy. There was little time for the colonial Government to take stock of the situation, for powerful forces were now attacking its very existence while in many areas of administration it had already been supplanted by rival organisations, especially the parallel executive structure of the Indian National Congress.

This was true in the economic as well as the political sphere. The origins of a national planned economy for India can be traced back to a speech by Shanmukham Chetty in the 1930 budget debate in the Central Legislative Assembly. His proposal, that something similar to the British Economic Advisory Committee should be created, spanning both official and non-official opinion, was taken up by the Finance Member. Preliminary meetings were held in March and April 1930, but the scheme collapsed when it became clear that Indian businessmen and politicians would participate only if they could control policy, while most officials would consent only to a research-orientated body to co-ordinate existing departmental activity.[6] This mutual distrust on political and racial grounds continued to frustrate Schuster's initiatives during the depression and, even in 1944–5, the Government of India's attempts to formulate a post-war economic policy for reconstruction were hampered by the antagonism between metropolitan, expatriate and indigenous interests.[7] The field was thus left open to others and the Congress, at Nehru's prompting, took the initiative by appointing a National Planning Committee of party workers, economists and businessmen in 1938 which, by 1940, had produced a series of detailed reports on the needs of the major sectors of the economy. Not surprisingly, Nehru stressed that 'such planning could only take place in a free National Government strong enough to be in a position to introduce fundamental changes in the social

The Economics of Decolonization

and economic structure'.[8] The most complete survey of India's postwar economic requirements, and the fullest statement of the planning needed to attain them, that had appeared by 1947 was an authoritative non-official pamphlet, the 'Brief Memorandum outlining a Plan for the Economic Development of India', published in Bombay in 1944 by Sir Purshottamdas Thakurdas, J. R. D. Tata, G. D. Birla, Sir Shri Ram, Kasturbhai Lalbhai, A. D. Shroff and John Matthai, most of whom had closer links with the Congress than they had with the Government of India. Furthermore, one consequence of the Government of India's failure to implement policies to mitigate the impact of the Great Depression on the Indian economy had been to strengthen the tendency among Indian businessmen to regard the Congress, rather than the Government, as the body best able and most willing to secure for them the place in the domestic economy and polity that they desired.

It was not only at the national level that the Congress was thus able to supplant the bureaucracy; events in the agrarian sector followed the same pattern, especially over relations between landlords and tenants and rural creditors and debtors.[9] The collapse of agrarian prices in the early 1930s had severely disrupted the customary relationships on which the rural economy had been based during the previous decades of steady growth. Tenants now found it hard to pay rent and landlords and owner-occupiers had difficulty in paying land revenue, while many debtors defaulted and creditors became unwilling to invest money with little prospect of return. Patterns of credit supply had traditionally provided much of the framework of social control in rural areas; now that the flow of money on which they depended had dried up, unrest and disorder became widespread. Landlords, moneylenders and even substantial peasant farmers became the target for attacks by their erstwhile dependents, who could no longer afford to pay the price of their dependency. With the customary ties of social control weakening, all those who had something to lose closed ranks and began to look for a new framework for stability and to Government to intervene in their favour. As an official observer in the United Provinces commented in 1934:

> Before the fall in prices occurred, tenants were mainly interested in obtaining heritable rights and security of tenure; landlords in prolonging the term of settlement. . . . [Now] the idea of expropriation [of zamindari holdings] makes little headway: the tenant

is interested in a 'payable' rent, the landlord in wresting further concessions from Government in revenue remissions.[10]

In Tamil Nadu the abolition of zamindari was more widely canvassed, but here it attracted the support of some of the zamindars themselves. One such landlord noted:

> The Zamindars themselves have been hard hit during the period of depression and they would not be unwilling to part with their zamindaris provided reasonable and equitable compensation is paid to them for the loss of their property.[11]

Moneylenders, too, became eager for compromise. Loans extended on the security of land were virtually irrecoverable as the value of land dropped with the fall in prices, while legal proceedings provided a slow and expensive method of recovering debts. In Madras a Government report observed: 'The moneylender wants a stay of all proceedings against land for a definite period for recovery. He is eager for a settlement of debts, for he has learned a bitter lesson'.[12]

In the depths of the depression provincial governments and local revenue officials did what they could by revenue remissions and personal contacts to relieve distress. But by the mid-1930s, with many zamindars withdrawing from the rental market, with the pool of rural credit stagnant and with many of those who had supplied it moving to the cities or looking to other sectors for investment opportunities, something had to be done to replace the relationships that had collapsed. In addition, there was the problem that the financial institutions that had expanded to fill the gap left in the rural economy were largely those – joint-stock banks, urban merchants and the like – which had no customary basis for their new dealings with much of the rural economy. Neither custom nor the law could now provide a satisfactory framework within which agriculture could be organised. Instead, new mediating institutions were needed and the Congress organisations, with their superior legitimacy based on the ideology of nationalism, their closer knowledge of, and contact with, the local political and social structure and their control over local and provincial government in many areas after 1937, were much better able to provide these than were the bureaucracy. In the mid-1930s the Congress organisations in the United Provinces and Bihar tried to place themselves between those battling over tenancy rights and the Government, as did other political movements that sought to rival the Congress in rural areas, such as the Bihar Kisan Sabha. Once the Congress came to power in these provinces in 1937 it produced Tenancy Acts that were, broadly, acceptable to landlord and tenant alike. In the early 1930s most provincial administrations had passed emergency legislation to scale down agrarian indebtedness or to prevent the distraint of holdings for failure to pay interest. By the end of the decade, however, it was becoming clear that the recovery of agriculture was being hampered because no one was prepared to lend to cultivators on these terms. Between 1937 and 1939, therefore, most Congress provincial governments, and the popular non-Congress governments in other provinces, sought to provide machinery for debt conciliation that would encourage moneylenders to inv :s. in agriculture while limiting the burden on debtors.

The available evidence suggests that this legislation was largely unsuccessful, for the flow of rural credit was not re-established. After 1945 further legislation by Congress governments to abolish zamindari (which also affected the market and mortgages in land) and to regulate more closely the relations between creditors and debtors aggravated the problem, and it has only been resolved by the supply of capital inputs for agriculture by official agencies. With the Congress party organisation the most effective channel of communication between the ruled and the rulers in the 1950s and 1960s it is hardly surprising that, in the words of one commentator, 'India may not have achieved an expanding economy [since Independence] . . .; it has, however, experienced *an expanding polity*'.[13] Political relationships have largely replaced the customary ones of previous generations; it is the ability to provide a political system of this type that distinguishes the national Government from the colonial Government of India.

Many historians have argued that in the nineteenth century British rule was converting India into an economic satellite, a supplier of raw materials for, and a purchaser of the products of, dynamic sectors of the metropolitan economy. In the first half of the twentieth century the structure of the British economy was changing and important industries were emerging that had little use for India unless she could be developed industrially. For a number of reasons this could never happen under colonial rule, and thus the logic of British economic forces was working towards a developing, independent India. The proceedings and pamphlets of the Federation of British Industries indicate that some British businessmen were beginning to see this by the 1940s,[14] but there is little evidence that they had any direct influence on the official mind. Yet in many ways, the central purpose of British rule in India – the maintenance of the imperial commitment without causing political upheaval – was frustrated by the inability of the Government of India to develop the economy satisfactorily. With hindsight, we can see that the death-knell of the Raj was rung as early as the 1920s when the failure of New Delhi's industrial policy for India combined with the terms of trade turning against her, and an increase of 50 per cent (thanks to reforms, pay increases and re-equipment) in the army budget. As a non-industrial, depressed peasant economy India was to prove herself of as little use, in the long run, to the British Government as she was to the leaders of Britain's industrial revival. By 1942 Ernest Bevin, at least, was happy to contemplate an independent and industrially developing India, provided that Britain, rather than the United States, supplied her with capital goods.[15]

India remained an important market for British goods and capital after 1947. Although she had a visible balance of trade surplus with Britain in the 1950s, she was still the best customer for iron and steel products, aircraft and parts, various types of machinery and electrical goods, and was among the top three purchasers of British chemicals, ships, textile machinery and general categories of electrical and non-electrical machinery.[16] British investment in India may well have been larger after Independence than before it;[17] certainly South Asia remained a financial asset to Britain after 1947. In 1963 India and Pakistan combined held the fifth largest share of the private investment abroad of British companies (excluding oil, banking and insurance) and were the fourth largest source of such companies' investment income from abroad.[18]

Despite these continuities, it would be wrong to argue that the transfer of power saw a simple switch of official British policy from imperial to 'neo-colonial' exploitation. In the first place, the ties of post-imperial capitalist control have sometimes been exaggerated. As John Strachey, an ex-Communist and ex-Labour Cabinet Minister, has pointed out in criticism of Professor Baran's classic exposition of neo-colonialism, *The Political Economy of Growth*:

The Economics of Decolonization

No impartial observer would wish to deny that it is possible to carry on imperial control and exploitation of an undeveloped country without retaining it as, or making it into, a direct and formal colony.... Every experienced imperialist will tell Professor Baran, however, that such indirect rule and exploitation is by no means the same thing as possession of the country in question as a direct colony. Once an even nominally sovereign local government is established, forces are inevitably set in motion which tend in the direction of genuine independence. Imperialist control can go on, often for some time, but it becomes more and more precarious. To say that the advent of even partial political independence makes no difference is a grotesque oversimplification.[19]

Secondly, the existence of the sterling area and of India's non-convertible sterling balances has distorted the apparent degree of interdependence of the British and Indian economies in the 1950s. Furthermore, British Governments of the late 1940s and the 1950s showed great reluctance to commit resources to India, urging that aid under the Colombo Plan be confined to technical assistance and that the regular release of the sterling balances was as much as she had a right to expect. While it is possible to argue that the development aid that has been given to India since Independence had been 'a normal, permanent and vital stimulant of the growing international society' and the most recent manifestation of 'the historic processes of migration, investment and trade that for four hundred years have been at work creating an international economy',[20] it must also be remembered that the grant of one of Britain's first major pieces of economic aid to India, the $108 million loan through the Export Credit Guarantee scheme in 1958, had a motive that would have appealed to the official mind of 1914–47: as the *Financial Times* commented, this loan was 'a hard-headed and useful piece of economic assistance' because the sterling area could 'much better afford such a loan than it could afford the effect on the pound of any crisis for the rupee'.[21]

Notes

PREFACE

1. R. E. Robinson and J. A. Gallagher, 'The Imperialism of Free Trade', *Economic History Review* VI (1953), pp. 5–6.
2. A. G. Hopkins, 'Imperial Connections', in Clive Dewey and A. G. Hopkins (eds.), *The Imperial Impact: Studies in the Economic History of Africa and India* (London, 1978), p. 2.

CHAPTER 1

1. See S. B. Saul, *Studies in British Overseas Trade 1870–1914* (Liverpool, 1960), Ch. VIII.
2. See ibid. and Committee on Industry and Trade, *Survey of Textile Industries* (London, 1928).
3. See Saul, op. cit. and Committee on Industry and Trade, *Survey of Metal Industries* (London, 1928).
4. 'Great Britain's Capital Investments in Individual Colonial and Foreign Countries', *Journal of the Royal Statistical Society* LXXIV Pt. II (1911) pp. 167–200 and 'The Export of Capital and the Cost of Living', *The Statist* 14.2.14 (supplement), pp. i–viii.
5. Review of T. Morrison, *The Economic Transition in India*, *Economic Journal* XXI (1911), p. 430.
6. H. F. Howard, *India and the Gold Exchange Standard* (Calcutta, 1911), pp. 92ff.
7. See A. K. Banerji, *India's Balance of Payments 1921–2 to 1938–9* (London, 1963), pp. 176–9.
8. *Statistical Abstract for British India 1902–3 to 1911–12* (Cd. 7078 of 1913), p. 261.
9. See Saul, op. cit., Chs. III and VIII.
10. The burden of taxation per capita (excluding land revenue) rose only from 2·1d in 1900–1 to 2·1·2d in 1909–10; with land revenue added these figures were 38·5d and 41·6d. See *Statistical Abstract for British India 1900–01 to 1909–10* (Cd. 6017 of 1911), p. 74.
11. For a graphic description of these defects see *Indian Industrial Commission Report 1916–18* (Cmd. 51 of 1919), para. 8.
12. *Census of India 1921, Volume 1 Part 1*, pp. 261–2.
13. See M. L. Dantwala, *Marketing of Raw Cotton in India* (Bombay, 1937), p. 35; *Indian Central Banking Enquiry Committee 1931, Volume 1 Part 1 – Majority Report* (Calcutta, 1931), paras. 108, 112 and 273, and forthcoming work by Dr C. J.

Baker of Queen's College, Cambridge on Madras and by Mr S. Epstein of St Anthony's College, Oxford on Bombay.

14. On the workings of international firms in India in this period, see *Report on the Conditions and Prospects of British Trade in India at the Close of the War* (Cmd. 442 of 1919), pp. 10–18. By 1919 American and Japanese export houses were moving into the jute export trade as well.
15. The following analysis is based on the evidence presented to the Indian Currency Committees of 1893 and 1898 and to the Royal Commission on Indian Finance and Currency of 1913.
16. *The Gazetteer of India Volume III: Economic Structure and Activities* (New Delhi, 1975), p. 806.
17. Letter of J. H. Sleigh in *Indian Currency Committee, 1898: Index and Appendices to the Evidence taken before the Committee* (Cd. 9376 of 1898), p. 70.
18. *Central Banking Enquiry Committee, Vol. I Pt. I*, para. 277.
19. Ibid., paras. 108, 112, 114, 250, 319, 621–2 and 637–8.
20. See W. J. MacPherson, 'Economic Development in India under the British Crown, 1858–1947', in A. J. Youngson (ed.), *Economic Development in the Long Run* (London, 1972), p. 184 and T. Timberg, 'Three Types of Marwari Firm', *Indian Economic and Social History Review* IX (1973).
21. *Central Banking Enquiry Committee, Vol. I Pt. I*, para. 266. Using Wadia and Joshi's figures of agricultural production in 1913 of Rs. 1100 crores (*Wealth of India* (London, 1925), p. 98) and export values from official statistics, the proportion is 17 per cent in 1913–14. The figures supplied by K. M. Mukerji (*Levels of Economic Activity and Public Expenditure in India* (London, 1962), Table 3) which show that 30 per cent of the value of total agricultural production was exported in 1913, seem to be dubious.
22. Saul, *Studies in British Overseas Trade*, p. 200.
23. This paragraph follows the argument developed by MacPherson in Youngson, op. cit., pp. 164–76 and 180–9.
24. *Indian Industrial Commission Evidence, Volume III* (Cmd. 234 of 1919), p. 51.
25. *Indian Industrial Commission Report 1916–18*, para. 286.
26. Ibid., paras. 281–6.
27. See T. D. Rider, 'The Tariff Policy of the Government of India and its Development Strategy 1894–1926' (Ph.D. thesis, Minnesota, 1974), pp. 63–76. The analysis of tariff policy which follows is based on Chapters III–V of this work.
28. S. K. Sen, *Studies in Industrial Policy and Development of India 1858–1914* (Calcutta, 1964), p. 98.
29. Ibid., pp. 47–50 and 112–3.
30. C. J. Dewey, 'The End of the Imperialism of Free Trade: The Eclipse of the Lancashire Lobby and the Concession of Fiscal Autonomy to India', in Dewey and Hopkins (eds.), *The Imperial Impact*, pp. 49–63.
31. Y. S. Pandit, *India's Balance of Indebtedness 1898–1913* (London, 1937), pp. 34 and 103. Pandit's direct estimates suggest that India's interest payments were slightly larger than the amount of new investment (pp. 100 and 127).
32. The following account of Indian currency policy is based on J. M. Keynes, *Indian Currency and Finance* (London, 1913); H. S. Jevons, *Money, Banking and Exchange in India* (Simla, 1922); G. Findlay Shirras, *Indian Finance and Banking* (London, 1920); P. A. Wadia and G. N. Joshi, *Money and the Money Market in*

Notes to pages 16–31

      India (London, 1926) and on my own research work on a later period.
33. Pandit, op. cit., pp. 62 and 103.
34. The classic account of the Council Bill mechanism is in Keynes, op. cit., pp. 102ff.
35. *Report of the Committee on Indian Exchange and Currency 1920, Volume I* (Cmd. 527 of 1920), para. 8.
36. *Statistical Abstract for the British Empire 1913 and 1924–9* (Cmd. 3919 of 1931), pp. 90 and 125.
37. *Royal Commission on Indian Finance and Currency: Final Report of the Commissioners* (Cd. 7236 of 1914), p. 20.
38. See, for example, C. N. Vakil and S. K. Muranjan, *Currency and Prices in India* (Bombay, 1927), pp. 73–103, 310–46 and 397–426; Wadia and Joshi, *Money and the Money Market*, pp. 203–15 and 225–50, and M. de Cecco, *Money and Empire: The International Gold Standard 1890–1914* (Oxford, 1974), Ch. 4.
39. Keynes, *Indian Currency and Finance*, p. 178.
40. See E. Johnson (ed.), *The Collected Writings of John Maynard Keynes Volume XV: Activities 1906–1914, India and Cambridge* (London, 1971), pp. 90–1 and 94–5.
41. De Cecco, op. cit., pp. 63–75 and 121–2.
42. *Royal Commission on Indian Finance and Currency: Interim Report, Appendix III* (Cd. 7070 of 1913), p. 97; *Statistical Abstract for the United Kingdom 1913 and 1915 to 1928* (Cmd. 3465 of 1930), p. 122.
43. De Cecco, op. cit., p. 71.
44. R. S. Sayers, *The Bank of England 1891–1944, Volume I* (Cambridge, 1976), pp. 39–40.
45. See Keynes, *Indian Currency and Finance*, pp. 125, 126 and 169–72.
46. *Royal Commission on Indian Finance and Currency: Final Report of the Commissioners*, p. 22.
47. Keynes, *Indian Currency and Finance*, pp. 138–9.
48. *Royal Commission on Indian Finance and Currency: Final Report of the Commissioners*, pp. 27, 37–9.
49. See Keynes, *Indian Currency and Finance*, pp. 57–8 and K. C. Chaudhuri, 'India's International Economy in the Nineteenth Century: A Historical Survey', *Modern Asian Studies* 2 (1969), pp. 49–50.
50. See C. J. Baker and D. A. Washbrook, *South India: Political Institutions and Political Change 1880–1940* (Delhi, 1975), pp. 205–7; P. J. Thomas, *The Growth of Federal Finance in India* (Oxford, 1939), pp. 141–92; F. C. R. Robinson, *Separatism among Indian Muslims* (Cambridge, 1974), pp. 46–8.
51. See F. C. R. Robinson, 'Consultation and Control: the United Provinces' Government and its Allies 1860–1906', *Modern Asia Studies* 5 (1971), p. 325 and Anil Seal, *The Emergence of Indian Nationalism* (Cambridge, 1968), p. 153.
52. Quoted in Seal, op. cit., p. 161.
53. *Royal Commission Upon Decentralisation In India, Volume 1, Report* (Cd. 4360 of 1908), p. 25.

CHAPTER 2

1. See League of Nations, *Review of World Trade* (annual).
2. This analysis is based on the figures in S. Subramanian and P. W. R.

Homfray, *Recent Social and Economic Trends in India* (New Delhi, 1946), pp. 47–50.
3. Government of India, *Report of the Fiscal Commission 1949–50*, Volume 1, p. 36.
4. See C. H. Lee, 'The effects of the depression on primary producing countries', *Journal of Contemporary History* 4, 4 (1969), pp. 148–55.
5. United Nations Department of Economic and Social Affairs, *Processes and Problems of Industrialization in Under-Developed Countries* (New York, 1955), p. 139.
6. C. Markovits, 'The Indian Business Class and National Politics 1934–1939', dissertation submitted for the annual election of Fellows, Trinity College, Cambridge 1976, pp. 33–4. I am grateful to Dr Markovits for allowing me to make use of this manuscript, on which his Ph.D. thesis, 'Indian Business and Nationalist Politics 1931–39' (Cambridge, 1978), is largely based.
7. A. K. Bagchi, *Private Investment in India 1900–1939* (Cambridge, 1972), p. 80.
8. Government of India, *First Census of Manufactures India – 1946*, Volume 1, p. 141.
9. *Industrialization in Under-Developed Countries*, p. 138.
10. See below pp. 61–3.
11. See summary tables in *Recent Social and Economic Trends in India*, pp. 33–7. There are useful general discussions of the progress of agriculture in Bagchi, op. cit., Ch. 4 and D. R. Gadgil, *The Industrial Evolution of India in Recent Times 1860–1939* (Bombay, 1971), Ch. XV.
12. International Institute of Agriculture, *World Trade in Agricultural Products* (Rome, 1940), pp. 261–3.
13. Bagchi, op. cit., p. 287 fn 70.
14. Gadgil, op. cit., p. 215.
15. The percentage of exports to production (by weight) of Indian staples in 1924–9, 1930–4 and 1935–9 were as follows: rice, 5·2, 4·6 and 3·4; raw cotton, 62, 65 and 63; raw jute, 45, 41 and 41; groundnuts, 20·9, 23·1 and 17·4; other oil-seeds, 9·2, 5·6 and 6·3; tea 93, 90 and 91. See League of Nations, *Statistical Year-Book* (annual) and *World Trade in Agricultural Products*.
16. Comparing the period 1929–30 to 1938–9 with 1919–20 to 1928–9, the acreage in British India under cotton fell by 3·3 per cent, that under jute by 1·2 per cent, that under gram by 0·6 per cent and that under jower and bajra by 0·5 per cent; the acreage under rice rose by 1 per cent, that under wheat by 8·3 per cent, that under sugar by 23 per cent and that under groundnuts by 74·5 per cent. See Dharm Narain, *Impact of Price Movements on Areas under Selected Crops in India 1900–1939* (Cambridge, 1965), pp. 170, 172, 181, 188, 196, 204 and 215.
17. See below, pp. 83–6.
18. K. M. Mukerji, *Levels of Economic Activity and Public Expenditure in India* (London, 1962), p. 92. These figures are based only on circulating currency and deposits in Westernised banks.
19. For a good analysis of the financial problems of Indian industries in the 1920s see P. Lokanathan, *Industrial Organization in India* (London, 1935), Ch. IV.
20. Reserve Bank of India, *Banking and Monetary Statistics of India* (Bombay, 1955), pp. 693 and 713–14.
21. Mukerji, op. cit., p. 92.
22. See Lokanathan, op. cit., Ch. IV and *Central Banking Enquiry Committee*, Vol. I

Pt. I, Ch. XVI.
23. Banking and Monetary Statistics, p. 269.
24. *The Gazetteer of India, Volume III: Economic Structure and Activities* (New Delhi, 1975), p. 886.
25. *Central Banking Enquiry Committee, Vol. I Pt. I*, p. 527.
26. Ibid., para. 137.
27. Reserve Bank of India, *All-India Rural Credit Survey (1955–7) Volume II*, p. 179.
28. Ibid., Vol. I Pt. 2, p. 681.
29. Ibid., p. 677.
30. Ibid., p. 674.
31. J. S. G. Wilson, *Monetary Policy and the Development of Money Markets* (London, 1966), p. 249 and 'The Business of Banking in India' in R. S. Sayers (ed.), *Banking in the British Commonwealth* (London, 1952), pp. 177–86.
32. In 1930 there were 1534 such companies at work with a paid-up capital of Rs. 12·81 crores; in 1935 there were 1930 companies with Rs. 15·92 crores capital; in 1939 there were 2045 companies with Rs. 14·69 crores capital. See *Banking and Monetary Statistics*, p. 784.
33. *Central Banking Enquiry Committee, Vol. I Pt. I*, para. 48.
34. Ibid., para. 574.
35. Ibid., para. 581.
36. Ibid., para. 580.
37. Ibid., para. 581.
38. G. P. Gupta, *The Reserve Bank of India and Monetary Management* (Bombay, 1962), pp. 85–96 and 100–2.
39. N. G. Ranga, *Economic Organisation of Indian Villages I* (Bezwada, 1926), pp. 35–6, quoted in C. J. Baker, *The Politics of South India 1920–1937* (Cambridge, 1976), p. 185.
40. Ibid., pp. 185–9; Markovits, op. cit., pp. 50–3. See also Timberg, 'Three Types of Marwari Firm', *Indian Economic and Social History Review* IX (1973). Estimates of the profitability of Indian industries in the 1930s can be found in *Recent Social and Economic Trends*, p. 67; M. Gopal, *The Theory of Excess Profits Taxation* (Mysore, 1947), pp. 96–7 and M. C. Munshi, *Industrial Profits in India: an Inductive Study* (New Delhi, 1948).
41. League of Nations, Economic, Financial and Transit Department, *Industrialization and Foreign Trade* (1946), p. 31.
42. As Frank has claimed for Latin America. See A. G. Frank, *Capitalism and Under-Development in Latin America* (New York, 1969), p. 213.
43. A. K. Banerji, *India's Balance of Payments 1921–2 to 1938–9* (London, 1963), pp. 29, 90, 147.
44. B. R. Mitchell and P. Deane, *Abstract of British Historical Statistics* (Cambridge, 1962), pp. 325–7.
45. In 1913 Britain supplied 64 per cent of India's imports and bought 23·5 per cent of her exports; these proportions were 44·7 and 24·3 in 1928–9 and 36·3 and 36·3 in 1938–9 (see *Statistical Abstract of the British Empire*). The standard study of this subject, H. Venkatasubbiah, *The Foreign Trade of India 1900–1947* (Bombay, 1946), is of limited use for the late 1930s as no account is taken of the separation of Burmese trade from the Indian trade statistics from 1937. On the course of inter-imperial trade in general see I. M. Drummond, *British*

Notes to pages 45–53   173

Economic Policy and the Empire 1919–1939 (London, 1972), Ch. 1.
46. *Report of the Fiscal Commission 1949–50, Volume 1*, p. 39.
47. For Britain's balance of payments in the 1920s see Mitchell and Deane, op. cit., p. 355 and D. E. Moggridge, *British Monetary Policy 1924–1931* (Cambridge, 1972), p. 118. India's current balance of payments with Britain can be calculated from material in Banerji, op. cit. and the *Statistical Abstracts of the British Empire*.
48. See *Accounts Relating to Trade and Navigation of the United Kingdom 1938*.
49. D. H. Aldcroft and H. W. Richardson, *The British Economy 1870–1939* (London, 1969), pp. 64–5.
50. For example, Aldcroft and Richardson, op. cit., Chs. 6–8; Moggridge, op. cit., pp. 113–7 and A. E. Kahn, *Great Britain and the World Economy* (London, 1946).
51. For a summary and critique of these estimates, see Banerji, op. cit., pp. 149–68 and Reserve Bank of India, *Census of India's Foreign Liabilities and Assets as on 30th June 1948* (Bombay, 1950), Appendix I.
52. Banerji, op. cit., pp. 182 and 192.
53. Bagchi, *Private Investment*, p. 80.
54. Sir Robert Kindersley, 'British Overseas Investment in 1931', *Economic Journal* XLIII (1933), p. 200 and T. Balogh, *Studies in Financial Organisation* (Cambridge, 1938), pp. 249–51. An alternative method of calculation rates India and Ceylon as the largest recipient area of British overseas investment in 1930 – see Royal Institute of International Affairs, *The Problem of International Investment* (London, 1937), p. 142.
55. B. R. Tomlinson, 'Private Foreign Investment in India 1920–1950', *Modern Asian Studies* (1978), forthcoming.
56. *Report on the Condition and Prospects of British Trade in India* (1919), p. 19.
57. Ibid., pp. 10–18, 43–4.
58. This is true at least for Madras and the Punjab in the late 1920s. Dr C. J. Baker has supplied the information for Madras; for the Punjab see *Central Banking Enquiry Committee, Vol. I Pt. I*, p. 772.
59. Ibid., para. 456.
60. See the returns of these companies filed with the Registrars of Joint-Stock Companies in Calcutta and Bombay.
61. For example, Greaves Cotton & Co. with Crompton Parkinson, Octavius Steel with G. E. C., Gillanders Arbuthnot with Goodlass wall, Barry & Co. with Jensen & Nicholson and Turner Morrison with Pinchin Johnson. See Tomlinson, 'Private Foreign Investment', Appendix II.
62. This happened earliest in Bombay where an integrated, indigenous modernised economic and financial sector had emerged by the 1920s. See Markovits, op. cit., pp. 9–12. On the general trend, see the case studies in R. K. Hazari, *The Corporate Private Sector* (New Delhi, 1966).
63. Markovits, op. cit., p. 39 and Appendix III.
64. See the evidence of Sir Victor Sassoon in *Report of the Royal Commission on Indian Currency and Finance 1926, Vol. III*.
65. See correspondence in Government of India Finance Department files 1(8)F and 1(10)F of 1931 and in Thakurdas Papers file 145.
66. P. J. Grigg to H. V. Hodson 24.1.39 in Grigg Papers file 2/11.
67. Hazari, op. cit., p. 60.

68. M. Kidron, *Foreign Investment in India* (Oxford, 1965), p. 10. But see also Banerji, op. cit., p. 177 for a different interpretation.
69. Quoted in *Census of India's Foreign Liabilities 30.6.48*, p. 15.
70. See Hazari, op. cit., pp. 11–13.
71. For more information on the managing agency system see Lokanathan, *Industrial Organisation* and S. K. Basu, *Industrial Finance in India* (Calcutta, 1950).
72. Markovits, op. cit., p. 199.
73. Tomlinson, 'Private Foreign Investment', Appendix II.

CHAPTER 3

1. For a useful summary of these developments, see *Moral and Material Progress and Condition of India 1917–18*, Ch. 3.
2. Throughout the war Indian industry was dependent on imported machinery, the real value of which fell by nearly 80 per cent between 1913–14 and 1918–19 (see Bagchi, *Private Investment*, p. 80).
3. Lord Chelmsford to George V, 21.7.17 in Chelmsford Papers, Vol. 1.
4. *Report of the Indian Industrial Commission 1916–18, Volume 1* (Cmd. 51 of 1919), pp. 229–42.
5. Ibid., pp. 4–5.
6. See C. J. Dewey, 'The Government of India's New Industrial Policy 1900–1925: Formation and Failure', in C. J. Dewey and K. C. Chaudhuri (eds.), *Economy and Society: Studies in Indian Economic and Social History* (New Delhi, 1978), forthcoming.
7. See A. D. Clow, *The State and Industry* (Calcutta, 1928).
8. See *Report on Indian Constitutional Reform 1918* (Cmd. 9109 of 1918), pp. 113, 116.
9. *Report of the Committee Appointed by the Secretary of State for India to Enquire into the Home Administration of Indian Affairs, 1919* (Cmd. 207 of 1919), p. 873.
10. See Dewey, 'The End of the Imperialism of Free Trade', in Dewey and Hopkins (eds.), *The Imperial Impact*.
11. For a discussion of the theoretical basis of the Fiscal Commission's report see Rider, 'Government of India Tariff Policy', pp. 363–76. The report was based largely on the views of J. C. Coyajee, for which see his *The Indian Fiscal Problem* (Calcutta, 1924).
12. *Report of the Indian Fiscal Commission 1921–2* (Cmd. 1764 of 1922), pp. 110–39.
13. See *Gazetteer of India, Volume III*, pp. 465–6 and *Report of the Fiscal Commission 1949–50, Volume 1*, pp. 49–51.
14. *Report of the Fiscal Commission 1949–50, Vol. 1*, Ch. V.
15. *Gazetteer of India, Vol. III*, pp. 468–9.
16. Government of India Department of Industries and Labour (henceforth G.o.I.I. & L.) files S–217(67) of 1929 K.W. and S–217(98) of 1931 Appendix.
17. S. K. Sen, *Studies in Economic Policy and Development in India 1848–1939* (Calcutta, 1972), p. 183.
18. G.o.I.I. & L. (Railways/Stores Branch) file 39/15/1/S of February 1939.
19. Rider, op. cit., p. 393.
20. The Government of India was responsible for the costs of Indian units at

Notes to pages 64–72   175

home and the Imperial Government for their costs abroad.
21. *Reports of the Operations of the Currency Department* (annual).
22. Viceroy (Finance Department) to Secretary of State 17.7.17 in Government of India Finance Department Proceedings (Accounts and Finance Branch) (henceforth G.o.I.F.D. Procs. (A. & F.) 583–7A of August 1917.
23. G.o.I.F.D. Procs. (A. & F.) 779–91A of August 1918, *Report of the Committee on Indian Exchange and Currency* (henceforth Babington-Smith Committee) *Volume I* (Cmd. 527 of 1920), para. 22.
24. Note by J. B. Brunyate 2.12.15 in G.o.I.F.D. Procs. (A. & F.) 74–121A of February 1916.
25. Note by M. S. S. Gubbay 6.2.17 in ibid., 637–799A of October 1917.
26. The direct expenditure of the Government of India increased from Rs. 98 crores in 1913–14 to Rs. 187 crores in 1919–20, and its revenue from Rs. 102 crores to Rs. 164 crores. Treasury Bills were issued to cover the deficit and as security against new notes. In 1913–14 the Government of India's total long-term public debt in India was Rs. 178 crores, with £144 million in Britain; in 1919–20 these figures were Rs. 381 crores and £193 million.
27. D.O. Officiating Secretary, Government of. India Finance Department, to Officiating Controller of Currency no. 2410–F 5.9.19 in G.o.I.F.D. Procs. (A. & F.) 33–55A of April 1920.
28. Ibid.
29. 'Memorandum from Government of India concerning price movements 16.8.19', *Babington-Smith Committee, Vol. III*, Appendix XXVIII.
30. Ibid., Vol. II, minutes of evidence of Sir David Barbour no. 2103.
31. Ibid., minutes of evidence of Manu Subedhar.
32. Ibid., Vol. I, *Minority Report*, para. 12.
33. Ibid., *Report*, paras. 37–41.
34. Note by E. M. Cook 17.1.20 in G.o.I.F.D. Procs. (A. & F.) 77–98A of April 1920.
35. *Babington-Smith Committee Vol. II*, minutes of evidence of Sir Lionel Abrahams no. 1181.
36. Ibid., Vol. I, *Report*, para. 35.
37. Ibid., Vol. II, minutes of evidence of Sir Brien Cockayne no. 2554.
38. Ibid., nos. 2525–8, 2554–5 and 2585–6.
39. *The Times* 29.12.19; the banker was Lord Inchcape.
40. *Babington-Smith Committee, Vol. II*, minutes of evidence of F. H. Lucas nos. 4108–15.
41. Ibid., Vol. I, *Report*, para. 56.
42. There is a good account of it in Jevons, *Money, Banking and Exchange in India*.
43. *Reports of the Controller of Currency* (annual).
44. *Report of the Royal Commission on Indian Currency and Finance 1926* (henceforth Hilton-Young Commission), *Volume IV*, minutes of evidence of Sir Basil Blackett no. 10481.
45. *Report of the Controller of Currency 1920–1*, para. 20.
46. *Hilton-Young Commission, Vol. II*, Appendix 3, 'Memorandum giving the History of the Indian Currency System', by A. C. MacWatters, paras. 19–23.
47. See papers in G.o.I.F.D. Procs. (A. & F.) 60–126A of May 1923 and file 42(F) of 1925; also Indian Office Finance Department (henceforth I.O.F.D.) files L/F/6/1026 of 1921, L/F/7/204 Finance Collection 23/27.

48. *Hilton-Young Commission, Vol. IV*, minutes of evidence of Sir Basil Blackett no. 10487.
49. Note by Blackett 1.8.24 G.o.I.F.D. file 46–II–F of 1924.
50. See papers in G.o.I.F.D. files 86–F of 1926, 4–IX–F of 1927 and 8(IX)F of 1927.
51. Survey by A. Fergesson and Company for Bombay Millowners Association 5.3.24, quoted in D.O. Secretary Bombay Millowners Association to Department of Commerce no. 890/85A 4.7.24 in G.o.I.F.D. file 105–F of 1924.
52. See letters Deputy Controller of Currency to Secretary, Finance Department May 1925 in G.o.I.F.D. file 64–F of 1925.
53. Deputy Controller of Currency to Secretary, Finance Department 25.5.25 in ibid.
54. *Hilton-Young Commission, Vol. IV*, minutes of evidence of Sir Victor Sassoon nos. 5014–20.
55. Ibid., Vol. II, Appendix 46.
56. Ibid., Vol. IV, minutes of evidence of Sir Victor Sassoon nos. 5014–53.
57. Ibid., minutes of evidence of Sir Basil Blackett nos. 10427–9.
58. See ibid., minutes of evidence of Sir Victor Sassoon no. 5041.
59. Ibid., minutes of evidence of Prof. C. N. Vakil, B. M. Madon and Dr Balkrishna.
60. Ibid.
61. Ibid., minutes of evidence of Prof. Vakil nos. 4050–4.
62. Ibid., minutes of evidence of D. P. Khaitan nos. 8153–9.
63. Speech by Sir Basil Blackett at Delhi University 23.11.26, copy in G.o.I.F.D. file 8(X)F of 1927.
64. *Legislative Assembly Debates 1927*, p. 2555.
65. *Hilton-Young Commission, Vol. IV*, minutes of evidence of Sir Basil Blackett nos. 16–19, 117, 122, 9931–4, 10480–3 and 10246.
66. Note by A. Ayangar (undated, but January 1927) in G.o.I.F.D. file 8(I)F of 1927, Appendix II.
67. *Hilton-Young Commission, Vol. IV*, minutes of evidence of Sir Basil Blackett nos. 9981–4.
68. *Legislative Assembly Debates 1927*, p. 1753.
69. See *Hilton-Young Commission, Vol. II*, memoranda submitted by Blackett, MacWatters and Denning. These proposals were not official, but were made by the three top men in the Government of India Finance Department in a personal capacity.
70. *Ibid., Vol. I, Report*, p. 15.
71. See correspondence and notes in Treasury Papers (henceforth T.) file 176/25B.
72. *Hilton-Young Commission, Vol. I, Report*, p. 24.
73. See Viceroy (Finance Department) to Secretary of State 14.7.27 in I.O.F.D. file L/F/7/2291 Finance Collection (henceforth F.C.) 375/19/2.
74. *Hilton-Young Commission, Vol. I, Report*, pp. 33–66.
75. Ibid., pp. 37–8.
76. See I.O.F.D. files L/F/7/2290–6 F.C. 375/19–22.
77. *Hilton-Young Commission, Vol. I, Report*, p. 45.
78. Quoted in *Central Banking Enquiry Committee, Vol. I Pt. II*, p. 289, footnote.

Notes to pages 80–90 177

79. See Sir Purshottamdas Thakurdas to Sir Basil Blackett 9.8.27 in Thakurdas Papers file 61.
80. Viceroy (Finance Department) to Secretary of State 13.9.27 in I.O.F.D. file L/F/7/2292 F.C. 375/19/3.
81. C. H. Kisch to Sir Campbell Rhodes 26.7.26 in I.O.F.D. file L/F/7/2286 F.C. 375/15.
82. Secretary of State to Viceroy (Finance Department) 19.9.27 in I.O.F.D. L/F/7/2292 F.C. 375/19/3.
83. Note by G. H. Baxter in ibid.
84. For the strength of his feelings on this issue see Secretary of State to Viceroy (Finance Department) 11.8.27 in I.O.F.D. file L/F/7/2291 F.C. 375/19/2.
85. The following account is highly compressed and it has not been possible to give detailed references; it is based on a number of Finance Department files, notably G.o.I.F.D. files 13(X)F of 1927, 5(1)F of 1928, 1(2)F of 1930, 1(8)F of 1931 and 1(10)F of 1931. On the London end of events, see below pp. 126–8 and my 'Britain and the Indian Currency Crisis 1930–32', *Economic History Review* (1979), forthcoming.
86. Viceroy (Finance Department) to Secretary of State 9.5.31 in G.o.I.F.D. file 1(8)F of 1931.
87. 'Note on Finance and Currency' by Sir George Schuster, sent as Private and Personal Telegram Viceroy to Secretary of State 8.9.31 in Templewood Papers, Vol. 11, Bundle 2.
88. Mukerji, *Economic Activity and Public Expenditure*, p. 92. From October 1931 to March 1932 the currency was expanded by the proceeds of gold sales.
89. Sir Frederick Leith-Ross to Sir Findlater Stewart 1.1.31 in I.O.F.D. L/F/7/2396 F.C. 381/4.
90. Sir George Schuster to Sir Henry Strakosch 5.10.31 in Templewood Papers, Vol. 8.
91. For further details, see below pp. 128–31. This interpretation corrects the false impression of the 1934 Reserve Bank Act given in my 'India and the British Empire 1880–1935', *Indian Economic and Social History Review* XII (1975), pp. 375–6.
92. G.o.I.I. & L. file I–258(204) of 1931.
93. G.o.I.I. & L. file I–276(63) of 1932, J. B. Taylor to Sanjiva Rao 12.8.38 in G.o.I.F.D. file 21(92)F of 1938.
94. G.o.I.F.D. file 16(IV)F of 1930.
95. On cotton, see Government of India Department of Education, Health and Lands (henceforth G.o.I.E.H. & L.) Agriculture branch Procs. 130–3B of April 1931. On jute, see G.o.I.F.D. file 17(65)F of 1931.
96. Note by Schuster November 1933 in G.o.I.F.D. 2(120)F of 1933.
97. Sir George Schuster, 'Indian Economic Life: Past Trends and Future Prospects', *Journal of the Royal Society of Arts* 83 (1935), pp. 656–7.
98. Note by Schuster in Government of India Commerce Department (henceforth G.o.I.C.D.) Procs. A no. 1 of March 1934 file 7–C(1) of 1933.
99. 'Proceedings of Conference with the Financial Secretaries of Provincial Governments August 1930 – Third Day, 23.8.30' in G.o.I.F.D. file 16(IV)F of 1930.
100. See G.o.I.E.H. & L. Agriculture branch Procs. 176B of March 1931 and G.o.I.F.D. files 2(120)F of 1933 and 15(7)F of 1937.

101. Banking and Monetary Statistics of India, pp. 873–4.
102. P. J. Grigg to Sir Findlater Stewart 14.5.34 in Grigg Papers file 2/20.
103. Note by P. J. Grigg 18.7.35 in G.o.I.I. & L. I–276(96) of 1935.
104. P. J. Grigg to Sir Findlater Stewart 16.6.34 in Grigg Papers file 2/20.
105. Draft speech in G.o.I.F.D. file 17(65)F of 1935.
106. P. J. Grigg to Neville Chamberlain 17.8.34 in Grigg Papers file 2/2.
107. See G.o.I.I. & L. file I–353(10) of 1935.
108. For an expansion of this point see my 'India and the British Empire 1935–1947', *Indian Economic and Social History Review* XIII (1976), pp. 335–8.
109. The following account is based on N. Mansergh *et al.* (eds.), *India: The Transfer of Power 1942–7* (henceforth *Transfer of* Power), Volumes I–VI (London 1970–6); N. Prasad, *Expansion of Armed Forces and Defence Organisations 1939–1945* (Calcutta, 1956); N. C. Sinha and P. N. Khera, *Indian War Economy (Supply, Industry and Finance)* (Calcutta, 1962); H. Duncan Hall and C. C. Wrigley, *Studies in Overseas Supply* (London, 1953); R. S. Sayers, *Financial Policy 1939–1945* (London, 1956); S. L. M. Simha, *History of the Reserve Bank of India 1935–51* (Bombay, 1970); A. R. Prest, *War Economies of Primary Producing Countries* (Cambridge, 1948); G. P. Gupta, *The Reserve Bank of India and Monetary Management* (Bombay, 1962); R. N. Poduval, *Finance of the Government of India Since 1935* (Delhi, 1951); B. R. Shenoy, *The Sterling Assets of the Reserve Bank of India* (New Delhi, 1946); B. Dhar, *The Sterling Balances of India* (Calcutta, 1956); C. N. Vakil, *The Economic Consequences of a Divided India* (Bombay, 1948); T. R. Sharma and S. D. Singh Chauhan, *Indian Industries* (Agra, 1960); U. J. Lele, *Foodgrain Marketing in India* (Cornell, 1971); H. Knight, *Food Administration in India 1939–1947* (Stanford, 1954); Reserve Bank of India, *Reports on Indian Currency and Finance* (annual) and *Government of India Budgets* (annual).
110. Poduval, *Finance of the Government of India Since 1935*, pp. 119–20.
111. Quoted in Sinha and Khera, *Indian War Economy*, p. 403.
112. Prest, *The War Economies of Primary Producing Countries*, pp. 43–4.
113. Poduval, op. cit., pp. 108–10.
114. Linlithgow to Amery 26.12.42 in *Transfer of Power III*, no. 297.
115. Quoted in Sinha and Khera, op. cit., p. 49.
116. Quoted in Knight, *Food Administration in India 1939–1947*, p. 244.
117. See *Transfer of Power III*, Chapter 7; *IV*, Chapter 7; *V*, Chapter 7; also Secretary to Governor-General's Executive Council file 28/C.F./45.
118. Prest, op. cit., pp. 81–2.

CHAPTER 4

1. Useful books on constitutional policy, narrowly defined, are S. R. Mehrotra, *India and the Commonwealth 1880–1929* (London, 1963); P. J. Robb, *The Government of India and Reform 1916–21* (London, 1976); R. J. Moore, *The Crisis of Indian Unity 1917–1940* (Oxford, 1974); 'The Making of India's Paper Federation 1927–35' and 'British Policy and the Indian Problem 1936–40' in C. H. Philips and M. D. Wainwright (eds.), *The Partition of India: Policies and Perspectives* (London, 1970); V. P. Menon, *The Transfer of Power in India* (Princeton, 1957) and H. V. Hodson, *The Great Divide: Britain-India-Pakistan*

Notes to pages 104–11   179

(London, 1969). On tariff policy there is I. M. Drummond, *British Economic Policy and the Empire 1919–1939* (London, 1972), Chapter IV. Nothing worthwhile has been published on monetary or currency policy since Keynes, *Indian Currency and Finance* and Jevons, *Money, Banking and Exchange in India*. On defence policy M. Howard, *The Continental Commitment* deals with India only as part of a larger problem and the British and Indian *Official Histories of the Second World War* concentrate on the period after 1939. One recent book which attempts to cover all aspects of British India policy is P. S. Gupta, *Imperialism and the British Labour Movement 1914–1964* (London, 1975) but this deals only with Labour Governments.

2. See Howard, *Continental Commitment*, pp. 13–20 and *Moral and Material Progress of India 1911–12*, p. 327.
3. Quoted in 'Memorandum on India's Contribution to the War in men, material and money August 1914 to November 1918' January 1920 in Government of India Department of Revenue and Agriculture Proceedings General 16(127)B of February 1920.
4. Ibid., Tables 5 and 10; *Moral and Material Progress of India 1917–18*, p. 5.
5. 'India's Contribution to the War', loc. cit., Table 23.
6. Including Lord Salisbury, the author of this famous remark, which ran in full:

> Having regard to the future, I do not like India to be looked upon as an English barrack in the Oriental seas from which we may draw any number of troops without paying for them. It is bad for England, because it is always bad for us not to have that check upon the temptation to engage in little wars which can only be controlled by the necessity of paying for them.

Parliamentary Debates (Commons) 1867 no. 190 Col. 406. But, of course, Lord Salisbury was in opposition when he made this speech.

7. Secretary to the Treasury to Under-Secretary of State for India 27.2.1885, printed in *Correspondence between the Government of India and the Secretary of State in Council regarding the incidence of the cost of Indian troops when employed out of India* (Cd. 8131 of 1896), p. 6.
8. This debate is summarised in I.O.F.D. file L/F/7/783 F.C. 456/1.
9. *Final Report of the Royal Commission on the Administration of the Expenditure of India* (Cd. 131 of 1900), p. 139.
10. See 'India's Contribution to the War', loc. cit., paras. 71–83.
11. Appendix B to memorandum by W. M. Hailey 30.12.31 in G.o.I.F.D. Procs. (A. & F.) 47–74A of June 1922.
12. *Statistical Abstract for British India 1911–12 to 1920–21* (Cmd. 2033 of 1924), p. 196; *Banking and Monetary Statistics of India*, p. 872.
13. Cabinet Office Papers (henceforth CAB) 23/1, War Cabinet no. 24 of 1.1.17 and no. 48 of 30.1.17.
14. See Robb, *The Government of India and Reform*, pp. 49–50 and 58ff.
15. See P. J. Robb, 'The British Cabinet and Indian Reform 1917–19', *Journal of Commonwealth and Imperial History* IV (1976).
16. CAB 27/17, GT 1199, memorandum on Indian Reform by Lord Curzon 27.6.17.
17. CAB 23/6, Note by Mr Montagu, in appendix to War Cabinet no. 428 of 17.6.18.

18. CAB 23/3, War Cabinet no. 214 of 14.8.17.
19. CAB 23/29, Conference of Ministers 9.2.22.
20. *Report of the Committee appointed by the Secretary of State for India to advise on the question of the Financial Relations between the Central and Provincial Governments in India* (Cmd. 724 of 1920), pp. 3–8.
21. *Moral and Material Progress of India 1920*, p. 107; Lord Reading, *Rufus Isaacs 1914–1935* (London, 1945), p. 212.
22. This section covers ground first explored by Prof. J. A. Gallagher in the 1974 Ford Lectures.
23. CAB 27/24, shorthand notes of Eastern Committee meeting 9.12.18.
24. See CAB 23/20, conclusions of Conference of Ministers 23.1.20; CAB 23/22, ditto 18.6.20; CAB 23/23, 69(20) of 13.12.20.
25. See CAB 23/22, conclusions of Conference of Ministers 18.6.20; CAB 23/23, ditto 1.12.20.
26. See telegrams between Secretary of State for India and Viceroy (Army Department) in CAB 6/4, 119–D.
27. Ibid.
28. CAB 6/4, 118–D, 'Indian Military Expenditure', memorandum by Secretary of State for India 24.12.20.
29. *Report of the Army in India Committee* (Cmd. 943 of 1920), Part I.
30. Ibid., p. 3.
31. CAB 6/4, 119–D, Viceroy (Army Department) to Secretary of State 3.9.20.
32. Ibid., 122–D, Viceroy (Army Department) to Secretary of State 30.3.21.
33. Ibid., 130–D, 'Report of the Sub-Committee on Indian Military Requirements as Amended and Approved by His Majesty's Government'.
34. Viceroy (Army Department) to Secretary of State 6.6.21 in India Office Military Department file L/MIL/3/2513 of 1921. I am grateful to Mr K. Jeffrey, late of St John's College, Cambridge, for this reference.
35. Secretary of State to Viceroy (Commerce Department) late December 1923, undated copy in Baldwin Papers file E 1 93 Imperial B.
36. See summary of working of Fiscal Autonomy Convention in CAB 24/66, C.P. 299(24) of 24.5.24.
37. *Report of the Joint Select Committee on the Government of India Bill 1919* (Cmd. 203 of 1919), p. 11. My italics.
38. W. K. Hancock, *Survey of British Commonwealth Affairs, Vol. II Part 1* (London, 1940), pp. 97–8.
39. *Imperial Economic Conference, Record of Proceedings and Documents* (Cmd. 2009 of 1923), p. 14, 'Resolution 3 on Imperial Preference'.
40. See note by G. Hardy 26.12.29 in G.o.I.C.D. Procs. (Tariffs) A no. 1–29 of June 1930 file 341–T (85).
41. Quoted in Appendix to note by E. S. Turner, enclosed with Turner to Kershaw 12.1.32 in G.o.I.C.D. Procs. B March 1933 file 42–C(11).
42. See memoranda by Worthington-Evans, Amery, Darling and others in CAB 24/104, 105 and 108.
43. *Hilton-Young Commission, Vol. I Report*, p. 25.
44. Banerji, *India's Balance of Payments*, Table II.
45. Ibid., Table III; *Statistical Abstract for British India 1922–3 to 1931–2* (Cmd. 4835 of 1934–5), Table 65.
46. Bagchi, *Private Investment*, p. 238.

Notes to pages 123-30

47. Statistical Abstract for British India 1922-3 to 1931-2, Table 65.
48. CAB 23/63, 9(30)2 of 7.2.30.
49. CAB 24/129, C.P. 18(31) of 2.2.31 and C.P. 35(31) of 22.2.31.
50. CAB 23/63, 9(30)2 of 7.2.30.
51. CAB 23/68, 58(31)3 of 17.9.31.
52. See Sir Samuel Hoare to Lord Willingdon 2.10.31 and 1.4.32 in Templewood Papers, Vol. 1.
53. CAB 23/68, 58(31)3 of 17.9.31.
54. Secretary of State to Viceroy 18.9.31 and 21.9.31 in Templewood Papers Vol. 13; ditto 25.9.31 in Ibid. Vol. 11 and CAB 23/68, 62(31)9 of 22.9.31.
55. Viceroy to Secretary of State 26.9.31 in Templewood Papers, Vol. 11 and Lord Willingdon to Sir Samuel Hoare 6.10.31 in ibid., Vol. 5.
56. Neville Chamberlain to John Taylor 13.1.32 in T. 172/1779.
57. See above, pp. 37-8 and Tomlinson, 'Britain and the Indian Currency Crisis 1930-32', *Economic History Review* (forthcoming).
58. G. D. Birla to Sir Purshottamdas Thakurdas 16.1.31 in Thakurdas Papers file 42(vii).
59. See correspondence in Ibid., file 145.
60. Lord Willingdon to Sir Samuel Hoare 31.10.33 in Templewood Papers, Vol. 6.
61. Undated memorandum enclosed in Schuster to Irwin 9.9.30 in G.o.I. Reforms Office file 67/X/30 R.
62. CAB 27/470, BDG(30)29, Viceroy to Secretary of State 1.1.31.
63. 'Secret Memorandum on Financial Safeguards' by R. A. Mant, H. Strakosch, L. J. Kershaw and C. H. Kisch 17.6.31 in I.O.F.D. L/F/7/2396 F.C. 381.
64. Private note by C. K. [isch] December 1930 in ibid.
65. Unsigned, undated note (pencil) of late September 1931 on Prime Minister's notepaper in T. 160 Box 519/12471/05/1. Italics in original.
66. See note by P. S. (Philip Snowden) on memorandum by Sir Frederick Leith-Ross of 30.12.30 in T. 160 Box 399/12471 Annex 1 Part 1 and unsigned brief for Chancellor of Exchequer (Neville Chamberlain) 23.11.31 in T. 160 Box 519/12471/05/2.
67. See notes by R. V. N. H. (Sir Richard Hopkins) 31.10.32 and 31.12.32 in T. 175/45.
68. Unsigned, undated note (late November 1932, in S. D. Waley's handwriting) in T. 160 Box 474/12471/09/7.
69. Sir Samuel Hoare to Lord Willington 20.10.32 in Templewood Papers, Vol. 2.
70. CAB 23/73, 65(32)5 of 7.12.32 and Neville Chamberlain's remarks of November 1932 as quoted in note by S. D. Waley 3.3.33 in T. 160 Box 510/12471/05/4.
71. *Proposals on Indian Constitutional Reform* (Cmd. 4268 of 1933), pp. 13-17.
72. Details of this process will be found in a number of official files, especially I.O.F.D. L/F/7 319-22 F.C. 32/8-11 and G.o.I.F.D. 7(18)F, 7(52)F and 7(26)F of 1933, 7(4)F of 1934, 7(44)F and 7(86)F of 1935. See also Thakurdas Papers file 498.
73. *Reserve Bank of India Act (Act II of 1934)* Preamble.
74. J. B. Taylor to C. H. Kisch 9.10.33 in I.O.F.D. file L/F/7/322 F.C. 32/11.
75. Taylor to Kisch 29.5.33 in G.o.I.F.D. file 7(52)F of 1933; Viceroy (Finance

Department) to Secretary of State 1.10.33 and 5.10.33 and Taylor to Kisch 9.10.33 in I.O.F.D. file L/F/7/322 F.C. 32/11.
76. Proceedings of Executive Council on Indian Statutory Commission Report, 24th meeting of 6.9.30 in G.o.I. Reforms Office file 67/V/30 R. & K.W. For a later statement of the same view see note by J. B. Taylor 14.5.34 in G.o.I.F.D. file 7(86)F of 1935.
77. C. H. Kisch to Montagu Norman 26.2.34 in I.O.F.D. file L/F/7/322 F.C. 32/11.
78. R. S. Sayers, *History of the Bank of England, Volume 2* (Cambridge, 1976), p. 519 footnote.
79. G. D. Birla to Sir Purshottamdas Thakurdas 16.1.31 in Thakurdas Papers file 42(vii).
80. Quoted in Appendix to note by E. S. Turner, enclosed with Turner to Kershaw 12.1.32 in G.o.I.C.D. Procs. B March 1933 file 42–C(11).
81. Note by G. L. C. [orbett] 16.5.31 in G.o.I.C.D. Procs. A June 1932 file 175(1) T. & E. (Tr.). Italics in original.
82. Ibid.
83. CAB 24/227, C.P. 25(32). See also Sir Samuel Hoare to Lord Willingdon 19.1.32 and 28.1.32 Templewood Papers, Vol. 5.
84. Note by J. C. B. Drake 25.5.32 in G.o.I.C.D. Procs. A September 1933 file 752–T(S).
85. Drummond, *British Economic Policy and the Empire*, p. 131; Bagchi, *Private Investment*, p. 91.
86. Drummond, op. cit., pp. 132–4.
87. These are summarised in Drummond, op. cit., pp. 132–40 and explored in great depth in B. Chatterji, 'Lancashire Cotton Trade and British Policy in India 1919–1939' (Ph.D. thesis, Cambridge, 1978).
88. Quoted in Drummond, op. cit., p. 139.
89. On the nature and working of the Exchange Equalisation Account in the 1930s see Sayers, *Bank of England 2*, Chapters 18 and 19, 'The Exchange Equalisation Account; its origins and development', *Bank of England Quarterly Review* (December 1968) and S. K. Howson, 'The Managed Floating Pound', *The Banker* 126 (1976).
90. See notes by H. Denning and A. Parsons 16.5.32, note by G. Schuster 17.5.32 and Private and Personal Telegram XX Viceroy to Secretary of State May 1932 in G.o.I.F.D. file 17(36)F of 1932.
91. Sir Frederick Phillips to C. Kisch 5.5.32 in I.O.F.D. file L/F/7/675 F.C. 57/10.
92. Memorandum on 'Future Policy' by Phillips 24.2.32 in T. 175/57. The best summary of this debate is in S. K. Howson, *Domestic Monetary Management in Britain 1919–1939* (Cambridge, 1975), pp. 79–89 and Appendix 4.
93. Phillips to Leith-Ross 31.2.32 in T. 188/48.
94. Phillips to Henderson 26.2.32 in T. 175/57.
95. I. M. Drummond, *Imperial Economic Policy 1917–1939* (London, 1974), pp. 228–9; Sayers, *Bank of England 2*, pp. 450–1. On the currency discussions at Ottawa see 'Confidential Report on the Discussions of Monetary and Financial Questions at the Imperial Economic Conference, Ottawa, 1932' by Sir Henry Strakosch and Sir George Schuster 23.9.32 in I.O.F.D. file L/F/9/13.

96. See Sayers, *Bank of England 2*, Ch. 19.
97. *Return of the Budget of the Governor-General of India in Council for 1934–5, 1935–6, 1936–7, 1937–8, 1938–9, 1939–40.*
98. For British defence planning in the 1930s, see Howard, *The Continental Commitment*, pp. 115–39.
99. See N. Prasad, *Expansion of Armed Forces 1939–1945*, pp. 10–13 and Lord Zetland to Lord Linlithgow 31.7.39 in Linlithgow Papers, Volume 8.
100. See S. T. Das, *Indian Military, Its History and Development* (New Delhi, 1969), p. 117 and Sinha and Khera, *Indian War Economy*, pp. 14–18.
101. See P. J. Grigg to H. J. (Sir Horace Wilson) 16.1.38 in Grigg Papers file 2/23.
102. The account which follows is based on B. Prasad, *Defence of India: Policies and Plans* (Calcutta, 1963), Ch. 1.
103. Chatfield Committee Report paragraph 72, quoted in ibid., p. 10.
104. See ibid., pp. 54–5 and 63.
105. See above pp. 92–3.
106. Chatfield Committee Report paragraph 20, quoted in B. Prasad, op. cit., p. 9.
107. Findlater Stewart to Grigg 15.9.34 in Grigg Papers file 2/20.
108. Note by Cripps 2.9.42 in *Transfer of Power II* no. 678. See also papers in Premier's Office Papers (henceforth PREM) 4/46/5.
109. See Tomlinson, *The Indian National Congress and the Raj 1929–42* (London, 1976), pp. 27–31.
110. PREM 1/414, Linlithgow to Zetland 21.12.39.
111. A clear statement of this idea will be found in *Indian Statutory Commission Report, Volume I* (Cmd. 3568 of 1929–30).
112. See Tomlinson, *Indian National Congress*, Chapters 3 and 4.
113. On the use of treaties in the Middle East see M. Fitzsimmons, *Empire by Treaty* (London, 1965), J. Marlowe, *Anglo-Egyptian Relations 1880–1953* (London, 1954) and E. Monroe, *Britain's Moment in the Middle East* (London, 1964).
114. Note by Irwin, enclosed in Irwin to Baldwin 26.11.29 in Baldwin Papers file E 5 103.
115. Amery to Linlithgow 2.3.42 in *Transfer of Power I* no. 218.
116. Quoted in H. Dalton to Pethick-Lawrence 11.3.46 in ibid. *VI* no. 517. For Indian views on this, see *Sardar Patel's Correspondence 1945–50, Volume III* (Ahmedabad, 1972), pp. 210–27.
117. See 'The Treaty', note by Pethick-Lawrence 23.2.46 in *Transfer of Power VI* no. 465.
118. Sir L. Hollis to Sir D. Monteath 13.3.46 in ibid. no. 521.
119. Conclusions of a meeting of ministers 13.3.46 in ibid. no. 524.
120. Hollis to Monteath 13.3.46, loc. cit.
121. Conclusions of a meeting of ministers 13.3.46, loc. cit.
122. Wavell to Pethick-Lawrence 11.3.46 in ibid. no. 512.
123. Hollis to Monteath 13.3.46, loc. cit.
124. See Record of Discussion at Chequers 24.2.46 in ibid. no. 468.
125. See H. J. Tinker, *Experiments with Freedom* (London, 1967), p. 112 and 'Jawaharlal Nehru at Simla, May 1947', *Modern Asian Studies* 4 (1970); C. H. Philips, 'Introduction' to Philips and Wainwright (eds.), *The Partition of India* pp. 19–21 and S. Gopal, *Jawaharlal Nehru: A Biography, Volume One* (London, 1975), pp. 346–9. On the dropping of the treaty see Hodson, *The Great Divide*,

pp. 289–321; Menon, *The Transfer of Power in India*, pp. 350–86 and A. Campbell-Johnson, *Mission with Mountbatten* (London, 1951), pp. 68–73 and 83–113.
126. P. Moon (ed.), *Wavell: The Viceroy's Journal* (Oxford, 1973), p. 396.
127. H. Dalton, *High Tide and After* (London, 1962), p. 211.
128. See Hodson, op. cit., pp. 513–16 and Gupta, *Imperialism and the British Labour Movement*, pp. 287–98.
129. The reasons for India's decision are discussed at length in M. Brecher, 'India's decision to remain in the Commonwealth', *Journal of Commonwealth and Comparative Politics* XII (1974). On the 1949 negotiations see H. D. Hall, *Commonwealth* (London, 1971), pp. 831–68.
130. *Parliamentary Debates (Commons) 1946–7* no. 431, Cols. 1493–4.

CHAPTER 5

1. A. G. Hopkins, *An Economic History of West Africa* (London, 1973), Chs. 5–8.
2. Ibid., p. 170.
3. Ibid., p. 171.
4. Memorandum by Sir George Schuster 21.5.30 in I.O.F.D. file L/F/7/319 F.C. 32/8.
5. See Hopkins, op. cit. and G. A. Maguire, *Toward 'Uhuru' in Tanzania* (Cambridge, 1970).
6. See Schuster's 'Note of Economic Policy' 22.5.30 in G.o.I.E.H. & L. (Agriculture) Procs. B March 1931 no. 176.
7. See *Transfer of Power III*, Chapter 7; *IV*, Chapter 7; *V*, Chapter 7 and Secretary to Viceroy's Executive Council file 28/C.F./45.
8. See Jawaharlal Nehru, *The Discovery of India* (London, 1946), p. 336 and K. T. Shah (ed.), *Report of the National Planning Committee* (Bombay, 1949), Appendix III.
9. The argument put forward in the following paragraphs is only tentative. It is based on the annual *Administration Reports* of the provincial governments of the United Provinces and Bihar; Tomlinson, *Indian National Congress*, pp. 53–5, 77–9 and 93–102; Baker, *South India*, pp. 175–84 and 'Tamilnad Estates in the Twentieth Century', *Indian Economic and Social History Review* XIII (1976); W. J. Neale, *Economic Change in Rural India* (London, 1962); D. N. Dhanagare, 'Congress and Agrarian Agitation in Oudh 1920–2 and 1930–2', *South Asia* 4 (1975); K. G. Sivaswamy, *Legislative Protection and Relief of Debtors in India* (Bombay, 1939) and a series of articles on rural indebtedness by a number of authors in *Indian Journal of Economics*, 19 (1938–9), pp. 515–674.
10. A. A. Waugh, *Rent and Revenue Problems* (Naini Tal, 1934), p. 1.
11. This was written in 1937 and is quoted in Baker, 'Tamilnad Estates', pp. 40–1.
12. W. R. S. Sathyanathan, *Report on Agricultural Indebtedness* (Madras, 1935), pp. 16–17, quoted in Baker, *South India*, p. 179.
13. D. F. Miller, 'What Price Politics? – In India', *South Asia* 1 (1972), p. 33. Italics in original.
14. I am grateful to Dr B. Chatterji, late of Selwyn College, Cambridge, for pointing this out to me.

15. See Gupta, *Imperialism and the British Labour Movement*, p. 282.
16. Central Office of information, *Economic Co-operation between India and the United Kingdom* (1963), pp. 6–7.
17. The available figures show that there was Rs. 232·3 crores' worth of privately invested British capital in India in 1938, Rs. 230·14 crores in 1948, Rs. 376·8 crores in 1955 and Rs. 441·6 crores in 1960 – although these figures mean little because they are in unadjusted historical values and because the 1955 and 1960 totals are for direct investments only, but include reinvestment of profits and investments in kind (see Banerji, *India's Balance of Payments*, p. 175; *Census of India's Liabilities 30.6.48*, p. 86 and Reserve Bank of India, *Bulletin* (April 1960), p. 477). This last source gives direct British investment in 1948 as Rs. 206 crores; the *Census* figure for this is Rs. 189 crores.
18. *Board of Trade Journal 15.11.63*, pp. 1080 and 1086.
19. J. Strachey, *The End of Empire* (London, 1959), p. 233.
20. Ronald Robinson, 'Introduction' to R. E. Robinson (ed.), *International Cooperation in Aid* (Cambridge, 1969), p. 4.
21. Quoted in K. M. Kurian, *Impact of Foreign Capital on Indian Economy* (New Delhi, 1966), p. 129.

Bibliography

1 GOVERNMENT RECORDS

Cabinet Office Papers (Public Records Office, London)
Government of India Departmental Papers (National Archives of India):
    Commerce Department
    Department of Education, Health and Lands
    Department of Industries and Labour
    Department of Revenue and Agriculture
    Finance Department
    Railways Department
    Reforms Office
    Secretary to Viceroy's Executive Council files
India Office Departmental Papers (India Office Library):
    Finance Department
    Secretary of State's Private Office
Premier's Office Papers (Public Records Office, London)
Treasury Papers (Public Records Office, London)
Returns deposited with Registrars of Joint-Stock Companies, West Bengal and Maharastra (Calcutta and Bombay)

2 PRIVATE PAPERS

Baldwin Papers (University Library, Cambridge)
Chelmsford Papers (India Office Library)
Grigg Papers (Churchill College, Cambridge)
Linlithgow Papers (India Office Library)
Templewood Papers (India Office Library)
Thakurdas Papers (Nehru Memorial Library, New Delhi)

3 OFFICIAL PUBLICATIONS

British Government:
Accounts Relating to Trade and Navigation of the United Kingdom (annual)
Censuses of Production
Conditions and Prospects for United Kingdom Trade in India (annual)
Correspondence between the Government of India and the Secretary of State in Council regarding the incidence of cost of Indian troops when employed out of India (1896)
Committee on Industry and Trade, *Survey of Metal Industries* (1928)
Committee on Industry and Trade, *Survey of Textile Industries* (1928)
Constitutional Relations between Britain and India: The Transfer of Power 1942–7, Editor-in-chief, N. Manseroh (1970–)
Economic Co-operation Between India and the United Kingdom (1963)
Imperial Economic Conference, Record of Proceedings and Documents (1923)
India: Review of Commercial Conditions 1945
Indian Currency Committee 1893
Indian Currency Committee 1898
Indian Industrial Commission Report 1916–8
Indian Statutory Commission (1930)
Moral and Material Progress and Condition of India (annual)
Papers laid before the Colonial Conference, 1907
Parliamentary Debates (Commons)
Proposals for Indian Constitutional Reform 1933
Report of the Army in India Committee (1920)
Report of the Committee on Indian Exchange and Currency 1920
Report of the Committee appointed by the Secretary of State for India to advise on the question of the Financial Relation between the Central and Provincial Governments in India (1920)
Report of the Committee appointed by the Secretary of State for India to enquire into the Home Administration of Indian Affairs, 1919
Report on the Conditions and Prospects of British Trade in India at the close of the War (1919)
Report of the Financial Enquiry Committee by Sir Otto Neimeyer (1935)
Report on Indian Constitutional Reform 1918
Report of the Joint Select Committee on the Government of India Bill, 1919
Report of the Joint Select Committee on Indian Constitutional Reform 1933–4

Bibliography

Royal Commission on the Administration of the Expenditure of India (1900)
Royal Commission on Agriculture in India (1928)
Royal Commission upon Decentralisation in India (1908)
Royal Commission on Indian Currency and Finance 1926
Royal Commission on Indian Finance and Currency 1914
Statistical Abstract for the British Empire (annual)
Statistical Abstract for British India (annual)
Statistical Abstract for the United Kingdom (annual)

Government of India:
Census of India, 1921 and 1931
First Census of Manufactures, India – 1946
Indian Central Banking Enquiry Committee (1931)
Joint-Stock Companies in British India (annual)
Legislative Assembly Debates
Provincial Governments' Administration Reports (annual)
Recent Social and Economic Trends in India (by S. Subramanian and P. W. D. Homfrey) (1946)
Report of the Enquiry into the Rise of Prices in India (by K. L. Datta) (1914)
Report of the Fiscal Commission 1949–50
Report of the Foreign Capital Committee (1924)
Report of the Indian Fiscal Commission 1921–2
Report of the Indian Retrenchment Committee (1923)
Report of the Controller of Currency (annual)
Report on the Operations of the Currency Department (annual)
Reserve Bank of India Act (1934)
Return of the Budget of the Governor-General of India in Council (annual)
Revenue and Expenditure Accounts (annual)
Scheme for an Economic Census of India (by A. L. Bowley and D. H. Robertson) (1934)
The Gazetteer of India, Volume III: Economic Structure and Activities (1975)
The History of the Indian Tariff (by B. N. Ardarkar) (1940)
The State and Industry (by A. G. Clow) (1928)

International Agencies:
League of Nations:
Economic, Financial and Transit Department, Industrialization and Foreign Trade (1945)
Review of World Trade (annual)
Statistical Year-Book (annual)

United Nations:
  Department of Economic and Social Affairs, *Processes and Problems of Industrialization in Under-Developed Countries* (1955)
Reserve Bank of India:
  All-India Rural Credit Survey (1956–7)
  Banking and Monetary Statistics of India (1954)
  Bulletin (annual)
  Census of India's Foreign Liabilities and Assets as on 30th June 1948 (1950)
  Foreign Collaboration in Indian Industry: Survey Report (1968)
  Report on Indian Currency and Finance (annual)

4 PERIODICALS

Bank of England Quarterly Bulletin
Board of Trade Journal
Calcutta Stock Exchange Official Year-Book
Capital
The Economist
Indian Annual Register
Indian Investors' Year-Book
Indian Journal of Economics
Journal of the Parliaments of the Empire
London Stock Exchange Official Year-Book
Sankhya
Statist
Thakur's Directory of Commerce and Industry
The Times
The Times Trade Supplement

5 UNPUBLISHED SECONDARY SOURCES

B. Chatterji, 'Lancashire Cotton Trade and British Policy in India 1919–1939', Ph.D. thesis, Cambridge, 1978.

C. Markovits, 'The Indian Business Class and National Politics 1934–9', dissertation submitted for the annual election of Fellows, Trinity College, Cambridge, 1976.

T. D. Rider, 'The Tariff Policy of the Government of India and its Development Strategy 1894–1924', Ph.D. thesis, University of Minnesota, 1974.

6 PUBLISHED SECONDARY SOURCES: ARTICLES, BOOKS AND PAMPHLETS

J. H. Adler (ed.), *Capital Movements and Economic Development* (London, 1967).
D. Aldcroft, *From Versailles to Wall Street 1919–1929* (London, 1977).
—— and H. W. Richardson, *The British Economy 1870–1939* (London, 1969).
G. C. Allen, *British Industries and their Organization* (5th edn.) (London, 1970).
All-India Manufacturers' Organization, *Heavy Industries in British India* (Bombay, n.d.).
V. Anstey, *The Economic Development of India* (London, 1952).
A. K. Bagchi, *Private Investment in India 1900–1939* (Cambridge, 1972).
C. J. Baker, 'Tamilnad Estates in the Twentieth Century', *Indian Economic and Social History Review* XII (1976).
——, *The Politics of South India 1920–1937* (Cambridge, 1976).
—— and D. A. Washbrook, *South India: Political Institutions and Political Change 1880–1940* (Delhi, 1975).
G. B. Baldwin, *Industrial Growth in South India* (Glencoe, Illinois, 1959).
T. Balogh, *Studies in Financial Organisation* (Cambridge, 1938).
A. K. Banerji, *India's Balance of Payments 1921–2 to 1938–9* (London, 1963).
S. K. Basu, *Industrial Finance in India* (Calcutta, 1950).
G. Blyn, *Agricultural Trends in India 1891–1947* (Philadelphia, 1966).
M. Brecher, 'India's Decision to Remain in the Commonwealth', *Journal of Commonwealth and Comparative Politics* XII (1974).
D. H. Buchanan, *The Development of Capitalistic Enterprise in India* (New York, 1934).
A. Campbell-Johnson, *Mission with Mountbatten* (London, 1951).
M. de Cecco, *Money and Empire: The International Gold Standard 1870–1914* (Oxford, 1974).
B. Chandra, *The Rise and Growth of Economic Nationalism in India* (New Delhi, 1966).
K. C. Chaudhuri, 'India's International Economy in the Nineteenth Century: A Historical Survey', *Modern Asian Studies* 2 (1968).
R. Coupland, *Indian Politics 1936–1942* (Oxford, 1943).
J. C. Coyajee, *The Indian Fiscal Problem* (Calcutta, 1924).

Bibliography

H. Dalton, *High Tide and After* (London, 1962).
M. L. Dantwala, *Marketing of Raw Cotton in India* (Bombay, 1937).
S. T. Das, *Indian Military, Its History and Development* (New Delhi, 1969).
C. J. Dewey and K. C. Chaudhuri (eds.), *Economy and Society: Studies in Indian Economic and Social History* (New Delhi, 1978).
C. J. Dewey and A. G. Hopkins (eds.), *The Imperial Impact: Studies in the Economic History of Africa and India* (London, 1978).
D. N. Dhanagare, 'Congress and Agrarian Agitation in Oudh 1920–2 and 1930–2', *South Asia* 4 (1975).
B. Dhar, *The Sterling Balances of India* (Calcutta, 1956).
I. M. Drummond, *Imperial Economic Policy 1917–1939* (London, 1974).
——, *British Economic Policy and the Empire 1919–1939* (London, 1972).
J. H. Dunning, *Studies in International Investment* (London, 1970).
R. C. Dutt, *India in the Victorian Age* (London, 1904).
R. P. Dutt, *India Today* (Bombay, 1949).
M. Fitzsimmons, *Empire by Treaty* (London, 1965).
A. G. Frank, *Capitalism and Under-Development in Latin America* (New York, 1969).
D. R. Gadgil, *The Industrial Evolution of India in Recent Times 1860–1939* (Bombay, 1971).
L. F. Giblin, *The Growth of a Central Bank: The Development of the Commonwealth Bank of Australia 1924–1945* (Melbourne, 1951).
M. Gopal, *The Theory of Excess Profits Taxation* (Mysore, 1947).
S. Gopal, *Jawaharlal Nehru: A Biography, Volume One* (London, 1975).
K. Gough and H. Sharma (eds.), *Imperialism and Revolution in South Asia* (New York, 1973).
H. G. Grubel, *The International Monetary System* (London, 1972).
G. P. Gupta, *The Reserve Bank of India and Monetary Management* (Bombay, 1962).
P. S. Gupta, *Imperialism and the British Labour Movement 1914–1964* (London, 1975).
D. N. Gurtoo, *India's Balance of Payments (1920–1960)* (Delhi, 1961).
H. Duncan Hall, *Commonwealth* (London, 1971).
—— and C. C. Wrigley, *Studies in Overseas Supply* (London, 1953).
W. K. Hancock, *Survey of British Commonwealth Affairs, Volume II*, Part I (London, 1940).

R. K. Hazari, *The Corporate Private Sector* (New Delhi, 1966).
H. V. Hodson, *The Great Divide: Britain-India-Pakistan* (London, 1969).
A. G. Hopkins, *An Economic History of West Africa* (London, 1973).
H. F. Howard, *India and the Gold-Exchange Standard* (Calcutta, 1911).
M. Howard, *The Continental Commitment* (London, 1972).
S. K. Howson, *Domestic Monetary Management in Britain 1919–1939* (Cambridge, 1975).
——, 'The Managed Floating Pound', *The Banker* 126 (1976).
G. E. Hubbard, *Eastern Industrialization and its Effect on the West* (London, 1938).
International Institute of Agriculture, *World Trade in Agricultural Products* (Rome, 1940).
H. S. Jevons, *Money, Banking and Exchange in India* (Simla, 1922).
E. Johnson (ed.), *The Collected Writings of John Maynard Keynes, Volume XV: Activities 1906–1914, India and Cambridge* (London, 1971).
W. A. Johnson, *The Steel Industry of India* (Cambridge, Mass., 1966).
A. E. Kahn, *Great Britain and the World Economy* (London, 1946).
J. M. Keynes, *Indian Currency and Finance* (London, 1913).
——, review of T. Morrison, *The Economic Transition in India*, *Economic Journal* XXI (1911).
M. Kidron, *Foreign Investment in India* (London, 1965).
Sir Robert Kindersley, 'British Overseas Investment in 1931', *Economic Journal* XLIII (1933).
C. P. Kindleberger, *The World Depression 1929–1939* (London, 1973).
H. Knight, *Food Administratin in India 1939–1947* (Stamford, 1954).
K. M. Kurian, *The Impact of Foreign Capital on the Indian Economy* (New Delhi, 1966).
S. S. Kuznets *et al.* (eds.), *Economic Growth: Brazil, India, Japan* (Durham, North Carolina, 1955).
C. H. Lee, 'The effects of the depression on primary producing countries', *Journal of Contemporary History* 4,4 (1969).
U. J. Lele, *Foodgrain Marketing in India* (Cornell, 1971).
W. Arthur Lewis, *Economic Survey 1919–1939* (London, 1949).
P. Lokanathan, *Industrial Organization in India* (London, 1935).
P. Lovatt, *The Mirror of Investment* (Calcutta, 1925).
G. A. Maguire, *Towards 'Uhuru' in Tanzania* (Cambridge, 1970).
A. Maizels, *Industrial Growth and World Trade* (Cambridge, 1963).
J. Marlowe, *Anglo-Egyptian Relations 1880–1953* (London, 1954).

Bibliography

S. R. Mehrotra, *India and the Commonwealth 1880–1929* (London, 1963).
Asoka Mehta, *Who Owns India?* (Hyderabad, 1950).
V. P. Menon, *The Transfer of Power in India* (Princeton, 1957).
D. F. Miller, 'What Price Politics? – In India', *South Asia* 1 (1972).
B. R. Mitchell and P. Deane, *Abstract of British Historical Statistics* (Cambridge, 1962).
K. L. Mitchell, *Industrialization of the Western Pacific* (New York, 1942).
D. E. Moggridge, *British Monetary Policy 1924–1931* (Cambridge, 1972).
E. Monroe, *Britain's Moment in the Middle East* (London, 1964).
P. Moon (ed.), *Wavell: The Viceroy's Journal* (Oxford, 1973).
R. J. Moore, *The Crisis of Indian Unity* (Oxford, 1974).
R. Mukerjee and H. L. Dey (eds.), *Economic Problems of Modern India* (London, 1941).
K. M. Mukerji, *Levels of Economic Activity and Public Expenditure in India* (London, 1962).
D. Naoroji, *Poverty and Un-British Rule* (London, 1901).
D. Narain, *Impact of Price Movements on Areas Under Selected Crops in India 1900–1939* (Cambridge, 1965).
W. J. Neale, *Economic Change in Rural India* (London, 1962).
J. Nehru, *The Discovery of India* (London, 1946).
R. K. Nigam, *Managing Agencies in India: First Round, Basic Facts* (New Delhi, 1957).
R. Owen and B. Sutcliffe (eds.), *Studies in the Theory of Imperialism* (London, 1972).
Sir George Paish, 'Great Britain's Capital Investments in Individual Colonial and Foreign Countries', *Journal of the Royal Statistical Society* LXXIV Pt. II (1911).
——, 'The Export of Capital and the Cost of Living', *The Statist* 14.12.14 (Supplement).
Y. S. Pandit, *India's Balance of Indebtedness 1898–1913* (London, 1937).
Sardar Patel's Correspondence 1945–1950, Volume III (Ahmedabad, 1972).
C. H. Philips and M. D. Wainwright (eds.), *The Partition of India: Policies and Perspectives 1935–1947* (London, 1970).
R. N. Poduval, *Finance of the Government of India since 1935* (Delhi, 1951).
B. Prasad, *Defence of India: Policies and Plans* (Calcutta, 1963).

N. Prasad, *Expansion of Armed Forces and Defence Organizations 1939–1945* (Calcutta, 1956).
A. R. Prest, *War Economies of Primary Producing Countries* (Cambridge 1948).
M. G. Ranade, *Essays on Indian Economics* (Bombay, 1899).
N. G. Ranga, *Economic Organization of Indian Villages* I (Bezwada, 1926).
P. Ray, *India's Foreign Trade since 1870* (London, 1934).
R. K. Ray, 'The Crisis of Bengal Agriculture 1870–1927', *Indian Economic and Social History Review* X (1973).
Reading, (Lord) *Rufus Isaacs 1914–1935* (London, 1945).
P. J. Robb, 'The British Cabinet and Indian Reform 1917–18', *Journal of Imperial and Commonwealth History* IV (1976).
P. J. Robb, *The Government of India and Reform 1916–1921* (Oxford, 1976).
F. C. R. Robinson, 'Consultation and Control: the United Provinces' Government and its Allies 1860–1906', *Modern Asian Studies* 5 (1971).
——, *The Growth of Separatism among Indian Muslims* (Cambridge, 1974).
R. E. Robinson, *International Co-operation in Aid* (Cambridge, 1969).
—— and J. A. Gallagher, 'The Imperialism of Free Trade', *Economic History Review* VI (1953).
D. Rothermund, *The Phases of Indian Nationalism* (Bombay, 1970).
N. S. R. Sastry, *A Statistical Survey of India's Industrial Development* (Bombay, 1947).
W. R. S. Sathyanathan, *Report on Agricultural Indebtedness* (Madras, 1935).
S. B. Saul, *Studies in British Overseas Trade 1870–1914* (Liverpool, 1960).
R. S. Sayers, *Banking in the British Commonwealth* (London, 1952).
——, *Financial Policy 1939–1945* (London, 1956).
——, *The Bank of England 1891–1944* (Cambridge, 1976).
Sir George Schuster, 'Indian Economic Life: Past Trends and Future Prospects', *Journal of the Royal Society of Arts* 83 (1935).
A. Seal, *The Emergence of Indian Nationalism* (Cambridge, 1968).
S. K. Sen, *Studies in Economic Policy and Development in India* (Calcutta, 1972).
——, *Studies in Industrial Policy and Development in India 1858–1914* (Calcutta, 1964).

K. T. Shah (ed.), *Report of the National Planning Council* (Bombay, 1949).
——, *Sixty Years of Indian Finance* (London, 1927).
S. L. Sharma, *Trends of Capitalist Concentration in India* (Aligarh, 1955).
T. R. Sharma and S. D. Singh Chauhan, *Indian Industries* (Agra, 1960).
B. R. Shenoy, *The Sterling Assets of the Reserve Bank of India* (New Delhi, 1946).
G. K. Shirakov, *Industrialisation of India* (Moscow, 1973).
G. Findlay Shirras, *Indian Finance and Banking* (London, 1920).
S. L. N. Simha, *History of the Reserve Bank of India 1935–1951* (Bombay, 1970).
V. B. Singh (ed.), *Economic History of India* (Bombay, 1965).
N. C. Sinha and P. N. Khera, *Indian War Economy (Supply, Industry and Finance)* (Calcutta, 1962).
K. G. Sivaswamy, *Legislative Protection and Relief of Agriculturalist Debtors in India* (Bombay, 1939).
N. V. Sovani (ed.), *Reports of the Commodity Prices Board* (Poona, 1948).
D. L. Spencer, *India: Mixed Enterprise and Western Business* (The Hague, 1959).
J. Strachey, *The End of Empire* (London, 1959).
S. Strange, *Sterling and British Policy* (London, 1971).
Sir Purshottamdas Thakurdas et al., *A Brief Memorandum Outlining a Plan for the Economic Development of India* (Bombay, 1944).
P. J. Thomas, *The Growth of Federal Finance in India* (Oxford, 1939).
T. Timberg, 'Three Types of Marwari Firm', *Indian Economic and Social History Review* IX (1973).
H. J. Tinker, *Experiments with Freedom* (London, 1967).
——, 'Jawaharlal Nehru at Simla, May 1947', *Modern Asian Studies* 4 (1970).
B. R. Tomlinson, 'Britain and the Indian Currency Crisis 1930–2', *Economic History Review* (1978–9), forthcoming.
——, 'India and the British Empire 1880–1935', *Indian Economic and Social History Review* XII (1975).
——, 'India and the British Empire 1935–1947', *Indian Economic and Social History Review* XIII (1976).
——, 'Private Foreign Investment in India 1920–1950', *Modern Asian Studies* (1978), forthcoming.

B. R. Tomlinson, *The Indian National Congress and the Raj 1929–1942: the Penultimate Phase* (London, 1976).
Sir Harry Townend, *A History of Shaw Wallace & Co.* (Calcutta, 1965).
C. N. Vakil, *The Economic Consequences of a Divided India* (Bombay, 1948).
——, S. C. Bose and P. V. Deolalkar, *Growth of Trade and Industry in Modern India* (Bombay, 1931).
—— and S. K. Muranajan, *Currency and Prices in India* (Bombay, 1927).
H. Venkatasubbiah, *The Foreign Trade of India 1900–1940* (Bombay, 1946).
M. Vivesvaraya, *A Planned Economy for India* (Bangalore, 1934).
P. A. Wadia and G. N. Joshi, *Money and the Money Market in India* (London, 1927).
——, *The Wealth of India* (London, 1925).
D. A. Washbrook, *The Emergence of Provincial Politics: The Madras Presidency 1870–1920* (Cambridge, 1976).
A. A. Waugh, *Rent and Revenue Problems in India* (Naini Tal, 1934).
D. Williams, 'London and the 1931 Financial Crisis', *Economic History Review* XV (1963).
——, 'The 1931 Financial Crisis', *Yorkshire Bulletin of Economic and Social Research* 15 (1963).
J. S. G. Wilson, *Monetary Policy and the Development of Money Markets* (London, 1966).
A. J. Youngson, (ed.), *Economic Development in the Long Run* (London, 1972).
T. Zinkin, *Foreign Investment in India* (n.p., n.d.).

Index

Abrahams, Sir Lionel, 19, 68
Agriculture, Indian, investment in, 11–12, 43, 163–5; problems of 1919–39, 34–5
All-India Rural Credit Survey, 40
Anglo-Indian Trade Agreement, 135
Army in India Committee (1913), 106
Army in India Committee (1919–20), 115–16, 145
Asbestos Cement Company, 55
Associated Cement Company, 55
Attlee, Clement, 147, 152
'August Offer' (1940), 146

Baldwin, Stanley, 124, 146
Bank of Chettinad, 41
Baran, Prof., 166
Barbour, Sir David, 67
Baring, Sir Evelyn, 26, 27
Benn, Wedgwood, 118, 123
Bevin, Ernest, 166
Birla, G. D., 163
Blackett, Sir Basil, 74, 76, 78
Bomanji, S. K., 67
Bombay Millowners' Association, 74
Bowley, Prof. A. L., 90
Britain, aid to India of, 167
British economy, links with India of, 2–6, 45, 155–6, 165–7
British Government, demands made on India by, defence, 105, 113–18, 138–41, 147–9, 150; monetary policy, 21–2, 120–1, 124–31, 135–7, 159–60, 167; tariffs, 118–19, 123–4, 133–5
British investment in India, 3–5, 48–50, 166
British trade with India, 2–3, 5–6, 46–7, 135, 166

Bunbury, E. J., 125

Cabinet Mission (1946), 148–9
Central Banking Enquiry Committee, 39–40, 42
Chamberlain, Neville, 124, 128
Chartered Bank of India, 51–2
Chatfield Committee, 139–40
Chelmsford, Lord, 58, 110–11
Chetty, Shanmukham, 162
Chiefs of Staff, British, 147–9
Colombo Plan, 167
Colvin, Sir Aukland, 26
Committee on Indian Exchange and Currency (1919), 66–9
Commonwealth model of decolonization, *see* Dominion Status
Corbett, Sir Geoffrey, 120
Council Bills, 17, 19, 25, 72
Cripps, Sir Stafford, 142
Cripps Mission (1942), 146–7
Curzon, Lord, 114

Dalal, Dadiba, 67
Dalton, Hugh, 149
Defence Expenditure Agreement, 92–3
Defence of India Plan (1937), 138, 148
Derby, Lord, 123
'Discriminating protection', 61–4; *see also* Government of India, economic policy of
Dominion Status, role in India policy of, 145–6, 147, 150–1

Economic Adviser, 90
'Emergency currency', 71–2
Exchange banks, role in money market of, 8, 84

Index

Expatriate firms, role in Indian economy of, 9, 52–5
Export Credit Guarantee Scheme, 167

Fazl-i-Husain, Sir, 88
Federation of British Industries, 166
Fiscal Autonomy Convention, 60–1, 118, 123–4
Foreign firms, role in Indian economy of, 9, 50–2
Fowler Committee, 18–19, 20

Garran Tribunal, 139
Gold, imports to and exports from India of, 1, 9, 10, 16, 19–21, 37–9, 87, 160–1
Gold Standard Reserve, 21, 22–3
Government of India, budgetary problems of, 26–7, 34, 36; defence expenditure of, 92–4, 107–10, 139; economic policy of, industrial, 14, 16, 58–60, 162, 166; monetary, 16–23, 25, 36–7, 66–88, 96–8, 124–7; price support schemes, 89; rationing, 96–100; stores, 14–15, 34, 62–3; tariffs, 15–16, 60–2, 88, 110, 113, 118–20, 122–4, 133–5; impact of economic policy on Indian economy, 13, 16, 25–6, 34, 101–3, 159–60, 161,162–3; financial constraints on, 113, 122–3, 124–5, 137–8; imperial commitment of, 27–8, 105–52 *pass.*; remittance problems of, 17–18, 36, 82–3; and economic development, 142, 159–60, 162–3, 166; and economic planning, 13–14, 89–91, 100, 103; and political containment, 142–4, 151–2
Government of India Act (1919), 110–11, 111–13, 143–4, 146
Government of India Act (1935), 126–31, 143–4, 146
Great Depression, impact on empire of, 121–2, 131–4, 138; impact on India of, 34–44, 86–7, 88–90, 121–31, 160–1, 163–4
Grigg, Sir James, 90–1

Herschell Committee, 18–19, 20
Hoare, Sir Samuel, 123–4

Holland, Sir Thomas, 58–9
Home Charges, 17–18
Howard, H. F., 4

Imperial Bank of India, 42, 71, 81, 83, 89
Imperial Economic Conference (1923), 119–20
Imperial Economic Conference (1932), 45, 132–4, 136–7, 145
Imperial Preference, 61, 119–20, 131–5
Import Duties Act, 133
India and international economy, 1–3, 5–6, 16, 30–1, 44–6, 158–9, 165–7
Indian Army, role of in imperial defence, 106–10, 113–17, 138–40, 145
Indian economy, institutional linkages of, *see* Exchange banks, Expatriate firms, Foreign firms, Government of India economic policy, Imperial Bank of India, Indigenous bankers, Joint-Stock banks, Markets and marketing, Money market, Money supply and Presidency banks
Indian Fiscal Commission, 61–2
Indian Industrial Commission, 58–9
Indian Munitions Board, 58–9, 107
Indian National Congress, 144, 146, 147, 151, 162–5
Indian Tariff Board, 61–2, 63–4
Indian war economy, 1914–18, 57–8; 1939–45, 92–3
Indigenous bankers, role in money market of, 9–10, 39–43; unwillingness of to invest in industry, 10, 11–12
Industrial finance, problems of, 10–12, 36, 43, 73–4
Industrialisation in India, course of, 10–11, 14–15, 31–4, 43, 94–6
Irwin, Lord, 123, 126, 145–6

Joint-Stock banks, role in money market of, 8–9, 37–9, 40–2, 102

Keynes, J. M., impact of economic theories of, 78, 90; work on India of, 4, 21, 24
Khaitan, D. P., 76

Index

Lalbhai, Kasturbhai, 163
Land revenue, problems of, 163–5
Law, Sir Edward, 19
Lees-Mody Pact, 134
Linlithgow, Lord, 144, 149
Local government, reforms in structure of, 26

MacDonald, Ramsay, 127–8
Managing Agency system, 52–4
Markets and marketing in India, 6–8, 86, 98–9, 101, 164
Matthai, John, 163
Meston Award, 112
Money market, Indian, structure of in 1913, 8–13, 23–5; changes in after 1914, 35–44, 101–2, 160–1, 164
Money supply, Indian, determinants of, 10, 24–5, 36; fluctuations in, 23–4, 36–7, 93–7, 97–8
Montagu, Edwin, 110–11, 118, 145
Mookerjee, Sir Rajendra, 53, 75
Muslim League, 147

National Planning Committee, 162
Nehru, Jawaharlal, 149, 162–3

'Open' and 'closed' economies, effect of on course of imperial rule, 157–61, 162

Paper Currency Reserve, 21
Peel, Lord, 118
Paish, Sir George, 4
Political mobilisation in India, 163–5
Presidency banks, role in money market of, 8–9, 71
Provincial government, reforms in structure of, 26–7, 110–12, 137–8, 142–4

Ram, Sir Shri, 163
Reserve Bank of India, establishment of, 79–81, 88, 125, 128–31; role in money market of, 42, 92, 102,
Robertson, Dr D. H., 90

Royal Commission on Administration of Expenditure of India, 108
Royal Commission on Decentralisation, 27
Royal Commission on Indian Currency and Finance (1926), 73, 74–6, 78–80
Royal Commission on Indian Finance and Currency (1914), 20, 22–3
Rupee, crisis of 1931–2, 83–7; exchange rate of, xii, 17, 65–71, 72–8; exchange standard of, 16–17, 17–20, 66–9, 78–9, 87, 120–1, 135–7
Rural debt, problems of, 164–5

Sassoon, Sir Victor, 74, 77–8
Schuster, Sir George, 85, 86–7, 88–9, 126, 159–60, 162
Sharma, S. K., 67
Shroff, A. D., 163
Smith, Sir Osbourne, 131
Snowden, Philip, 128
Sterling area, 135–7, 145, 167
Sterling balances, Indian, 131, 140, 147, 167
Sterling debt, Indian, 127–8, 131, 140
Strachey, John, 166–7
Subedar, Manu, 67

Tata, J. R. D., 163
Tata Iron and Steel Company, 51, 63, 134
Thakurdas, Sir Purshottamdas, 76, 163
Treaty-making, role in India policy of, 144–5, 146–9

Vakil, Prof. C. N., 75

Wavell, Lord, 148, 149
Webb, Montagu, 21
Willingdon, Lord, 124, 176
Wilson, J. S. G., 40
World War I, impact on India of, 57–8, 64–5, 66, 106–11
World War II, impact on India of, 92–100, 140–1, 160–1